"This invaluable book makes a vital contribution both to decolonising and to gendering desistance research. Through painstaking analysis of the trajectories through crime of young women and men in Chile, Droppelman reveals the ambivalences, inconsistencies and liminality of their transitions to maturity and social integration. Social and psychological factors interact in these transitions and to understand them, we must also situate them in their cultural and structural contexts. This book is a must-read for anyone interested in understanding and supporting desistance – not just in Chile and Latin America, but everywhere".

–Fergus McNeill, Professor of Criminology and Social Work at the University of Glasgow, Centre for Crime and Justice Research and in Sociology

"The study of desistance from crime, like most areas of criminology, has lacked a strong engagement with the Global South, and this neglect has been to the detriment of theory development. So, Droppelmann's ground-breaking new study of desistance in Chile is a hugely welcomed contribution to the field that will hopefully be a catalyst for new work across Latin America and beyond".

–Shadd Maruna, Professor of Criminology, Queen's University Belfast

"This book represents major analysis of late adolescence and crime in Latin America. Drawing on precepts of Southern Criminology, and the cultural nuances that this entails, the author delves deeply into the lives of young people to offer insights into both pathways into crime but particularly *pathways out of crime*, motivations, challenges and transformational processes. This is hugely insightful and invaluable reading for all involved in supporting young people, and in correctional practice and penal reform".

–Professor Loraine Gelsthorpe, Director, Institute of Criminology, University of Cambridge

"In this fine book, Catalina Droppelmann offers an excellent review of the research literature as well as a pioneering research study of late adolescent offenders in Chile. Her research highlights the uncertainties and difficulties often experienced by would-be desisters from crime, and therefore cautions against drawing neat distinctions between 'desisters' and 'persisters'. Her analysis raises important issues for both researchers and practitioners".

–Sir Anthony Bottoms, Emeritus Wolfson Professor of Criminology, University of Cambridge

Transitions Out of Crime

This book contributes to our knowledge of desistance in a developing country. Offering an intercultural dialogue with mainstream explanations, *Transitions Out of Crime* analyses the transition from crime to conformity among a group of Chilean juvenile offenders.

Desistance from crime is not just the cessation of criminal activity itself, but a process of acquiring roles, identities, and virtues; of developing new social ties; and of inhabiting new spaces. This book offers new evidence that shows that the traditional binary between the "reformed desister" and the "anti-social persister" is inaccurate and that the road to desistance contains various oscillations between crime and conformity. Furthermore, this study shows the role that gender plays in shaping, limiting, and structuring pathways away from crime.

Written in a clear and direct style, this book will appeal to those engaged in criminology, sociology, penology, desistance, rehabilitation, gender studies, and all those interested in the transition from crime to conformity outside the Anglo-American orthodoxy.

Catalina Droppelmann is lecturer at the Social Science Faculty and leads the Centre for Studies on Justice and Society at the Pontificia Universidad Católica de Chile. She has worked for more than 20 years researching and teaching on justice, crime, and social exclusion. She holds a BA in Psychology from the University of Valparaíso and an MPhil and a PhD in Criminology at the University of Cambridge. Her interests are on criminal desistance from crime, re-entry policies, and youth justice.

International Series on Desistance and Rehabilitation

The *International Series on Desistance and Rehabilitation* aims to provide a forum for critical debate and discussion surrounding the topics of why people stop offending and how they can be more effectively reintegrated into the communities and societies from which they came. The books published in the series will be international in outlook, but tightly focused on the unique, specific contexts and processes associated with desistance, rehabilitation and reform. Each book in the series will stand as an attempt to advance knowledge or theorising about the topics at hand, rather than being merely an extended report of specific a research project. As such, it is anticipated that some of the books included in the series will be primarily theoretical, whilst others will be more tightly focused on the sorts of initiatives which could be employed to encourage desistance. It is not our intention that books published in the series be limited to the contemporary period, as good studies of desistance, rehabilitation and reform undertaken by historians of crime are also welcome. In terms of authorship, we would welcome excellent PhD work, as well as contributions from more established academics and research teams. Most books are expected to be monographs, but edited collections are also encouraged.

Governing delinquency through freedom
Control, rehabilitation and desistance
Géraldine Bugnon

Prison education and desistance
Changing perspectives
Geraldine Cleere

Rethinking what works with offenders
Probation, social context and desistance from crime
Stephen Farrall

Transitions out of crime
New approaches on desistance in late adolescence
Catalina Droppelmann

For more information about this series, please visit: www.routledge.com/criminology/series/ISODR

Transitions Out of Crime

New Approaches on Desistance in Late Adolescence

Catalina Droppelmann

Routledge
Taylor & Francis Group
LONDON AND NEW YORK

First published 2022
by Routledge
2 Park Square, Milton Park, Abingdon, Oxon OX14 4RN

and by Routledge
605 Third Avenue, New York, NY 10158

Routledge is an imprint of the Taylor & Francis Group, an informa business

British Library Cataloguing-in-Publication Data
A catalogue record for this book is available from the British Library

Library of Congress Cataloging-in-Publication Data
A catalog record has been requested for this book

ISBN: 978-0-367-75030-5 (hbk)
ISBN: 978-0-367-75031-2 (pbk)
ISBN: 978-1-003-16080-9 (ebk)

DOI: 10.4324/9781003160809

Typeset in Bembo
by Newgen Publishing UK

Contents

Figures

Tables

General Editor's introduction

The International Series on Desistance and Rehabilitation aims to provide a forum for critical debate and discussion surrounding the topics of why people stop offending and how they can be more effectively reintegrated into the communities and societies from which they came. The books published in the series will be international in outlook, but tightly focused on the unique, specific contexts and processes associated with desistance, rehabilitation, and reform. Each book in the series will stand as an attempt to advance knowledge or theorising about the topics at hand, rather than being merely an extended report of specific a research project. As such, it is anticipated that some of the books included in the series will be primarily theoretical, whilst others will be more tightly focused on the sorts of initiatives which could be employed to encourage desistance. It is not our intention that books published in the series be limited to the contemporary period, as good studies of desistance, rehabilitation and reform undertaken by historians of crime are also welcome. In terms of authorship, we would welcome excellent PhD work, as well as contributions from more established academics and research teams. Most books are expected to be monographs, but edited collections are also encouraged.

Rooted in her own experiences of working with young people in her native Chile, Catalina Droppelmann's contribution to this series is another which extends our thinking and insight into processes of reform outside of the overly familiar contexts of North America and key European countries with strong criminological research traditions (such as the United Kingdom, many of the Nordic nations, Spain, and Germany, to name a handful). Based on a still rare combination of both quantitative and qualitative data sources, Catalina is able to show how a number of the assumptions of theories developed in the global north do not easily survive the journey into the global south. Along the way we are given an insightful exposition on the role of gender and of gendered processes in desistance (still being debated and discussed of course) and into the ways in which Chile's adoption of neo-liberalism has provided a background for the processes of desistance which the men and women whose lives she studied. All in all, this is another powerful study of desistance in a South American context and can be read alongside earlier contributions to this series by Géraldine

Bugnon on Brazil and Carolina Villagra (also on Chile, and included in The Architectures of Desistance edited collection). I welcome Catalina's study to the growing corpus of work on desistance which this series is developing.

Stephen Farrall,
Sheffield,
July 2021.

Acknowledgements

This book is the result of my PhD research, which was possible thanks to the support of the Institute of Criminology at the University of Cambridge. Loraine Gelsthorpe, my supervisor, was a key support in this research. I also especially want to thank Anthony Bottoms, for his generous and continuous advice along the process.

I gratefully acknowledge my financial support from the Becas Chile Scholarship, awarded by the Chilean Ministry of Education; the Simon Bolivar Award, provided by the Centre for Latin American Studies at the University of Cambridge; the Society of Latin American Studies Postgraduate Award and from ANID/Fondecyt.[1]

Profound thanks are due to the Centre for Studies on Justice and Society of the Pontificia Universidad Católica de Chile. For the work undertaken in the Trajectories Study, I deeply thank Eduardo Valenzuela, Paloma del Villar and Estefania Simonetti. I also thank Tommo Fowler for his support editing and proofreading the drafts of this book. I would like to acknowledge Corporación Opción for facilitating access to the probation centres; to Sename and to the National Office for the Defence Attorney, which granted me access to conviction data. The most heartfelt thanks go to Javier, my partner and friend, who gave me the encouragement I needed to conduct this study in the first place.

But my greatest debt of gratitude is to the participants of the study, who so generously shared with me their life experiences, who placed their trust in me, and who taught me the most through the writing of this book. To each one of you, thank you.

Note

1 ANID/FONDECYT Regular 1212047 and 1121107.

Introduction

The internal motivation towards action is often a nebulous, multifarious thing. Behind any academic work, for instance, one may find various motivations to write; indeed, George Orwell (1946) recognised enough stimuli that he formed the basis of a whole book titled *Why I Write*. Of course, Orwell was concerned with the process of writing in general, not specifically academic research – but the questions his book asks the reader are the same: "What motivates you to do what you do?" This question was also the starting point for the present research: I interrogated several young people who had violated the law about their motivations for doing so – their motivations to start committing crimes, leave crime behind, or continue offending (among other things). Therefore, I will start this introduction by explaining my own motivations behind this book and the research which I conducted that is part of it, since it stems from a step-change in my outlook – both academic and social.

Prior to my undertaking of the research for this book, I had come to know many adolescent offenders, drug addicts, and people with mental health disorders. I learned a lot during the years that I worked directly with them, supporting them in their processes of change and integration into society. At that time, strongly shaped by my positivist social scientific academic training, it never occurred to me to ask myself what should happen so that they could change. Nor did I wonder in those days if they felt capable of change – or, indeed, if they even wanted to. I was guided by an impetus for reform, transformation, and integration; in other words, a search for normalisation in which mainstream social values and lifestyles were granted a superior ontology.

However, over time I came to understand that the limits separating my own social sphere and that of offenders ("us" and "them") were far more diffuse than I had imagined. I started to understand, as Young (2007) points out, that "they" were not simply the inversion of the norm – their deviance could not be neatly identified as the result of a moral or material deficit that could be reverted merely by providing them with opportunities for change. Rather, this was an oversimplification of crime abandonment – a process in fact of manifold complexity – and that teasing out its specific intricacies and nuances would be the key to the improvement of correctional practice.

DOI: 10.4324/9781003160809-1

It was in this context, that I first saw in the criminological literature an articulation of my central question: "what makes individuals stop committing crimes?". At first, I thought the answer was very simple – presumably, the opposite of what makes them reoffend. However, I realised that focusing on the changing process rather than the causes of recidivism allowed for a number of other lines of enquiry to emerge.

Desistance is not just the cessation of criminal activity itself but also a process of acquiring roles, identities, and virtues, developing new social ties, and inhabiting new spaces. It is the process of learning to live a new life – not necessarily eradicating the old one, but reconciling the two within the singular personhood of a profoundly complex individual. Such a reframing of the issue undoubtedly has extremely important implications for correctional practice, and this was precisely what provided my motivation to study the process of leaving crime behind.

The decision to orient my research towards late-adolescent offenders partially resulted from my prior familiarity with them (outlined earlier); it was also, as I will discuss fully in the body of the book, because adolescence is a key period for the abandonment of criminal behaviour. Late adolescence is a critical stage for the expression of resilience – particularly in the case of adolescent delinquents, who are normally immersed in contexts of high risk and adversities. Moreover, individuals in late adolescence (by which I mean the period between the ages of 16 and 21) are exposed to a higher variance of possibilities for life decisions than in other life periods, and there is an accumulation of opportunities that may have the transformative potential.

I also chose to conduct my research in Latin America – specifically in Chile, my home country. Latin America has several particularities in the manifestations of crime and the strategies to control it. As in previous years, in 2020, Latin America and the Caribbean was the region where people felt least safe (Gallup, 2020). Crime is the second major public concern (Latinobarómetro, 2018) and there is widespread mistrust of the police, the judiciary, and the excessive levels of impunity for those with high social capital, leaving citizens feeling extremely vulnerable. These issues have strongly influenced public opinion and demands for punitive interventions: more than half of citizens think that the best solutions for tackling crime are increasing the presence of police force on the streets and implementing harsher penalties (Latinobarómetro, 2018). Within this context, the embrace of neoliberal ideologies (to varying degrees) has led to crime being viewed as a free, purposeful behavioural choice; it apparently therefore requires little structural change to tackle it, and the paradigm of controlling crime with measures thought to be tough, smart, and cost-effective persists. Policies for crime prevention have primarily simply been imported imitations of practices developed in non-Latin-American countries; the adoption of these policies has been strongly characterised by the "what works" approach, reflecting an assumption of universal applicability that denies the need for any cultural adaptation (Droppelmann and Trajtenberg, 2021.

This has also had a strong impact on criminological research in Latin America, which has been mainly based on empirical and theoretical references derived from Anglophone countries. The approach has therefore neglected both the specific historical and societal issues from the Global South and the particular ways in which crime has been affected by culture and gender.[1] Southern Criminology (see Connell, 2007; Carrington et al., 2018),[2] which has strongly influenced the present research, has contended the Anglophone intellectual hegemony, challenging its universal applicability and validity, and encouraged the development of research, knowledge, and theory on crime from developing countries. Consistently, I decided to embark personally on a primary data collection effort; I was interested in gathering the life stories of the young offenders by myself, becoming deeply immersed in their environments, routines, and cultures in the process. The data that were collected, and the ways in which they were obtained, allowed me to pay special attention to structural, cultural, and gender issues that might shape the process of crime abandonment in Latin America. With this in mind, the book attempts to fill some of the gaps in our knowledge of desistance in developing countries and contribute to an intercultural dialogue with mainstream theories.

The aim of this book is to analyse the transition from crime to conformity among a group of Chilean juvenile offenders and discuss theoretical, policy and practice implications. For these purposes, the book is focused on examining three main areas: (1) the process of moving away from crime, its obstacles and challenges; (2) possible factors involved in the transition from crime to conformity; and (3) the particularities of gender in the desistance process, focusing on young female offenders. The book draws on data from the Trajectories Study,[3] a longitudinal research project that uses mixed methods to explore the criminal and life trajectories within a panel of young offenders in Chile.

The findings marshal new evidence to show that the traditionally oppositional, binary tropes of the "completely reformed desister" and the "categorically antisocial and non-virtuous persister" are hardly found, and that several individuals can be better identified as halfway desisters/persisters who oscillate between crime and conformity. Regarding the factors involved in the process of crime abandonment, it is shown that although social control and routine factors are extremely important for the process of leaving crime behind, desistance is not simply the result of these factors that appear in life and promote changes without individuals being aware of it. Rather, individuals' orientations towards conformity may be critical throughout the process, supporting daily decisions of routine and lifestyle changes that allow them to avoid crime, facilitating coherence and sense of purpose that orients behaviour. Several transversal issues emerge as impacting the desistance process among young males – ambivalence, attachment, consumerism, and masculinity – affecting them bilaterally, capable of both pulling them away from crime and pushing them back towards it. Finally, the findings indicate that gender plays a relevant role in the desistance process shaping, limiting, and structuring pathways out of crime. These findings lead to interesting research and policy implications to counteract current correctional practice in Latin America and abroad, characterised by an excessive orientation towards compliance, redemption, and transformation.

Book structure

The book is structured in six chapters. Chapter 1 reviews the existing literature, and it is divided into four sections. The first section discusses how desistance might be defined and operationalised. I discuss how some current criminological definitions of desistance have been limited by the belief that desistance is an overnight change, implying clean-cut with criminal activity, and by the notion that a radical internal transformation towards conformity is a sine qua non condition for desisting from crime.

The second section discusses how and why late adolescence is a crucial life stage for desistance. It examines the relationship between crime and age and the transformative potential of late adolescence in terms of the emergence of transition-linked turning points, new social interactions, and psychosocial capabilities. The role that neurological changes and improvements in moral orientations might play in the process of crime abandonment is also critically discussed throughout this section.

The third section discusses the main explanations and factors associated with women's desistance, and the fourth and final section discusses the explanations for a decline in criminal activity available in the criminological literature. It includes an examination of ontogenic explanations, rational choice, social control, and phenomenological approaches. Finally, the main integrated explanations of desistance are reviewed, arguing that diverse desistance explanations might be needed to properly understand different experiences of individuals when leaving crime behind.

Chapter 2 presents general methodological issues relevant to an understanding of the study, explicating the research findings. The aims and research design of the study are presented, and the rationale for – as well as the limitations of – the chosen methodology is discussed. The data collection process is then explained, describing the data sources and the main characteristics of the participants of the study; this section aims to properly situate the reader within the cultural particularities that characterised the juveniles who participated in the study.

The following three chapters present the research findings for each aim of the book. Chapter 3 explores the process and failed process of crime abandonment among the young male offenders of the study. It aims to answer the first two questions of the present research: who desists and who persists? and how do the participants experience the process and failed process of moving away from crime? First, operationalisations of desistance as a continuous variable are explored, showing that desistance and persistence categories are far from absolute and are rather two ends of a continuum that individuals can move along fluidly. Second, the way in which participants experience desistance and persistence processes is discussed to illustrate how transversal issues appeared as impacting this process among young male offenders, affecting them bilaterally, capable of both pulling them away from crime and pushing them back towards it.

Chapter 4 analyses the factors that may be involved in the transition from crime to conformity among the sample. It investigates those factors that increase the probability of desisting from crime among the late adolescents from the study and explores how these factors change when different models and operationalisations of desistance are used.

Chapter 5 explores the gender particularities of the desistance process among a sample of female late-adolescent offenders – how gender shapes, limits, and structures women's pathways out of crime. I discuss some of the gender gaps in the literature, exposing the limitations of an approach that merely seeks to define the factors that trigger, impede, or have no effect on the process of women's desistance; it argues instead for the need to explore how gender intersects with these factors, causing them to operate as they do.

Finally, Chapter 6 recapitulates the aim of the book and discusses its conclusions and the main similarities and differences with studies conducted in Anglophone countries. Then, the chapter presents the theoretical and practical implications of the findings for crime policies and correctional practice.

Notes

1 "The Global South" is a term that has been emerging in studies regarding the cultural legacies of colonialism and refers to what may also be called "the developing world".
2 Southern Criminology is a theoretical project that challenges the power imbalances which have privileged knowledge produced in the Global North, "decolonizing and democratizing" the study of criminology (Carrington, Hogg, & Sozzo, 2016:3).
3 For more information about the study, see http://trayectoriasdelictuales.uc.cl/.

References

Carrington, K., Hogg, R. and Sozzo, M. (2016). Southern criminology. *British Journal of Criminology*, 56(1): 1–20.

Carrington, K., Hogg, R., Scott, J. and Sozzo, M. (2018). *The Palgrave Handbook of Criminology and the Global South*. Switzerland: Palgrave Macmillan.

Connell, R. W. (2007). The northern theory of globalization. *Sociological Theory*, 25(4): 368–385.

Droppelmann C. and Trajenberg, N. (2021). 'Crime and inequalities in Latin America'. In: P.B. Anand, Fennell and F. Comim (eds.), *The Oxford Handbook of BRICS and Emerging Economies*, pp. 713–745 Oxford: Oxford University Press.

GALLUP. (2020). Global Law and Order Report. Available from: www.gallup.com/analytics/322247/gallup-global-law-and-order-report-2020.aspx.

Latinobarómetro. (2018). Informe Latinobarómetro 2018. Available from: www.latinobarometro.org/lat.jsp.

Orwell, G. (1946). *Why I Write*. London: Gangrel.

Young, J. (2007). *The Vertigo of Late Modernity*. London: Sage.

Chapter 1

Desistance and youth crime

Defining and operationalising desistance from crime

In general terms, "desistance" is used consistently to define the cessation, suspension, pause, or remittal of a certain action; in the field of criminology, however, definitions of desistance are as varied as their authors – and they are rarely clear, precise, or straightforward. Even in those articles, which do manage to provide some clarity, it is almost always preceded by an author's statement about the difficulty of arriving at their definition. It has been noted that desistance definitions are so idiosyncratic that, in some studies, it is possible to find ones that are made only to match the research design, the available data, and other practical concerns (Laub & Sampson, 2001; Stouthamer-Loeber et al., 2004).

Laub and Sampson (2001) argue that the ambiguity found in definitions of desistance may be due to their dependence on an adequate independent explanation of an offender. This makes logical sense: without a clear understanding of who an offender is, it is not possible to understand who they are not. Yet even arriving at this initial definition is fraught with problems, since the boundary between crime and conformity can often be more porous than expected (Hopkins, 2009; Young, 2007). This chapter discusses these issues, exploring diverse ways to characterise desistance from crime.

Desistance and the criminal career approach

The criminal career approach divides criminal trajectories into three stages: emergence (onset), pattering (duration), and abandonment (desistance) (Soothill, Fitzpatrick, & Francis, 2009; Sullivan & Piquero, 2016). Although a key component in criminal career research, desistance has received less attention than persistence and onset (Bushway, Thornberry, & Kohn, 2003; Laub & Sampson, 2001; Piquero, 2004; Shover, 2004).

This has been partially justified by the fact that, from a public safety approach, it is more worthwhile to focus efforts on those prolific and chronic criminals who generate great costs for society than it is on those who have already stopped committing crimes. Furthermore, the Juvenile Justice Systems in many

DOI: 10.4324/9781003160809-2

countries have been continually ineffective in attempts to reduce crime, thereby enforcing the idea that prevention is better than cure. Thus, efforts to prevent crime have been more oriented to understanding the factors that provoke its onset (Van Der Put & Dekovic, 2011; Farrington, 2007; Farrington & Welsh, 2007; Lôsel & Beelmann, 2006).

Yet putting the focus merely on the causes of crime may limit criminal rehabilitation and indeed may accentuate the problematic issues that rehabilitation aims to diminish (McNeil, 2004). By identifying the process of crime abandonment, on the other hand, desistance research can open the way to thinking more prospectively about how and why people change – thus paving the way for a more successful method of crime prevention in the long term (Maruna, 2001).

Despite the limited attention that the criminal career approach has given to desistance, it has made great contributions to the field by providing relevant information about the patterns of crime along the life course (see Basto-Pereira & Farrington, 2020; Farrington et al., 2014; Piquero, Farrington, & Blusmstein, 2003, 2007). For instance, with data from official criminal records and self-reported crime, we now know that offending most typically starts between the ages of 8 and 14 and stops between the ages of 20 and 29 (Piquero, 2011) – though other studies have shown that desistance peaks earlier, around 18 years of age (see Bowles & Pradiptyo, 2005; Stouthamer-Loeber et al., 2004).

Nevertheless, it is worth asking whether the first and the last self-reported or recorded crime (including arrest or conviction) really represents the starting and the ending of an individual's criminal career. Does a criminal career stop after committing the last offence, or does it finish when one decides to stop? How long must an individual be away from crime to qualify as a desister? These questions have raised a debate regarding the understanding of desistance: whether the abandoning of a criminal career should be viewed as a fixed end point in offenders' lives, or whether it should rather be seen as a process that supports the termination of offending (Sampson & Laub, 2003).

Beyond the termination point: desistance as the process of moving away from crime

In almost all the studies carried out before the nineties (with the notable exception of Meisenhelder, 1977), desistance had always been defined in a static way as denoting the end of the criminal career (see Cusson & Pinsonneault, 1986; Farrington, 1986; Farrington & Hawkins, 1991; Glueck & Glueck, 1943). This trend has continued in more recent years, too. Shover (1996:121), in a study in which he explored criminal career changes among more than 50 persistent thieves in the United States, defined desistance as "the voluntary termination of serious criminal participation"; similarly, Stouthamer-Loeber et al. (2004:897) offered the following definition in their study of the factors triggering and inhibiting desistance: "desistance is defined here as an individual's stopping the commission of crime".

The first limitation of studying desistance as having a static end point arises when we attempt to determine precisely how and when an individual's criminal career has stopped. In strict terms, the study of desistance in this sense would need to follow individuals until their death to establish whether or not they had truly stopped committing crimes. Since this is not feasible, most studies have operationalised desistance as the presence of a certain period of time without any criminal offence. Nevertheless, this operationalisation implies at least three key methodological issues that need to be considered.

First, it is difficult to ascertain a sufficient amount of follow-up time, because some offenders show intermittent crime-free gaps throughout their criminal careers (Kazemian, 2007). This is not a new finding – indeed, several decades ago, Glaser (1969) argued that offenders follow a zigzag path in which they alternate between crime and non-crime along their lives. Even prior to that, West (1963:34) had referred to intermittency as "interludes of honesty", arguing that these periods coincided with circumstances (material or relationship-based) that provided offenders with shelter or support. More recently, several further studies gave support to the fact that individuals can experience periods of temporary desistance (see Barnett et al., 1989; Elliott, Huizinga, & Menard, 1989; Farrington, Barnett, & Blumstein; 2020; Horney et al., 1995), with advanced statistical techniques being developed to assess intermittency in criminal careers (Nagin & Land, 1993).

Second, the length of follow-up is also relevant to determine correctly the age from which desistance takes place. For example, Le Blanc and Fréchete (1989) found, when following individuals up to 25 years of age, that the average age of those who had achieved desistance was 19.9 years. However, when following individuals up to the age of 40, the average age at which the last conviction took place was 31 years. This occurred because individuals who were followed until the age 40 had more exposure time to commit crimes. More recently, Farrington (2019) with data from the Cambridge Study in Delinquent Development observed that the mean age of desistance tended to increase, as the duration of the criminal career increased.

Time of exposure can also be a problem when scholars define the cut-off time in their studies. In simple terms, when operationalising desistance as a period free of crime, scholars normally divide their samples into two time periods: to be defined as desisters, individuals who have offended in period one must not have offended in period two. The difficulty is that the age of individuals in both periods differs considerably between studies, making the timing and prevalence of desistance difficult to define and compare (Bushway, Thornberry, & Krohn, 2003).

The third key issue is the type of data available: desistance rates can vary markedly within a sample when considering official criminal records versus self-reported crime (Brame et al., 2004; Farrington, 1989; Farrington, Auty,

Coid, & Turner, 2013; Le Blanc & Fréchete, 1989; Sampson & Laub, 2003; Stouthamer-Loeber et al., 2004). A study in the mid-20th century found that many instances of self-reported crime were not detected by the criminal justice system (see Short & Nye, 1957) – a discrepancy which occurs variously because some crimes are not reported, the perpetrator is not found by the police, and/or the case is not officially processed and is subsequently diverted from the criminal justice system (Loeber & Le Blanc, 1990; Piquero, Hawkins, & Kazemian, 2012). The issue is starkly highlighted by Elliott (1994), who estimates that, per 100 self-reported violent offences, merely two arrests are made. Furthermore, in a study that analysed data from the Seattle Social Development Project,[1] Farrington et al. (2003) observed that while 85.9% of the juveniles admitted committing at least one offence, only 34% were referred to court for at least one offence. In a more recent article, Farrington, Auty, Coid, and Turner (2013) using data from the Cambridge Study in Delinquent Behaviour observed that on average there were 38 self-reported offences per conviction among the participants of the study, and that this ratio decreased with age.

One would, therefore, expect to find that desistance would occur later in life when assessed using self-reported rather than official data (Farrington, 2007), and that official records may over-represent desistance rates compared to self-reported crime (Farrington, 1989; LeBlanc & Fréchette, 1989; Stouthamer-Loeber et al., 2004). Indeed, Massoglia and Uggen (2007), in a study drawing on data from the Youth Development Study,[2] introduced different conceptualisations of desistance through comparison of official records with what they defined as "behavioural desistance".[3] When using official records, 85% of the sample had desisted at the age of 29–30, but this figure dropped to 65% when measuring behavioural desistance.

A further limitation of defining desistance as having a definite end point arises when we try to determine how that termination occurs. Does it happen when an individual commits their last crime? As mentioned previously, it is difficult (if not impossible) to establish when an individual commits their final offence – even if they are followed until their death.

Some scholars have argued that, instead of focussing on the last offence, the individual's decision to stop committing crimes should be considered as the moment at which desistance occurs (see Cusson & Pinsonneaukt, 1986). Yet the decision to desist does not necessarily imply that full crime abandonment will occur (Healy, 2010; Maruna, 2001). Bottoms and Shapland (2011:56), in the Sheffield Pathways out of Crime Study,[4] observed that – even though in the first interview 56% of the sample said that they "have made a definite decision to try to stop committing crimes" 79% of the sample was re-convicted for at least one offence in the following three years.

In a two-year longitudinal study with males who progressed from prison to community in England, Burnett (2004) used a "desistance optimism score" that measured offenders' pre-release expectations of possible future criminal outcomes. She observed that 44% of those offenders who were optimistic about desisting from crime persisted after release. Moreover, Leibrich (1993), in a study of 48 men and women on probation in New Zealand, observed that almost half of the sampled interviewees who stopped committing crimes had tried previously and failed.

Furthermore, it seems that the interval between the decision to stop committing crimes and the actual termination can be longer than expected. In fact, in the study of Leibrich (1993), the participants reported that the process of crime abandonment took them at least three years after their initial decision to stop committing crimes. Similarities may be observed in the field of addictions recovery, wherein the decision to stop using drugs can occur several years before the addict's cessation. Even though an individual can be determined to stop, recovery usually includes several relapses (Prochaska, Norcross, & DiClemente, 1994). As Maruna points out (2001:25):

> Like the person who makes a New Year's resolution to give up chocolate, the ex-offender who decides he or she wants to desist from a life of drugs and crime often loses his or her resolve when faced temptation and frustration.

With these aforementioned limitations in mind, it can be argued that, even if it is possible to follow offenders for a long period of time, an extensive crime-free gap does not guarantee the termination of a criminal career (Farrington, 1986). Moreover, in studies where desistance is operationalised with a definitive end and the follow-up period is short, "desistance is more likely to refer to a state of temporary non-offending" (Kazemian, 2007:11).

Given that the termination point may be not an identifiable or fixed moment in the offender's life and may take place at any time during the criminal career (Maruna, 2001; Mulvey et al., 2004) (indeed, in strict terms, termination could occur every time an individual decides to stop committing crimes, whether this break lasts for a day or a whole lifetime), it can be argued that it is more accurate and relevant to define desistance as the process of "moving away from crime", which can happen several times and at any stage during the criminal career.

A more nuanced definition of desistance

Even though it has been argued that desistance does not occur overnight, and that it can be better understood as the process of moving away from crime, it is still not clear how we can determine who is a desister and who is not. Is a desister a person who has not decided to stop doing illegal activities per se, but in fact just commits less crime, or a person who gets involved in illegal activities only in some specific situations? At what point can we say this person has changed? Can one be defined as a desister only when one has completely stopped committing crimes? Can an offender change without achieving a new non-offender status and identity?

Although research on desistance has given a relevant place to the process of change, these questions have not yet been answered. Nevertheless, it can be argued that desistance may not imply an absolute, clean-cut, and final break with criminal activity (Shover, 2004). As pointed out by Loeber and Le Blanc (1990:407), "Desistance refers to the process that leads to cessation of crime, either entirely or in part". Indeed, many offenders do not reach a zero crime point in their lives, and they continue to be engaged in different sorts of anti-social activities (Healy, 2010; Sampson & Laub, 2003). Even those who do stop committing crimes may never reach a lifestyle of absolute conformity or may never achieve a deep and radical internal transformation.

Whilst most of the literature about criminal trajectories considers intermittency, there have been only a few in-depth studies into the fact that desistance can include partial change. One notable exception is a study conducted by Farrall (2002) in which he operationalised desistance as a gradual process that transcended absolute terms and included the emergence of desistance as well.[5] Nevertheless, desistance has primarily been described in dichotomous terms as either the absence or the presence of criminal activities in an individual's life. We can see, then, that although several definitions of desistance put the emphasis on the maintenance process of a crime-free life rather than on the termination point, it still describes desistance in absolute terms. According to these descriptions, an individual can be an offender or a non-offender, but there is no definition of a "half-way" criminal – or, using phrasing of Healy (2010:102), of individuals "who exist in the liminal place betwixt and between crime and convention".

Before embarking on the discussion of partial changes towards conformity, the concept of a "liminal place" deserves some consideration. Etymologically, "liminality" comes from the Latin word limen, a threshold. In anthropology, it was initially introduced by Van Gennep (1960), who used it to describe rites of passage for individuals or social groups moving from one state to another (e.g. from childhood to adolescence in the case of individuals, or from peace to war in the case of societies). According to Van Gennep (1960), these rites are divided into three main phases: separation, limen, and segregation. In the liminal phase, the individual or group exists in an ambiguous state between the separation of previous practices and routines from their former group of reference, and the incorporation into a new group with a new identity and sense of being. In this space, social rules are suspended, because the individual does not belong to the old world and is not yet part of the new world. This concept was widely used by Turner (1967) in his studies with aboriginals, through which he observed that there are some rites of passage that have well-developed liminal periods. Liminality could equally be applied to the transition from crime to conformity, in which the individual may be in an ambiguous state that combines characteristics from the previous criminal stage with a number of practices from the subsequent stage of conformity.

It is interesting to note how several authors have used the idea of liminality as a way of describing "half-way" offenders – albeit with divergent terminology. Bottoms et al. (2004:383), for instance, employ the word continuum to describe the space wherein individuals move from criminal behaviour to conformity; several decades earlier, Matza (1964:28) used the term limbo to describe this space in which, according to him, adolescent delinquents exist.

Despite little scholarly attention having been paid to the idea that desisters do not fall into discrete categories, research does exist which demonstrates that desistance is hardly ever absolute. For example, Glaser (1969:31) argued that although it can be easier to divide offenders into those who ultimately succeed or fail in their intent to abandon crime, this division erases the great variation that can be observed in offenders' efforts to move away from crime:

> Those who have lived in both the criminal and the lawful world may walk a zigzag path between the two, although many of them eventually will make a clear turn into one or the other. Those who do not return to crime may be said to have made either a complete or a marginal reformation.

What can occur within the liminal space?

As per the above, desistance may be better understood as a continuous variable that includes not merely the stage of being a non-offender, but rather a wider range of partial changes towards conformity. A more nuanced operationalisation of desistance is explored in this section, taking into account declines and restrictions in criminal activities, as well as internal changes towards conformity.

Decline in criminal activity

It has been stated that, prior to or instead of total cessation, the process of moving away from crime involves gradual reductions of frequency, severity, and versatility of crime (Farrington, 2007; Le Blanc, 2011; Loeber & Le Blanc, 1998; Mulvey et al., 2004). Thus, when studying desistance, some scholars have not only demonstrated the absence of criminal behaviour for a reasonably long period of time, but they also have started searching for downward changes, such as (1) deceleration, (2) de-escalation, and (3) decline in the variety of criminal activities across time (Kazemian, Farrington, & Le Blanc, 2009; Le Blanc & Fréchete, 1989; Loeber & Le Blanc, 1998; Mulvey et al., 2004). These processes are discussed next.

Deceleration

Deceleration can be understood as "a slowing down in the frequency of offending" (Loeber & Le Blanc, 1990:382). It seems that, when looking at changes in the frequency of crime (dynamic measures) rather than at crime cessation (static measures) among the same group of individuals, the two measures identify different individuals as desisters. Such a divergence may be seen, for instance, in the data from the Rochester Youth Development Study (RYDS)[6]: From their sample, the static method suggested that 27.6% of individuals stopped committing crimes, while the dynamic method identified only 8.4% (Bushway, Thornberry, & Krohn, 2003). In addition, there was little overlap between the different measures, with an agreement of only 4.8% of the individuals. Moreover, 78% of the cases that were identified in the static measure as desisters were contrastingly identified by the dynamic measure as individuals who continued offending but at a low rate.

Similarly, in the Sheffield Pathways out of Crime Study (Bottoms & Shapland, 2011), results from the two measures revealed very different pictures: while only 20% of offenders stopped completely committing crimes during the follow-up period, the frequency of crimes for the whole sample decreased from a mean number of 8.2 offences per year to 2.6 – a statistically significant finding.

It is interesting to note that looking into declines in the frequency of offending not only allows us to observe a different picture of desistance but also opens the way to identify subgroups of individuals that follow different pathways in their criminal trajectories (see, for example, Mulvey et al., 2010 and Monahan et al., 2009). Bushway et al. (2001) proposed a technique initially developed by Nagin and Land (1993) which uses semi-parametric models to identify these groups, the main advantage of which being that it allows individuals to be grouped in such a way as to estimate the offending rates at each point in time. It, therefore, does not force the entire sample to follow the same pattern of change as in the survival models, and it estimates the proportion of the population belonging to each group.

Mulvey et al. (2010) used this technique to examine self-reported crime in a sample of 1,119 male offenders for a period of three years after court involvement. Interestingly, they distinguished five different groups of individuals, only one of which was composed of persisters (8.7% of the sample). The other four groups represented different kinds of desisters, each encompassing a different manifestation of declining criminal activity. While, for instance, the first group demonstrated almost zero levels of crime in the follow-up period, the second group showed a slighter decline, and the fourth group steadily decreased criminal activity. Even though the researchers did not find relevant causal factors that distinguished between these groups, they accurately showed that offenders can follow different paths to desistance.

De-escalation

De-escalation can be understood as the decrease in seriousness of criminal activity (Soothill, Fitzpatrick, & Francis, 2009) – or, in other words, "as the probability that subjects at time two will continue to offend, but in categories less serious than the ones in which they participated at time one" (Le Blanc, Coté, & Loeber, 1991:27).

Unfortunately, not many studies contain specific data regarding the nature of the offences committed by individuals which would be necessary for scholars to assess de-escalation and, as a result, research has been more oriented to the study of deceleration (Kazemian, Farrington, & Le Blanc, 2009; Le Blanc, 2012; Le Blanc, 2002; Loeber & Le Blanc, 1998; Piquero, Hawkins, & Kazemian, 2012). Nevertheless, it can be argued that there is relative agreement about the fact that although a minority of offenders increase the severity of their offending in late adolescence, others show patterns of de-escalation during the same period (Loeber & Farrington, 2012).

Glueck and Glueck (1943:225) were among the first scholars who pointed out that, beyond crime cessation, offenders could also follow de-escalation patterns in their criminal careers. In their study Unraveling Juvenile Delinquency,[7] they distinguished between offenders who progressed from serious to minor crimes and those who reformed entirely. Several years later, Robins (1966) recomputed data of Glueck and Glueck (1943) and observed that, while 45% of individuals in the sample de-escalated their criminal activity, only 17% of them abandoned crime completely.

Later, Le Blanc, Coté, and Loeber (1991) administered a self-reported crime questionnaire to a sample of normative adolescents and adolescent offenders over a two-year interval. Results showed that while a small proportion of the sample desisted entirely from crime during the follow-up period (0.8%), a far larger percentage of boys de-escalated in criminal activities (20.1%).

Qualitative studies of desistance have also highlighted de-escalation patterns (Glaser, 1969; Heally, 2010; Leibrich, 1992). For example, when interviewing 73 probationers in Ireland, Heally (2010) observed that over a third of her sample de-escalated in their criminal activity. These results must be considered with caution, however, since she measured de-escalation as comprising the adjudication of a less serious conviction, without considering the type of offence.

Although research has shown that de-escalation is a relevant phenomenon in criminal careers, it is still not clear what kind of paths of de-escalating individuals follow and why they pursue them. Le Blanc, Coté, and Loeber (1991) observed three different forms of de-escalation in criminal careers: from aggression to vandalism, vandalism to minor thefts, and thefts to state offences. Similarly, Loeber et al. (2008), observing sequences of offences, pointed out that theft generally precedes violent offences.

Loeber et al. (1991) explored correlates of de-escalation among a sample of boys. They observed that de-escalation was more marked among the older boys (who were 12–13 years old) than in the younger boys (who were 9–10 years old). They also demonstrated that low levels of disruptive behaviour were associated with decreases in the seriousness of offending.[8] Kazemian, Farrington, and Le Blanc (2009) also explored correlates of de-escalation with data from the

Cambridge Study in Delinquent Development and the Montreal Two Samples Longitudinal Study.[9] Specifically exploring the role of social bonds and cognitive predispositions, they observed that – although early measures of these variables were weak predictors of de-escalation – improvements in cognitive predispositions, job attachment and stability, and reductions in substance use correlated with de-escalation in criminal behaviour.

Furthermore, differences in correlates of de-escalation have been observed between males and females. For example, Ayers et al. (1999) observed, using data from the Seattle Social Development Project, that maternal bonding significantly correlated with de-escalation among females but not males. In addition, decline in antisocial interactions was associated with male de-escalation, but not with female. School bonding, meanwhile, significantly correlated with de-escalation for both, males and females.

Decline in the variety of criminal activities

The decline in the variety of criminal activities across time is sometimes used as a synonym of specialisation, understood as "the tendency to repeat the same offence type in successive arrests" (Blumstein et al., 1986:81). It can, for example, signify instances when an individual repeats the same four types of offence in period one and period two. The reference here is not to the repetition of the same type of offence, however, but to the process in which offenders narrow the repertoires of offence types that they commit. For example, a decline in the versatility of crime is seen when an offender commits four different types of crimes (e.g. thefts, burglary, motor vehicle theft, and personal attack) in period one, then in period two limits their criminal activity to one or two types of offence (e.g. theft and personal attack).

Although research on criminal careers has shown that offending is more versatile than specialised, it has also revealed that, generally, after reaching the age of 20 (the transition to adulthood), specialisation increases (DeLisi et al., 2018; Mazerolle & McPhedran, 2019; Piquero, 2011). There is still a good deal of controversy regarding specialisation, though – especially concerning how to define and measure it (see Piquero, Hawkins, & Kazemian, 2012; Soothill, Fitzpatrick, & Francis, 2009). It seems that specialisation can be highly sensitive to the type of data chosen, the selection or classification of criminal offences, and the length of follow-up period (among other factors).

Several studies have defined specialisation as the focus of criminal behaviour on one single crime, or into a group or a cluster of crimes over time (see Blumstein et al., 1986; Farrington, 1986; Loeber et al., 2008; Mazerolle et al., 2000; Nieuwbeerta et al., 2009; Piquero et al., 1999; Piquero, Hawkins, & Kazemian, 2012). Nevertheless, fewer studies have focused on the decline of the variety of offences as a possible measure of desistance. Using data from the Montreal Two Samples Longitudinal Study, which explored declines in offending versatility between adolescence and adulthood, Morizot and Le Blanc (2007) observed that there was a significant decline in the variety of criminal activities across time, decreasing by 0.08 offences at each wave of assessment: while the individuals from the sample reported an average of 2.5 types of offences at the age of 15, by the time they had reached 41 years old they reported only 0.41.

Restrictions in criminal activities: circumscribed deviance and displacement

Having now considered downward trends that can occur during the transition from crime to conformity, we turn to discuss the type of criminal and/or antisocial behaviour desisters continue to be engaged – or, the cases in which instead of abandoning criminal behaviour altogether, individuals replace it with other forms of antisocial behaviour.

Circumscribed deviance

It seems that, when moving away from crime, offenders can restrict their criminal activities to those that do not threaten their conventional social attachments, and which have low risks of being caught or getting a long sentence. For example, Goldweber et al. (2011), in a study using prospective longitudinal data from 937 offenders aged 14–17, observed an increasingly solo offender trajectory. Offenders who followed this path restricted their criminal behaviour to less spontaneous and more opportunistic activities with a low probability of detection.

Furthermore, Le Blanc (2012) has proposed that there exist three main criminal trajectories: persistent, transitory, and common. According to him, the common trajectory is characterised by individuals who avoid crime but continues to engage in occasional deviant behaviours such as vandalism, drug use, and other minor crimes. Indeed, some research has suggested that while assault and the use of physical violence decrease in line with offenders' age, minor offences remain stable (Fagan & Western, 2005; Le Blanc & Fréchete, 1989; Miranda & Corcoran, 2000).

Nagin, Farrington, and Moffitt (1995:132), using data from the Cambridge Study in Delinquent Development, observed that the individuals who were engaged in crime during adolescence but none thereafter (according to criminal records) continued to be engaged in what they called "circumscribed deviance". Indeed, they observed from self-reports that although these individuals performed well at work and had prosocial attachments, they nevertheless continued to engage in thievery, heavy drinking, and fighting. This duality of lifestyle allowed them to maintain bonds in both criminal and conformity settings and gain recognition and success on both sides (Glaserm, 1969). Indeed, Shover (1996:122) observed that some offenders, to avoid the complete abandonment of their criminal peers, moved to a different role within their gang, segueing from "frontline participants" to "background operators".

Displacement

Massoglia (2006) has used the term "displacement" to define shifts in offending that occur during the transition to adulthood. He differentiates the process of displacement from the deceleration of criminal activity examined previously, referring not only to changes in crime frequency but also to the display of new behaviours.[10]

Displacement is thus not about changes in the manifestation of a certain function but refers to the fact that "individuals engage in qualitatively different acts as they age" (Massoglia, 2006:217). Although there is a paucity of information regarding the specific qualities of the crimes, offenders can commit during the transition to conformity, it seems that they shift to more utilitarian and less hedonistic activities (Kazemian & Le Blanc, 2004). Bushway, Thornberry, and Krohn (2003) observed that although 8.6% of the juveniles from their sample decreased their offending rate to almost zero for a period of three years, they subsequently embarked upon a new type of criminal activity. Le Blanc and Fréchete (1989) and Langan and Farrington (1983) observed that, as they age, offenders progress to more profitable crimes that can satisfy their economic needs. This was also observed by Bottoms and Shapland (2011) in the Sheffield Pathways out of Crime Study, in which some offenders moved towards more purposeful offences, such as drug dealing and business robbery, among others.[11]

Furthermore, Barry (2012) observed in a Scottish Desistance Study that although among her sample crime started as a mean of obtaining status and social recognition, with time it stopped being a source of excitement.[12] Especially in the case of women, crime turned into a means to get money to sustain their drug habits.

Although displacement is to be differentiated from deceleration, it may perhaps overlap with de-escalation and with the changes in versatility outlined previously. For example, if an individual shifts their criminal behaviour from burglary to shoplifting, it would be possible to observe both de-escalation and displacement. Moreover, if the same individual not only committed burglary, but also motor vehicle theft and personal attack before a shift towards shoplifting, it could be argued that they displaced, de-escalated, and decreased the variety of their criminal offences.

Displacement is not a merely repetition of the concepts discussed previously, however, since it can occur regardless of de-escalation and decreases in the variety of criminal activities. It can, for example, occur in cases wherein an individual moves from selling crack to selling cocaine. Is it more serious to sell the former than the latter, or vice versa? To answer this question, the specific characteristics of the offence need to be taken into account. It might be, for instance, that individuals move to selling cocaine because it represents a higher status in the criminal culture; yet it is simultaneously a less risky activity, since the clients who buy cocaine are less dangerous than those who buy crack.

Moreover, it can be argued that displacement may not only be used in reference to the type of crime, but also to the type of target. For example, it could be possible that offenders who commit burglary displace the targets of their crimes from houses to shops. They may start looking for less risky targets, for instance, or those which would result in the crime producing less harm (see Piquero, 2004). In this case, it could be less harmful to rob a shop (where the seller might put up less resistance) than a house (where they may encounter families and children).

Internal changes towards conformity

In the preceding overview, only the changes in antisocial behaviour that can occur during the transition from crime to conformity have been discussed. Yet just because a person has ceased their criminal activity or antisocial behaviour – or has decreased or restricted it – it does not necessarily follow that they have changed in themselves (Maruna et al., 2009). As Christian et al. wrote: "Following a more nuanced view of desistance, simply living a crime-free life is not an adequate marker of success" (2009:13).

Indeed, the literature on desistance has a clear emphasis not only on the external changes in offenders' lives, but also the internal ones: those in the process of moving away from crime not only cease behaving as an offender, but they also stop being an offender. The abandonment of the offender's role may imply a reorganisation to new roles and an alteration of the individual's sense of self (Maruna et al., 2009), and understanding the process of moving away from crime should, therefore, have an internal dimension (changes in identity and values) as well as a behavioural one (changes in criminal behaviour).

Several scholars who have explored offenders' life narratives have pointed out that, during the transition from crime to conformity, individuals develop a more prosocial sense of self (Aresti, Eatough, & Brooks-Gordon, 2010; Christian et al., 2009; Farrall & Calverley, 2006; Giordano et al., 2002; Gove, 1985; Hill, 1971; Leibrich, 1993; Maruna, 2001; Paternoster & Bushway, 2009; Pressner & Kurth, 2009; Shover, 1996; Vaughan, 2007). Nevertheless, it is still not clear how far an individual must shift their identity to qualify as a desister. Do all desisters reach a radical conversion towards conformity? Must they leave their former identity completely behind? Can offenders stop committing crimes without an internal transformation? Do identity shifts always sustain changes in criminal activity?

Although there is no clear agreement among criminologists on these issues, there are four distinct areas of possibility for desisters: (1) the experience of radical internal transformation, (2) the experience of partial internal transformation, (3) cessation of criminal activity without the experience of internal transformation, and (4) continuation of criminal activity despite the experience of internal transformation. These possibilities are discussed next.

Radical transformations: replacement or reconstruction?

Perhaps the most idealised version we have of a desister is as a person who has completely reformed their life. Heroic stories, conversions, and broad and deep internal changes may come to mind when we think about individuals who have stopped committing crimes: these are cases of desisters who have recovered, reformed, or – in other words – achieved a radical internal transformation. They not only stop being an offender but start to be a completely new person. Although qualitative research on desistance has described many characteristics of these radical transformations (Christian et al., 2009; Gadd & Farrall, 2004; Giordano et al., 2002; Leibrich, 1993; Maruna, 2001; Pressner & Kurth, 2009; Shover, 1996), two main changes can be highlighted.

The first is a tendency on the part of the offender to overemphasise positive and prosocial personal qualities. As pointed out by Maruna (2001: 97) when describing the 66 Liverpudlian desisters in his study:

> The fathers I talked to were not just fathers, but super-fathers. The volunteers were super-volunteers [...] In the redemption narrative, making good is part of a higher mission, fulfilling a role that has been inherent in the person's true self.

Similarly, Presser (2008), using life stories of men who had perpetrated violent crimes in the United States, observed that they claimed their reform in heroic terms. The theme of this heroism was a constant struggle with societal foes such as addiction, the criminal justice system, and their own personality trends and attitudes. Indeed, the defeat of these "enemies", or forces that pull them away from conformity, was the basis for the development and maintenance of a prosocial identity.

It seems that the tendency of desisters to see themselves as examples of prosocial behaviour operates as a psychological strategy to maintain or recover their self-worth. Greenberg and Pyszczynski (1985) called this process "compensatory self-inflation" and argued that individuals inflate their self-image in an attempt to counteract and regulate negative emotions that arise when the self is in jeopardy. This mechanism may help ex-offenders to think and behave in accordance with their favourable self-image, thereby allowing them to show consistency in their new prosocial role.

The second change is the development of a moral orientation towards society (Farrall & Calverley, 2006; Harris, 2009; Maruna, 2001). Indeed, this group of desisters develops a desire to do good, to help others, to avoid selfish interests, and to be a part of – and contributor to – society. The following quotation, taken from an ex-offender in a study by Harris (2009:153), serves as a useful illustration of this idea:

> Transformation is a great connection movement. It is a movement geared towards seeing yourself as being part of a larger community. It means that you are obligated, responsible for being involved. [...] You not gonna be able to help everybody, but you have to contribute to the betterment of everyone around.

It can be argued that, in terms of moral reasoning theory of Kohlberg (1984),[13] these individuals may have reached a "conventional level" of moral development. At this level, moral decisions are taken from the perspective of society as a whole, and individuals obey rules even when there are no sanctions or rewards for obedience or disobedience. Similarly, according to Bottoms' (2002) mechanisms of legal compliance,[14] these individuals would be situated in a "normative level" of legal compliance; within this framework, conformity arises via the acceptance of society's values, through attachment to significant others that follow strong moral norms, or through the granting of legitimacy to social and legal authorities.[15]

Since these changes seem to be particularly radical, several scholars have argued that desisters leave their past antisocial self completely behind (Giordano et al., 2002; Harris, 2009; Paternoster & Bushway, 2009; Vaughan, 2007). As noted by Giordano et al. (2002:1001) at the beginning of their Theory of Cognitive Transformation: "cognitive transformation occurs when actors are able to envision and begin to fashion an appealing and conventional replacement self that can supplant the marginal one that must be left behind".

Similarly, Paternoster and Bushway have also argued that shifts towards conformist settings and activities will not take place until an ex-offender's new conventional identity replaces the former one. Although they suggest that this new self is connected in some way with past and current experiences, they understand desistance as occurring when offenders "literally break with the past" (Paternoster & Bushway, 2009:1106). Indeed, according to their theory, offenders do a cost-benefit analysis, through which a sense of dissatisfaction with their former self arises; as a result, the past self-stopping being a source of gratification and they leave it behind. Vaughan (2007) went slightly further, asserting that desisters disown their past self because of the shame that arises from reviewing their criminal life.

Yet evidence of a new identity supplanting the former is not apparent in all studies of desistance (Aresti, Eatough, & Brooks-Gordon, 2010; Gadd & Farrall, 2004; Glaser, 1969; Hundleby, Gfellner, & Racine, 2007; Irwin, 1970; Le Bel et al., 2008; Maruna, 2001; Maruna & Roy, 2007; Opsal, 2011). In their work with ex-prisoners from the United States and the United Kingdom, for example, Maruna and Roy (2007) observed that individuals did not necessarily "knife off" or deny their pasts when desisting from crime. Indeed, they included their former identities in the formation of a new non-offender self as a sort of reconstruction. Healy (2010) argued that this process occurs because real converts adopted an integrated narrative capable of incorporating the positive elements that had emerged from their past lives. Similarly, Hundleby, Gfellner, and Racine (2007), in a study exploring desistance among aboriginal females in Canada, observed that women who desisted from crime explored their past identities and integrated them within their new selves to help direct their current and future behaviour.

This is consistent with Swann's self-verification theory (1990), according to which individuals are motivated to maintain stability or continuity in their conception of self to achieve a sense of coherence and guidance. This sense of unification between past, current, and future selves also prevents individuals from suffering the anxiety that arises when the capacity to preserve a coherent and stable narrative of self-identity is threatened (Aronson, 1968; Giddens, 1991). Indeed, Maruna (2001) observed that ex-offenders desisting from crime build a coherent narrative to explain and justify their change. This narrative or "redemption script" has a logical structure that connects past and present experiences, rendering the current self as a consequence of past behaviour.

Mixed identities: when a radical transformation is not possible

Despite the argument proposed by Paternoster and Bushway (2009), that offenders leave their past identity behind because it stops being a source of gratification, it seems that a criminal identity is not as easy to surrender as these scholars suggest. Indeed, a number of studies (Ebaugh, 1988; Glaser, 1969; Irwin, 1970) have shown that some desisters do not develop or reconstruct a new identity at all; rather, they develop a mixed identity that contains elements of both delinquent and conventional worlds.

Several decades ago, Irwin (1970:202) described what he termed "marginal" offenders – those who, despite having terminated their criminal activity, maintained some components of their criminal identities. As he noted:

> the criminal identity does not disappear but submerges to a latency state … There is no denial of, or regret for, the past. In fact, past criminal life is locked back upon with pleasure and excitement.

Similarly, Glaser (1969) described the "marginal successes" which accounted for individuals who, although they had reduced their frequency of offending or stopped altogether, maintained vestiges of their antisocial self. For example, he grouped together individuals who maintained contact with the criminal world but simultaneously had legitimate occupations as "crime-contacting ex-criminals".

Perhaps one plausible explanation for the development of these mixed identities among desisters can be found in role exit theory of Ebaugh (1988). In her study *Becoming an Ex*, she explored the process of role exit in various spheres of social life, such as among ex-prostitutes, ex-convicts, ex-nuns, and transsexuals.

She observed that role acquisition was different for individuals who were ex-members of a certain role than for those who were non-members, because, unlike the latter situation, the former involved a tension between past, present, and future. It seems that, in such cases, individuals do not replace or reconstruct their former identity but maintain parts of it in the development of their sense of self. As Ebaugh (1988: 4–5) pointed out:

> What characterises the ex is the fact that the new identity incorporates vestiges and residuals from the previous role. [...] Exes tend to maintain role residuals or some kind of hangover identity from previous roles as they move into new social roles. This role residual is part of self-identity and must be incorporated into current ideas and self.

During the transition from crime to conformity, some individuals may experience inter-role conflicts (Ebaugh, 1988; Merton, 1957) that confront them with two different sets of role expectations: the one from their antisocial past and the one from their ex-offender prosocial status. Gross, Ward and McEachern (1966) have stated that individuals who experience these conflicts can resolve them in three main ways. First, those who have moral orientations will fulfil society's prosocial expectations, regardless of the sanctions and rewards that may be involved. This may be the case for desisters who experience the radical transformations outlined previously. Second, those who do not have moral orientations will be oriented towards minimising the sanctions that are involved in the conflict. This may also apply to the third group (explained next), in which individuals consider both the sanction and the legitimacy of the rule and try to balance these two dimensions through their behaviour.

This may be one of the reasons why such desisters hang in the balance between a criminal and a prosocial identity. Indeed, research into cultural identities (Cross & Gore, 2005) has shown that individuals exposed to different role sets can develop separate self-representations, and that the identities arising from the new roles can coexist with the old ones. Another reason may be found in the difficulties that ex-offenders encounter when trying to perform conventional roles (Matsueda & Heimer, 2004; Uggen, Manza, & Behrens, 2004). Despite the fact that the acquisition of conventional roles provides desisters with a "skeleton script" that gives guidance and makes available a set of behaviours for conformity settings,[16] opportunities to take on a new role successfully are limited for them. Indeed, social structure has a direct effect on role transitions and, consequently, a person with a lack of human and social capital would have access to very few new conventional social roles to replace or enrich the old ones (Farrall, 2010; Matsueda & Heimer, 2004; Bottoms & Shapland, 2011).

The capacity of ex-offenders to adopt new roles is also affected by stigma and a lack of trust from society at large. Members of society expect offenders to be rehabilitated, but they are not necessarily open to, including them in their communities, jobs, and schools (Veysey, Martinez, & Christian, 2009). Thus, for individuals who are strongly engaged in criminal subcultures, an identity replacement or reconstruction is less likely to occur, and they will probably develop – at least at the beginning of the desistance process – a mixed identity instead.

Stop committing crimes without an internal transformation

As mentioned previously, several scholars have argued that internal transformations are a key component of desistance. Indeed, Maruna and Farrall (2004) have differentiated between primary desistance (any crime-free gap during the criminal career) and the more radical secondary desistance (the movement from non-offending behaviour to self-identification as a non-offender). It has been argued that the latter implies a real change defined by the assumption of a new identity of a "reformed person" and, therefore, deserves more attention from research (Farrall & Calverley, 2006:2).

This sentiment has not been exempt from controversy, though, with other scholars contending instead that crime abandonment may occur regardless of internal transformations, and that primary desistance also deserves attention. For example, Bottoms et al. (2004) have suggested that a radical internal transformation may not be a sine qua non condition for desisting from crime. Moreover, Sampson and Laub (2003:278) have argued that offenders desist "by default", without experiencing any identity shift or cognitive transformation. Indeed, according to their age-graded theory of social control, offenders change without realising it, as a result of the capitalisation of the investment that they have made in a conventional life.

Although research on desistance (especially qualitative research) has strongly highlighted secondary desistance, some studies have stressed the possibility that desisters stop committing crimes without experiencing internal transformations. For example, Burnett (2004), in the Oxford study on recidivism,[17] constructed a desisters' typology of "avoiders" whose abandonment of crime was motivated only by personal and practical reasons, such as preventing the risk of being caught and imprisoned. Furthermore, Presser (2008) coined the term weak evaluators to describe those whose decision to stop committing crimes was based only on the costs of crime, regardless of considerations about the meanings of criminal activities on an internal and societal level.

It seems that there may be groups of offenders who are motivated to abandon crime only by a self-interested cost-benefit analysis, discounting any shift towards a more prosocial identity. We may question, then, whether this type of change is characteristic of an early stage of the desistance process: do such individuals show little commitment to abandon crime, or are they in fact as devoted to abandonment as individuals who experience radical transformations? Although there is still a lack of evidence to answer these questions, Bottoms and Shapland (2011) have observed among their sample that individuals who were less committed to stopping crime gave more practical reasons to explain their decision to desist. By contrast, those individuals who had made a definite decision to stop committing crimes gave reasons that were more moral than practical.

If we analyse this type of offender in terms of moral reasoning theory of Kohlberg (1984), in contrast to the group which experiences radical transformations, this group may be at a pre-conventional level. Indeed, Thoronton and Reid (1982) have demonstrated that offenders at a pre-conventional moral reasoning stage stop committing crimes only to avoid sanctions. If they consider others in their decision to stop, it is only insofar as they believe that they can obtain some kind of benefit from them. According to Bottoms' (2002) mechanisms of legal compliance typology, these individuals would be situated within an instrumental/prudential level of compliance, in which decisions are taken based on rational calculations of the direct effects of incentives and sanctions.

Conformist offenders

We have seen above that, when desisting from crime, individuals can either experience radical transformations, partially change their identity, or desist only as a result of self-centred cost-benefit analysis that does not imply internal shifts. We may now address the question of whether internal shifts towards conformity necessarily imply crime abandonment at all. Even though evidence is scarce, there are some studies that deserve some attention with regards to this issue.

For example, Bottoms and Shapland (2011) observed in the Sheffield Pathways out of Crime Study that although desistance was associated with more conformist values, these values did not prevent all the individuals in the sample from continuing to offend. Indeed, although several individuals had conformity aspirations and did not see themselves as offenders, they nevertheless continued committing crimes during the follow-up period. Furthermore, some scholars (Healy, 2010; Presser, 2008) have described a group of desisters who claim that they have always followed a steady moral orientation along their lives, despite their criminal pasts. Studies that have described offender typologies have also highlighted a similar process (Gibbons, 1965; Irwin, 1970; Murray, 2009). For example, Murray (2009) described a group of juveniles which she called "quasi-resisters", who kept a non-offender identity and continued committing crimes. Similarly, Healy (2010) and, some years earlier, Gibbons (1965) and Irwin (1970), described groups of offenders who, although they committed crimes, defined themselves as "non-delinquents".

Though it is not clear how to explain the dynamics that follow this group of so-called conformist offenders, it can be argued that such a discrepancy between values and behaviour is not new in social sciences. Indeed, several decades ago, Merton (1957) described a process called "anticipatory socialisation", wherein individuals identify themselves with the values, norms, and orientations of social groups in which they aspire to participate, but of which they are not yet members. Since they have not reached a complete transition, their behaviours and lifestyle continue in much the same way and are, therefore, inconsistent with their values and norms. This may be the case among the groups of offenders identified previously, whose prosocial identities are not strong enough to discourage them from continuing to commit crimes. Indeed, it seems that, for this to occur, internal changes also need to be supported and recognised at a societal level, facilitating a "civic integration" (Uggen, Manza, & Behrens, 2004:290). As Maruna notes, "Not only must a person accept conventional society in order to go straight, but conventional society must accept that person as well" (2001:155).

Summary and final comments

The aim of this section was to discuss how desistance might be defined and operationalised and to identify gaps in scholarship that this study intends to address.

We have seen how some current definitions of desistance in the field of criminology have been limited by three main issues: first, the belief that desistance is an overnight change; second, the idea that desistance necessarily implies a clean cut with criminal activity; and third, the notion that a radical internal transformation towards conformity is a sine qua non condition for desisting from crime.

Through discussion of these issues, I have prepared the way to formulate a more nuanced operationalisation of desistance that includes both a behavioural dimension (changes in criminal behaviour) and an internal dimension (changes in identity and values). Accordingly, during the transition from crime to conformity, individuals can decrease their criminal behaviour by reducing the frequency of their crimes, by committing less serious offences, and by narrowing the repertoires of the offence types that they commit.

Furthermore, desisters may circumscribe their criminal activities to occasional deviant behaviours that do not threaten their conventional social attachments, and in which the risks of being caught or getting a long sentence are low. In addition, some desisters may displace their behaviour towards more utilitarian and less hedonistic activities. Beyond changes in criminal behaviours, desisters may also experience internal changes towards conformity, which can range from radical to partial transformations.

Even though we have seen that several studies have supported the existence of the changes outlined previously, they have mostly been conducted separately and have not been adequately integrated into explanations of desistance. A more holistic exploration would allow for a more nuanced understanding that the transition from crime to conformity is not straightforward, and that contradictions and partial changes are more common than rare when we study desisters' lives. Addressing these complexities may lead us to a deeper and more accurate understanding of desistance.

Late adolescence as a propitious time for change

Late adolescence can be understood as a window in which social opportunities, interpersonal relations, and internal attributes come together, thereby triggering the redirection and reorganisation of life (Burt & Masten, 2010). Research has shown that this accumulation of transitional events has stronger implications for the life course than changes that occur outside this period (Berntsen & Rubin, 2004).

This section discusses how and why late adolescence functions as a crucial life stage for desistance to occur: the first part examines the relationship between crime and age, while the second discusses the transformative potential of late adolescence in terms of the emergence of transition-linked turning points, new social interactions, and psychosocial capabilities.

The relationship between crime and age

The relation between crime and age – known as the age-crime curve – has been one of the most studied topics in criminology (Piquero, Farrington, & Blumstein, 2003). Indeed, nearly two centuries ago, Quetelet (1834) observed crime peaks in adolescence – a finding that has been validated by many studies since. The age-crime curve is of great relevance not only to academic research, but also regarding its implication for crime policies (Loeber & Farrington, 2012). Although the age-crime curve offers relevant information to examine several trends and patterns in criminal careers – onset, duration, frequency, prevalence, and desistance (Farrington, Loeber, & Jolliffe, 2008) – the focus here is on what the curve can tell us about the decline of crime.

In several longitudinal studies (Loeber et al., 2008; Moffitt et al., 2001; Piquero, Farrington, & Blumstein, 2007), age-crime curves show a sharp increase in arrests during the early adolescent period, followed by a peak of arrests in the early adult years, and a subsequent decrease in arrests over the remainder of the age range (Ezell & Cohen, 2005; Loeber & Farrington, 2012). Thus, crime typically starts to decline during late adolescence and early adulthood, independently of the individual's age at the onset of their criminal behaviour (Loeber & Farrington, 2012). According to Blumstein and Cohen (1987), an estimated 85% of offenders desist from crime by the age of 28, though Loeber and Farrington (2012) argue that between 40% and 60% of juvenile offenders desist by early adulthood.

The variation of crime and age can be explored using cross-sectional or longitudinal methods (Bottoms & Shapland, 2011; Farrington, 1986). In the first case, offending is observed in a specific period of time (e.g. one year);

in the second, offending is observed over time for a specific offender group (e.g. the same persons at different ages). One might assume that these different methodologies could lead to different conclusions, yet the shapes of cross-sectional and longitudinal curves are not radically different (Bottoms & Shapland, 2011). Nevertheless, it is important to note that, to explore trends in individuals' desistance from crime (and other trajectories), longitudinal age-crime curves are better suited to estimating the relation of crime and age, offering more independence of cohort, age, and period effects than cross-sectional curves (Loeber & Farrington, 2012).[18]

Longitudinal age-crime curves can be constructed using different units of measurement, such as the prevalence or participation rate of the offender, or the frequency of offences; in addition, different types of data sets may be consulted, such as self-reported crime and official criminal records. Offender-based age-crime curves show how many individuals from a sample or group participate in crime at each age-point (each individual counts as one data-point). On the other hand, offence-based age-crime curves show the total amount of offences committed by the sample members at each age-point. This method has its detractors, however, with some researchers arguing that only the offences of those sampled individuals who are active during the observation period (i.e. not imprisoned) may be considered.

It seems that although early studies suggested that crime frequency did not vary with age in the same way as prevalence did (Farrington, 1986), recent studies have shown that both measures closely tracked each other (Loeber & Farrington, 2012). Piquero, Farrington, and Blumstein (2007), using data from the Cambridge Study in Delinquent Development, examined the variance in prevalence and frequency of offending over age. They observed that the peak age of offending was 17, declining in prevalence thereafter until the age of 23 (at which point it remained relatively stable until the age of 30). When examining the variation of the frequency of crime over age in the whole sample, a very similar pattern was observed (though it must be noted that, when considering only the frequency of those who were active offenders, the peak occurred at the age of 16). There is still a lack of information regarding the correlation of prevalence and frequency trends (Farrington, Loeber, & Jolliffe, 2008; Loeber & Farrington, 2012), and it has been argued that although they seem to not differ significantly, frequency trends show less consistency between different studies and are more sensitive to methodological issues (Piquero, Hawkins, & Kazemian, 2012).

Although most published age-crime curves have been constructed based on official criminal records (e.g. police contacts, arrests, convictions), they may also, as mentioned previously, be constructed using self-reported crime. It seems that, when comparing age-crime curves constructed with these different types of data, the peak ages of crime differ. In fact, although most studies indicate that crime peaks around the ages of 15–19 before starting to decline, the peak tends to occur earlier when using self-report measures (Moffitt et al., 2001; Piquero, 2011; Piquero, Hawkins, & Kazemian, 2012). This should not be surprising and may simply reflect the fact that crime committed at younger ages is less likely to be detected by the police (Loeber & Farrington, 2012) – or, perhaps, such offences may not end in arrests and convictions and thus are not represented in official records.

Even though the use of official and self-reported criminal records each has their advantages and disadvantages, both are biased methods (Farrington, 1986; Loeber et al., 2015). On the one hand, official records may have problems of reliability, since the variation in arrests and convictions may not be due to changes in the level of transgression at each age, but rather to variations in prosecution and surveillance strategies, among other factors (Bryman, 2004). On the other hand, although self-reports may be richer sources of information from which to detect patterns of criminal behaviour, they are biased by the willingness of individuals to admit their offences at different ages (Farrington, 1986).

Another relevant issue that must be considered when interpreting age-crime curves is the fact that they can vary according to the type of crime and population. When analysing the curve per type of crime, it can be observed that violent crimes tend to peak later than non-violent crimes and minor offences (Cline, 1980; Farrington, 1986; Farrington, Loeber, & Jolliffe, 2008; Piquero, Hawkins, & Kazemian, 2012).

Soothill, Francis, and Fliglstone (2002) analysed data from the Offender Index for England and Wales for a cohort of individuals born in 1953 and 1958, and, using latent class analysis (LCA),[19] they identified different clusters of offences among the cohort and observed sharp differences in the age-crime curve among those clusters. For example, in the case of males, while non-violent property crime and shoplifting peaked between the ages of 10 and 15 and declined thereafter, aggressive property offending and car crime peaked between the ages of 16 and 20 and showed a shallower decline thereafter.

Furthermore, desistance seems to occur later in life not only for violent crimes, but also for drug-related offences (Doherty & Bersani, 2018). Sampson and Laub (2003), with data from the study of Glueck and Glueck (1943), compared mean ages of desistance between violent, property, and drug/alcohol offences. While the mean age of desistance for property crimes was 26, it was 31 for violent crimes and 37 for drug/alcohol offences. This finding was reinforced by Le Blanc and Fréchette (1989), who found that the age of drug trafficking termination was higher than the age of desistance for minor offences.

Moreover, it seems that the curve peaks earlier for females than males, and the peak tends to be higher among males (Elliott, 1994; Fagan & Western, 2005; Graham & Bowling, 1995; Moffitt et al., 2001; Piquero, Hawkins, & Kazemian, 2012). Indeed, Graham and Bowling (1995), using a national British sample of juveniles aged 14–25, observed that female offending peaked at the age of 16 – five years younger than males, who peaked at the age of 21. Furthermore, Elliot

(1994), with data from the National Youth Survey,[20] observed that the decline of the curve was steeper for females, and that the gender differential became greater with time. Indeed, while at the age of 12 the male/female ratio was 2, it was 4 by the age of 21. Farrington (1986) observed similar gender differences, with a peak male/female ratio ranging from 7.5 to 9.5 between the ages of 16 and 22 for English offenders.

Gender differences have also been observed in the length of the criminal career. Prime et al. (2001), using a cohort of British males born between 1953 and 1978, observed that while the average criminal career length for males was 6.2 years, it was only 1.8 years for females. There is further evidence of female offenders desisting earlier than men (Flood-Page et al., 2000; Giordano et al., 2002; McIvor, Murray, & Jamieson, 2004), as well as having much lower reoffending rates (Kruttschnitt et al., 2002; Ministry of Justice, 2011).

Finally, although the relation between social disadvantage and crime has been extensively studied in criminology (Horney, Tolan, & Weisburd, 2012), there is a lack of information about the way in which it may affect the slope of the age-crime curve. Fabio et al. (2011), with data from the Pittsburgh Youth Study, compared age-crime curves of individuals from neighbourhoods with different levels of disadvantage. They observed that individuals from more disadvantaged environments reached higher peaks of violent behaviour, with desistance occurring at older ages among this group.

If we consider the above, and the fact that age-crime curve varies according to the type of crime and population, we can plainly see that its trends need to be interpreted with caution. Nevertheless, the study of the relationship between crime and age highlights relevant issues for the understanding of desistance from crime. Indeed, although desistance occurs across the whole age-crime curve, it is concentrated in the downward slope of the curve (Loeber & Farrington, 2012), which matches with late adolescence and young adult life periods. Thus, we can argue that individuals may experience some changes that trigger crime decline during these periods. These triggers are discussed next.

The transformative potential of late adolescence

Late adolescence is a critical stage for the expression of resilience – particularly in the case of adolescent delinquents, who are normally immersed in contexts of high risks and adversities. Resilience arises as a result of adaptive resources, such as future orientation and autonomy, and is a strong precursor of individual change (Burt & Masten, 2010).

Moreover, individuals are exposed in late adolescence to a higher variance of possibility for life decisions than in other life periods. When leaving home (or another social environment), individuals have the opportunity to explore new and perhaps better options, before engaging with the commitments of adult life. Yet this wide range of choices can also sometimes generate anxiety and uncertainty, since – as noted by Arnett (2004:3) – individuals at this stage are open to new freedoms and new fears.

Although it is possible to find many explanations of the peaking of the age-crime curve (see Agnew, 2003), there is less understanding of why it decreases following this peak. The concentration of desistance research on adulthood (though see Barry, 2006; Bottoms & Shapland, 2011; Mulvey et al., 2010) has certainly given rise to a clear account of the factors that maintain desistance in the long term, but it fails to give an adequate understanding of those variables that trigger crime abandonment in the first place – which we must assume are not linked simply by coincidence. Indeed, contrary to Gottfredson and Hirshi (1983), who have argued that the relation between crime and age is invariant, it is argued here that at least a significant proportion of the changes in criminal activity during this period can be related to what I will term "developmental capital".

This builds upon Hagan's (1998) idea of development as capitalisation, since it provides a means to account for the accumulation (or "stock") of opportunities that occur in the transition from adolescence to adulthood – more frequently than in other life periods – and may have a transformative potential. These opportunities can be grouped into three main categories: (1) transition-linked turning points and factors triggering desistance, (2) new social interactions, and (3) psychosocial capabilities.

Such a framework is consistent with explanations of desistance proposed by Rocque (2015) and Prior et al. (2011), who argue that different domains of maturation – such as changes in social roles, psychosocial, identity, civic, and cognitive domains – are additive in their effects on desistance. Indeed, an empirical study conducted by Rocque, Posick, and White (2015), with data from the Rutgers Health and Human Development Project,[21] showed that greater maturation through emerging adulthood was a factor influencing desistance.

Transition-linked turning points and factors triggering desistance

Transition-linked turning points (see Graber, Brooks-Gunn, & Galen, 1998:273) are simple life events that occur in late adolescence or early adulthood periods – more frequently than in other life periods – and may have a transformative potential. Although we may think that the achievements of transition events such as work and marriage are what define individuals as adults, research has shown that feelings of "being an adult" are based on more gradual and internal issues. Indeed, the top criteria for defining adulthood are accepting responsibilities, making independent decisions and becoming financially independent (Arnett, 2004, 2010; Facio & Micocci, 2003). This is consistent with "the respectability package" noted by Giordano et al. (2002:1013), who argue that what matters in crime reduction is the combination of turning points and the impact that the interdependence of role transitions has on individuals' lives.

Rocque (2017:181), based on Sampson and Laub's (1993) age-graded theory of informal social control,[22] labels this domain "Adult Social Role Maturation". He argues that informal social institutions, such as marriage and employment, are not causal mechanisms related to desistance, but in fact part of the process of becoming an adult. According to him, four factors might be part of this domain: adult relationships (i.e. marriage and children), markers of independence, finishing school, and employment.

Evidence regarding the association of turning points and different factors with desistance from crime comes primarily from studies conducted with young adult and adult male samples, and there is unfortunately little research with a specific focus on adolescent offenders (Nguyen & Loughran, 2018). Therefore, the evidence regarding these factors is not limited to adolescence; as a result, it must be interpreted with caution, accounting for the fact that some factors may either be less relevant or have a different impact on desistance when affecting a different life stage. As follows, I present a discussion of the main factors and turning points associated with desistance divided according to three main groups of explanations: social control theories, routine activity theories, and psychosocial factors.

Social control factors

Drawing upon social control theories (Hirshi, 1969), Sampson and Laub (1993) developed the age-graded theory of informal social control, which examines the effect that interactions with institutions of informal social control have on crime and desistance. According to these scholars, desistance occurs as a result of turning points (i.e. changes in the life course) prompted by life events that enhance social bonds. Using life story narratives from men who both desisted from and persisted in crime, they observed that four main turning points had a consistent impact on the desistance process: marriage, military service, correctional school, and neighbourhood change.

These turning points are well attested in the literature on desistance, with studies confirming the impact of marriage (Beaver et al., 2008; Theobald & Farrington, 2009) and military service (Bouffard & Laub, 2004; Sampson & Laub, 2003). Yet several other social control factors are also identified as being involved in crime abandonment, such as having a stable job (Farrall, 2002; Tripodi, Kim, & Bender, 2010; Wright & Cullen, 2004), the experience of parenthood (Kreager et al., 2010; Sampson & Laub, 1993, 2003), and spirituality (Giordano et al., 2008; Schroeder et al., 2009). Factors that are relevant for the present research are discussed next.

Employment not only provides a source of income but also can be a starting point for ex-offenders to rebuild both self-esteem and identity, engendering a sense of belonging within social institutions and community (Visher, Winterfield, & Coggeshall, 2005). It is arguably not simply having a job that explains crime reduction, however, but the specific characteristics of the employment.

According to Sampson and Laub (2003), job stability both creates a sense of commitment and promotes social bonds in the workplace, thereby encouraging desistance through increasing social controls. They argue that employers operate as social control agents by simultaneously restricting employees' behaviour, and investing, and believing in their capacities – thus creating reciprocal social ties. Similarly, Apel and Horney (2017) have also highlighted the role of commitment, arguing that the subjective experience of work is pivotal in reducing reoffending. Furthermore, Wright and Cullen (2004) suggested that a full-time job provides structure for individuals and limits their exposure to risk factors and delinquent peers. In a study using longitudinal data from a national sample in the United States, they found that offenders who established relations with prosocial co-workers consequently diminished their peer contact and restored social networks. Nevertheless, a more recent study conducted by Abeling-Judge (2020) observed that those prosocial networks did not influence crime reduction through employment.

The quality of a job has also been highlighted as playing a relevant role in desistance (Nguyen, Kamada, & Ramakers, 2020; Shover, 1996; Staff et al., 2010; Uggen, 1999). In a study with persistent thieves in the United States, Shover (1996) argued that the opportunity for employees to exercise intelligence and creativity in a job is critical to its efficacy as a factor of desistance.[23] Similarly, Uggen and Staff (2001), in their analysis of the National Supported Work Demonstration Project,[24] found that offenders who obtained high-quality jobs were less likely to commit crimes than their counterparts working in poor-quality jobs. Similarly, Nguyen, Kamada, and Ramakers (2020) highlighted the relevance of job quality, arguing that the instability and general autonomy associated with informal employment may provide opportunities to engage in deviant behaviour.

Some research has shown, however, that the age of the offender can affect the efficacy of employment as a factor of desistance – regardless of quality. For example, Uggen (2000) found that work provided a turning point in criminal careers only in offenders over the age of 26. Similarly, Graham and Bowling (1995), in a study using self-reported offending among 14–25 years old in England and Wales, found that young males' employment status bore no relation to desistance.

Marriage has also been highlighted as an important factor in the desistance process (Blokland & Nieuwbeerta, 2005; Capaldi, Kim, & Owen, 2008; Farrington & West, 1995). Since the prevalence of marriage has decreased in recent years, and young adults are often marrying at later ages (Bramlett & Mosher, 2002; Kennedy & Bumpass, 2008), research has investigated the effects of intimate relations and cohabitation on crime as well. In doing so, it has revealed that it is not marriage per se that has an effect on desistance: primarily, it is the intimate attachment developed with a partner that triggers the abandonment of crime (Bersani, Laub, & Nieuwbeerta, 2009; Farrington & West, 1995; Horney et al., 1995; Sampson & Laub, 1993).

Despite several studies showing the impact of marriage on desistance, there is a lack of knowledge regarding the mechanisms involved in this process (Bersani, Laub, & Nieuwbeerta, 2009). According to Sampson, Laub, and Wimer (2006), marriage fosters desistance because it creates social ties and responsibilities such as mutual obligations and support. In addition, marriage (as well as parenting) alters daily routines because more time is spent on family-based activities. It has also been argued that marriage might change individuals' perceptions of themselves and promote more conventional orientations (Giordano, Cernkovich, & Rudolph, 2002; Johnson & Giordano, 2020; Yamaguchi & Kandel, 1985). Similarly to the abovementioned evidence on the role of employers, partners can also operate as social control agents by exercising supervision, restricting risky activities, and dissolving unhealthy peer relationships. Indeed, Warr (1998) found that marriage precipitated a decrease in the exposure to delinquent peers, and indeed a decline in the time spent with friends more generally.

Some scholars have argued that the effects of marriage on desistance might be rather spurious, since "those who are more likely to benefit from marriage tend to be those who get married" (Theobald & Farrington, 2010:136). Nevertheless, several studies that have been designed to avoid selection bias (i.e. within individual analysis) have confirmed the connection (Siennick & Osgood, 2008). For example, Sampson, Laub, and Wimer (2006) found that the likelihood of their individuals in their sample committing a crime dropped by 35% when they were married as compared to when they were not. Similarly, King, Massoglia, and Macmillan (2007), with data from the National Youth Survey, found that marriage has an effect on crime reduction even when controlling for likelihood to marry. Finally, Theobald and Farrington (2009), using data from 162 convicted males from the Cambridge Study in Delinquent Development, found that marriages lasting more than five years were followed by a decrease in crime.

Research looking at **cohabitation** and other forms of **intimate relationships**, however, has generated conflicting results (Horney, Tolan, & Weisburd, 2012; Wyse, Harding, & Moreonff, 2014). While some studies have concluded that cohabitation is associated with desistance (Gottlieb & Sugie, 2018; Sampson et al., 2006; Savolainen, 2009), others have reported no effects on crime (Horney et al., 1995; Simons & Barr, 2014; Yamaguchi & Kandel, 1985). Simons and Barr (2014), using longitudinal data from a sample of 600 African American young adults, found that – again – quality is an important factor: while a romantic relationship per se had no effect on desistance, high-quality relationships were strongly associated with desistance from crime.

Interestingly, the exploration of associations between intimate relationships and crime undertaken by Forrest (2014) distinguished between episodes of cohabitation and marriage. He found that, while cohabitation was associated with reductions in crime rates but not with termination, marriage was consistently associated both with large reductions in crime rates and with crime abandonment. Capaldi et al. (2008) and later Gottlieb and Sugie (2018) looked at the effect of relationship stability on crime and found that continuity in romantic relationships was associated with desistance among male and women offenders.

Drawing on the fact that individuals are increasingly likely to become involved in sporadic romantic relationships during the transition from adolescence to late adolescence (Meier & Allen, 2009), Larson, Sweeten, and Piquero (2016) explored the connection between relationship dissolution and crime. Using data from the Pathways to Desistance Study, they confirmed the effect of break-ups on crime and observed that the impact was stronger for relationships that involved cohabitation.

Gender differences have also been explored, with research showing differences between men and women: while among men, romantic partnerships triggered desistance regardless of quality, for women it was only warm and supportive partners that prompted crime abandonment (but see Lee et al., 2020), bringing about cognitive changes in their views of conventional norms (Barr & Simons, 2015; Gottlieb & Sugie, 2018; Simons & Barr, 2014).

Finally, research on partners' attitudes towards deviance and its effects on desistance has also shown mixed results. While Simons et al. (2002), Herrera, Wiersman, and Cleveland (2010), and Lee et al. (2020) found that having an antisocial partner increased criminal activities, Theobald and Farrington (2010) found that the effects of marriage on crime were not affected by the partner's deviance.

Parenthood has been highlighted as a factor triggering desistance, since it restructures daily routines, increases the costs of crime, gives a sense of optimism and future orientation, and fosters the development of a prosocial identity through new role obligations (Giordano et al., 2011; Moloney et al., 2009; Sampson & Laub, 2003). Nevertheless, empirical research has not proved consistent results (Horney, Tolan, & Weisburd, 2012; Schinkel, 2019; Theobald, Farrington, & Piquero, 2015).

While some studies have identified no effect of parenthood on desistance – sometimes even having positive effects on crime (Blokland & Nieuwbeerta, 2005; Farrington & West, 1995; Sampson & Laub, 2003; Massoglia & Uggen, 2007) – others have found that parenthood is associated with crime abandonment (Maloney et al., 2009; Savolainen, 2009; Skardhamar & Lyngstad, 2009).

It seems that the effect of parenthood depends on many factors, such as the number of children, the quality of parental relationships, the timing of the transition, residence with a child and marital, and socio-economic status (Abell, 2018; Boonstoppel, 2019; Theobland, Farrington, & Piquero, 2015). Zoutewelle-Terovan et al. (2014), with data from a longitudinal study conducted in the Netherlands over 21 years, observed that parenthood reduced offending, especially when having the first child. Research has also shown that the quality of the parent's relationship with their child is relevant to the triggering of desistance. Ganem and Agnew (2007) observed that parents who had high-quality filial relationships were significantly less likely to persist with crime.

Perhaps related to this, these scholars also observed that having multiple children increased the likelihood of offending.

Giordanno et al. (2011) published evidence that the effect of parenthood on desistance was mediated by socio-economic status; indeed, highly disadvantaged young men were less likely to show lower levels of criminal behaviour after becoming a parent than more advantaged young people. Maloney et al. (2009), using interview data from 91 gang members in San Francisco, observed that fatherhood triggered relevant internal transformations towards desistance. Nevertheless, those changes were not sufficient to trigger full crime abandonment unless they were accompanied by changes in the amount of time spent on the streets and the ability to support the household through legal income. Finally, Savolainen (2009) observed that parenthood promoted desistance only among married couples.

Routine and lifestyle factors

Bottoms and Shapland (2014:7) have argued that "desistance is the process of learning to live a non-criminal life when one has been leading a largely criminal life". This means that, when desisting from crime, individuals have to change their routine, lifestyles, friends and generally resist the several temptations that they will encounter during their attempts to leave crime behind. To do so, according to Bottoms and Shapland (2011), offenders adopt tactics of "diachronic self-control" through which they purposely engage or avoid certain situations that might lead them to failure in their attempts to change. Indeed, actively staying away from former friends and risky places has been noted as a viable strategy that allows offenders to avoid the temptations associated with an antisocial lifestyle. It has been argued that women in particular end up experiencing periods of strong social isolation at the beginning of the desistance process (Giordano et al., 2003; McIvor, 2016; Nugent & Schinkel, 2016; Wright et al., 2013).

Evidence has shown that **unstructured socialising** (i.e. "hanging around") with peers in the absence of authority figures is a strong predictor of delinquency among young people (Anderson & Hughes, 2009; Hay & Forrest, 2008; Maimon & Browning, 2010; Miller, 2012). According to Osgood and Anderson (2004:520), "the presence of peers will make deviant acts easier and more rewarding, the absence of authority figures will reduce the potential for social control responses, and the lack of structure will leave time available for deviance". Therefore, role transitions that reduce the above (i.e. employment, parenthood, marriage) might promote desistance from crime (Laub, Sampson, & Sweeten, 2006; Siennick & Osgood, 2008).

Wikström (2004), in his Situational Action Theory, stresses the importance of the interaction between person and environment; he argues that people's exposures to situations, understood as the particular perception of action alternatives, are what triggers crime. Wikström, Mann, and Hardie (2018), with data from the Peterborough Adolescent and Young Adult Development Study (PADS+),[25] observed that engaging in unsupervised and unstructured activities with peers is strongly associated with crime. Also, they found that persons with higher criminal propensity are more vulnerable to unstructured socialising.

Nevertheless, research on desistance has shown that it is not just exposure to such settings that matters; the meanings that individuals impute are also relevant in the process of leaving crime behind (Hunt & Farrall, 2015). Routines, the places a person visit and the people with whom they associate all in some ways communicate the sort of person that they are (Goffman, 1963; Meisenhelder, 1977). In that sense, desisters who still spend time socialising in unstructured environments (e.g. bars) with the friends they had whilst offending will most probably communicate that they are still offending – regardless of how far along they are in the desistance process. Hunt and Farrall (2015), through a longitudinal study of 43 current and former drug users, explored the differences in the routines of continued offenders versus desisters. They observed that although offenders wanting to desist made efforts to avoid high-risk environments, these efforts were not merely physical – they also involved a cognitive process that helped them to reconstruct the emotional meanings of the spaces they inhabited.

During adolescence and late adolescence, one of the main factors that might obstruct lifestyle changes is the affiliation to **deviant peers** (Farrington, 1986; Farrington & Welsh, 2007; Monahan, Cauffman, & Steinberg, 2009; Steinberg & Monahan, 2007; Thornberry 1987; Warr, 2002). Developmental theories have suggested that these affiliations, and the susceptibility to peer influence, are important contributors to adolescent delinquency (Brown, 2004; Gardner & Steinberg, 2005; Moffitt, 1993; Thornberry & Krohn, 1997; Warr, 2002). However, less is known about the role played by association with deviant peers in the desistance process (but see Copp et al., 2019 and Turanovic, 2019). What is clear is that individuals' ability to resist peer influence increases significantly during late adolescence (Berndt, 1979; Erickson, Crosnoe, & Dornbusch, 2000; Farrington & Welsh 2007; Monahan, Steinberg, & Cauffman, 2009; Steinberg & Monahan, 2007; Steinberg & Silverberg, 1986; Warr, 2002), suggesting that the process of desistance from crime may be related to normative changes in peer relations that occur as individuals grow up.

Monahan, Steinberg, and Cauffman (2009), using longitudinal data from 1,354 antisocial juveniles in the United States, found that individuals from their sample started to become resistant to the influences of peers after the age of 20, and the impact of those peers on antisocial behaviour disappeared. Giordanno, Cernkovich, and Holland (2003) explored the role of peer associations using data from 180 offenders who were interviewed twice, in 1982 and 1995. Interestingly, they observed that perceived peer pressure declined significantly across the two waves of data, and that – over time – interviewees showed efforts to develop more conventional social ties. Although they did not specify whether these changes were causally related to desistance, they did discover that the changes were associated with other processes as well. Among them were gaining opportunities to perform conventional activities or receiving social support – both of which can give individuals the potential to access other mechanisms which may trigger desistance from crime in the long term. The above highlights a more agentic view of desistance, in which exogenous factors might operate due to changes in the individuals' choices or interests. This is consistent with Bottoms and Shapland (2014), who have argued that changes in individuals' social associations are always interconnected with their intentions to change.

Mac Donald and Shildrick (2007: 20) with data from the Teesside Studies of Youth Transitions and Social Exclusion,[26] observed that the most commonly cited factor among desisting youths was separation from peer groups. Indeed, the difficulty of abandoning the "street corner society" was the main obstacle to desistance, since it provided leisure, identity reassurance, a sense of belonging, and – for those who were addicts – it also provided access to drugs. By contrast, engagement with prosocial peers who could be trusted emerged as a key aspect of desistance from crime.

Similarly, Haynie et al. (2014) found that individuals have higher rates of criminal persistence if they are within networks that support and facilitate crime. Nevertheless, offenders are not only participants in social networks comprised of delinquent peers. Another study conducted by Haynie in 2002 showed that approximately half of the young offenders from his sample had a mixed association pattern: they were involved in social networks that included delinquent as well as non-delinquent peers. This latter mixed association group was made up of individuals who were significantly less involved in crime than those who were involved mostly with delinquent companions. Therefore, "it is not the absolute level of delinquency that is occurring in networks that is crucial, but rather the homogeneity of peer influences in the network" (Haynie, 2002:129).

Drug misuse has also been highlighted as a strong obstacle against desistance from crime (Hunt & Farrall, 2015; Mac Donald & Shildrick, 2007; Schroeder, Giordano, & Cernkovich, 2007; Stouthamer-Loeber et al., 2004). However, beyond the direct links between drug use and criminality (such as being caught using drugs, stealing to get money to buy drugs, or committing crimes under the influence of drugs), drug use also hinders the development of key factors promoting desistance (Schroeder, Giordano, & Cernkovich, 2007). Indeed, drug use negatively affects work stability (Mijares, 1997) and social bonds, since it is incompatible with the acquisition of conventional roles needed to desist from crime (Jessor, Donovan, & Costa, 1991; Yamaguchi & Kandel, 1985).

Schroeder, Giordano, and Cernkovich (2007), using three waves of data from the Ohio Life-Course Study (OLS),[27] observed not only that drug use had a sustained effect on life-course patterns of criminal offending, but also that it was associated with peer group deviance and romantic partner criminality (which in turn were significantly associated with persistence in crime). Coleman and Vander Laenen (2017), with data from the DESDRUG study,[28] explored the interconnectedness of desistance and recovery from drug use. Interestingly, most interviewees argued that their desistance process was subordinated to their recovery process, with the latter involving a deliberate intention to change and the former being an unconscious process that automatically derived from recovery.

Psychosocial factors

As discussed in the previous section, several scholars have pointed to the role that **identity shifts** have in the desistance process, but there is little agreement on the scope of these changes. While some scholars argue that shifts towards desistance will not take place until a new, conventional (i.e. non-offending) identity replaces the former one (Giordano et al., 2002; Harris, 2009; Paternoster & Bushway, 2009; Vaughan, 2007), others suggest that individuals do not necessarily deny their pasts, but include their former identities in the formation of a new non-offender self as a sort of reconstruction (Aresti, Eatough, & Brooks-Gordon, 2010; Gadd & Farrall, 2004; Glaser, 1969; Hundleby, Gfellner, & Racine, 2007; Irwin, 1970; Le Bel et al., 2008; Maruna, 2001; Maruna & Roy, 2007; Opsal, 2011).

As mentioned before, Sampson and Laub (2003:278) have argued that offenders desist "by default", without experiencing any identity shift or cognitive transformation. According to their age-graded theory of social control, offenders change as a result of the capitalisation of the investment that they have made in a conventional life – almost without realising it. Indeed, other studies have also highlighted the possibility that desisters stop committing crimes without experiencing internal transformations and are motivated only by instrumental and practical reasons such as lowering the risk of being caught (Burnett, 2004; Presser, 2008). Moreover, some research has identified a group of offenders who, although they have committed crimes, nevertheless define themselves as non-delinquents and claim that they have followed a steady moral orientation throughout their lives (Gibbons, 1965; Heally, 2010; Irwin, 1970; Murray, 2009; Presser, 2008).

The temporal order in which identity shifts occur along the process of desistance has also been a controversial issue. While Bushway and Paternoster (2013) place identity changes first in the sequence of transformations, Bottoms and Shapland (2014) have argued that, during the first stages of the desistance process, only a gradual change in identity occurs. Moreover, Giordanno (2016:15) has argued that although she had placed identity shifts at the end of the process in her initial model of desistance, further revisions of her theory have led her to the conclusion that "the idea of a series of steps is itself not all that helpful or accurate as a description of what occurs". Nevertheless, a study conducted by Lebel et al. (2008), with data from the Oxford Recidivism Study, produced some insights on the above. The analysis showed that the process of crime abandonment followed a "subjective-social model" in which subjective states measured before release had both a direct effect on recidivism and indirect effects on social circumstances experienced after release from prison.

Most evidence regarding the influence of identity shifts on desistance comes from qualitative studies which have assessed identity based on self-accounts (but see Codd 2020). Maruna (2001) observed that ex-offenders desisting from crime build a "redemption script" which has a logical structure that connects past and present experiences, presenting the current "good self" as a consequence of past behaviour. Similarly, Hundleby, Gfellner, and Racine (2007), in a study exploring desistance among aboriginal females in Canada, observed that women who desisted from crime explored their past identities and integrated them with their new selves to get directions for their current and future behaviour. Another study conducted in Northern Ireland by Byrne and Trew (2008) showed that identity was as much an element of pathways away from crime as it was of pathways into it.

More recently, the role of identity in the desistance process has been explored through quantitative methods. Na, Paternoster, and Bachman (2015) conducted an initial attempt to test the Identity Theory of Desistance (ITD), developed by Bushway and Paternoster (2012, 2013). The ITD's primary argument is that a change in identity is the major factor initiating the desistance process, unlocking the potential for turning points to operate effectively. According to Bushway and Paternoster (2012, 2013), antisocial identities only prevail until offenders start linking their negative outcomes and failures to their delinquent lifestyle. At this moment, a "feared self" of the kind of person one may turn out to be emerges, serving as an initial provocation that motivates the development of a conventional "possible self". The study, using longitudinal data from the Delaware correctional system, showed that one's identity and agentic moves (such as seeking help for drug and alcohol abuse) were related to the changes in offending outcomes over time, thereby promoting desistance.

Another study conducted by Paternoster et al. (2016), using the same data set, also showed that those offenders who changed their self-reported identity were more likely to desist from crime. However, it must be noted that both studies were limited by the absence of an appropriate measure of identity change. They captured the process of identity change by the self-reported status of "considering themselves as an addict", and agentic moves towards desistance were assessed through the seeking of help for substance use after release. Thus, although these studies reported interesting insights, their results cannot be considered as stemming from an empirical test of the role of identity changes in the desistance process. It also cannot, therefore, be extrapolated to countries where drug use is not criminalised.

As mentioned earlier, cognitive improvements in perspective-taking and interpersonal negotiation skills contribute to the development of other-oriented social interactions in late adolescence (Eisenberg et al., 2005). By this point, individuals are expected not only to be responsible for themselves and their actions, but also for others. Arnett (2004) has noted that learning **consideration for others** has been one of the key markers of adulthood in several studies. It opens the way to new forms of social demands, such as reciprocity and mutual care, which may be key in giving individuals the impetus to stop offending. Indeed, the belief that one can provide support and help is perhaps one of the deepest demonstrations of social recognition, since it implies the acknowledgement of one's capacity to perform according to the demands and standards of significant others. This is actually what occurs when "tertiary desistance" takes place – a term developed by McNeill (2016) to describe a crucial stage of desistance process in which others recognise that one has changed, and a sense of belonging therefore emerges. As Vaughan (2006:391) pointed out, "Emotional empathy and responsive-ness may help initiate a process of self-appraisal from which a different kind of person emerges".

Several studies on desistance have produced evidence supporting the above. Weaver and McNeill (2015), in a study exploring the interrelated narratives of the life stories of a friendship group of men in their 40s who offended together in their youth, observed that social relations that were characterised by solidarity and subsidiarity (i.e. the interchange of resources to support and help each other) strongly influenced desistance. Bottoms and Shapland (2014), with data from the Sheffield Desistance Study, observed that respondents started to develop greater empathy at a relatively advanced stage of the desistance process, evidenced through an understanding of the hurt felt by victims. McCuish, Lussier, and Rocque (2020), with data from the Pathways to Desistance Study, observed that measures of consideration for others were related to lower levels of offending and within-individual desistance, giving support to the integrated maturation theory of desistance developed by Rocque (2015).

Barry (2012:124) has demonstrated that one of the key issues in the desistance process is what she calls "capital expenditure". This term refers to a process in which individuals can give their own capital to others, by recognising others' needs and developing their capacity to address those needs. Maruna (2001) observed among his male sample in the Liverpool Study the so-called wounded healers: offenders who actively construct a conforming identity that supports desistance through helping other offenders to achieve change.

Similarly, Martinez (2009) and Boonstoppe (2019) also noted that support exchanges might trigger desistance by providing former offenders with an alternative identity, a sense of purpose and a role in life. He observed that the expectations of significant others accord individuals the status of a person who has "something to give". This is perhaps the reason for desisters to engage in what Maruna (2001, 2004) called "generativity" – a process drawn from Erickson's (1968) theory of development, which outlines the uniquely adult desire to "give something back" to subsequent generations.

As it is discussed in the next section, evidence suggests that the acquisition of **prosocial values** and the ability to exercise moral judgements are one of the key developmental tasks of late adolescence (Heaven, 2001). Moreover, research in different social contexts has highlighted that one of the markers of the social maturity which characterises the transition to early adulthood is the improvement of moral reasoning and prosocial orientation (Arnett, 2004; Eisenberg et al., 2005; Mayseless & Scharf, 2003).

Situational Action Theory also stresses the role of moral orientation towards crime. It is propounded by Wikström (2004), who understands crime as moral actions "which are guided by value-based rules of conduct specifying what is the right or wrong thing to do (or not do) in response to particular motivations in particular circumstances" (Wikström, Mann, & Hardie, 2018:12). Research to test his theory has shown that individuals with strong morals and the ability to exercise self-control afford themselves fewer opportunities to commit crime (Wikström, Mann, & Hardie, 2018).

Although not widely explored, desistance studies with young adult and adult samples have supported the contention that improvements in moral orientations might be associated with desistance from crime. King (2013:144) observed in research conducted with probationers in the United Kingdom that, when desisting from crime, individuals developed "moral agency" – a process through which they "question their attitudes, values and beliefs … and begin to reinterpret past actions as incongruent with the values that they wanted to live by in the future". Interestingly, he found that reorientations in moral agency were prompted by the experience of probation supervision. Similarly, Fowers (2006) observed that offenders' rehabilitation entails a "moral dialogue" between the offender and the service provider.

Bottoms and Shapland (2011) have claimed that desistance involves a process of "active maturation" during which individuals start thinking about their goals and ethical norms through reflection on what sort of person they "should" be. This kind of ethical reflection (described in Virtue Ethics Theory) stresses that individuals approach moral dilemmas not simply by considering the moral rule itself, but by their own dispositions and beliefs as embedded within a certain context. With data from the Sheffield Study on Desistance, they observed that, when individuals progress in their attempts to desist from crime, their moral orientations and understandings deepen. This was evident in – among other things – a more empathetic discursive tone, and an increase in expressions of shame and regret (Bottoms & Shapland, 2014). Although individuals' desires might contradict prosocial values at the beginning of the desistance process, they start to align with time, creating habits that individuals start to enjoy. According to Bottoms and Shapland, the above could be interpreted as a process of "acquiring virtue" that might be crucial to the development of desistance in the long term.

Several studies have pointed out that **agency** plays a crucial role in desistance (Albertson et al., 2020; Bottoms et al., 2004; Carlsson, 2016; Giordano et al., 2002; Healy, 2014; Maruna, 1999; Mulvey et al., 2004; Vaughan, 2006). Vaughan (2006) stated that the fallacy of the structural approach has been the idea that individuals have little or no participation in desistance, and that social opportunities trigger desistance by themselves. Similarly, Barry (2006) found when interviewing 40 juvenile offenders from the United Kingdom that several of them made an active decision to stop offending, and that turning points were not a cause of desistance but rather operated as a "push, rather than as a pull" (Barry, 2006:105).

Among the literature on desistance, agency has been understood in different ways, mixing sociological definitions (agency as free choice) and psychological ones (agency as self-efficacy). Accordingly, agency has been understood as not only the willingness of individuals to embrace change and independently make their own free choices (Giordano et al., 2002), but also as self-confidence in one's capacity to carry out particular actions (Mulvey et al., 2004).

Evidence emerging mainly from qualitative studies has shown that desistance might be triggered by agency, which moves individuals to adopt prosocial roles (Bottoms et al., 2004; Farrall & Bowling, 1999; Maruna, 2001; Vaughan, 2007). Nevertheless, as Bottoms (2014:18) pointed out, "agency must always be seen as operating within a given structural and cultural context". Indeed, some scholars (Carlsson, 2013; Lindegaard & Jackes, 2014) have suggested that criminal persistence could also – for individuals embedded in social contexts of extreme deprivation and poverty – represent an agentic move in the direction of transforming one's life through the acquisition of power and status (acquired through crime).

Although agency has been a pivotal concept in desistance research, some scholars (Carlsson, 2016; Heally, 2013; King, 2014) have warned against holding it in high regard. They have argued that neoliberalism may have led to an over-emphasis on agency not only by researchers, but also in the narratives of the individuals who took part in the studies on desistance. In a culture which sees individuals as responsible for their own failures and successes, there is a danger of skewing interpretation to exclude consideration of relevant structural issues.

New social interactions, new social expectations

As mentioned previously, from an interactionist perspective, significant others play a crucial role in the development of self-conceptions by providing norms and goals that individuals try to attain (Kemper, 1966). They also operate as a sort of standard for judging the legitimacy of one's life and actions. It can be argued that, in late adolescence, three main changes start to occur in the relationships between individuals and their significant others. First, regulations from parents and teachers are replaced by self-regulation based on the internalisation of rules and norms from wider social settings (Hoffman, 2000; Lynn, 2008). Second, cognitive improvements in perspective-taking and interpersonal negotiation skills contribute to the development of other-oriented social interactions (Eisenberg et al., 2005). Third, individuals enlarge their audiences because they get involved in new forms of relationships with their partners, peers, and families. Moreover, they start to play new roles at work and in their communities, developing ties and commitments with these new reference sets. Finally, and as consequence of the former changes, social expectations from the individuals' audiences start to change.

Although the changes outlined previously strongly influence the future of the life course in many ways, at least two main consequences can be highlighted that may be involved in crime decline. First, individuals begin to be more accountable for their actions and they start to be judged by adult standards.

This new set of expectations is normally incompatible with the delinquent lifestyle and identity starts to generate strong discrepancies that individuals may seek to diminish by performing the appropriate role behaviour (Stets & Burke, 2005). Second, individuals are expected not only to be responsible for themselves and their actions, but also for others. This opens the way to new forms of social demands, such as reciprocity and mutual care, which operate as an opportunity to be trusted and to perform roles that demand intimate social ties. As mentioned previously, several studies on desistance have produced evidence supporting the above (Barry, 2012; Maruna, 2001; Maruna et al., 2009). Indeed, Maruna et al. (2009) described a de-labelling process called the "Pygmalion effect", in which the social recognition of the desisting individual's changes leads to a greater sense of self and thus supports desistance from crime in the long term.

The development of psychosocial capabilities

Some scholars have argued that the desistance process might be strongly linked to an increase in cognitive capacity or rationality (Rocque, 2017). With similarities to deterrence theory, these explanations have portrayed desistance as a choice made by offenders as they start to consider the formal and informal costs of crime, such as the possibilities of being caught and the consequences of crime in their lives (see Cusson & Pinsonneault, 1986; Fagan, 1989; Patrenoster, 1989; Shover & Thompson, 1992).

During the last decades, a growing body of research into neuroimaging has shown that, in late adolescence, brain neuromaturation may trigger relevant changes in decision-making patterns and maturity of judgement (Johnson, Blum, & Giedd, 2009). According to Steinberg (2008), these changes may be explained by two main neurobiological processes.

First, although the brain mechanisms involved in perceptions of sanctions and rewards are not entirely clear (Reyna & Rivers, 2008), it has been argued that changes in the dopaminergic system decrease reward-seeking behaviour in the transition from adolescence to adulthood (Albert & Steinberg, 2011; Cauffman et al., 2010; Steinberg, 2008). Individuals, therefore, become less sensitive to variations in rewards during this period and are more able to forego immediate gratification (Cauffman & Steinberg, 2000). With age, individuals also seem to increase their capacity to learn from punishment and anticipate the negative consequences of their behaviour (Crone et al., 2005). These improvements in the capacity to weigh risks and benefits may trigger the long-term appreciation of criminal behaviour, and so may be associated with a decline in crime during late adolescence.

Although there is a paucity of research into the relationship between an individual's age and how they perceive the risks and rewards of criminal activity, there are some studies that have produced valuable evidence. Shover and Thompson (1992), in a study which followed 948 adult male inmates from

12 prisons in the United States for 36 months after their release, observed that the effect of age on crime was mediated by a decline in reward expectations associated with crime success.[29] Similarly, Ayers et al. (1999), using data from the Seattle Social Development Project, observed that adolescent desisters perceived fewer rewards from antisocial involvement than persisters. More recently, Loughran et al. (2012) used data from the Pathways to Desistance Study to examine changes in perceptions of risks, costs, and rewards regarding crime among adolescents in a 36-month follow-up period. They observed that, with age, perceptions of the risks and costs of crime increased or remained flat and that the perception of the rewards associated with crime decreased.

Giordano, Schroeder, and Cernkovich (2007), working instead within the field of emotions, argued similarly: in the transition from adolescence to adulthood, the negative emotions connected with crime increased and the positive ones decreased. Finally, Barry (2012) observed among juveniles from her sample that the transition to adulthood was a period in which individuals started realising that criminal activity was resulting in more costs than benefits. In particular, it started to become clearer to them that offending was making them lose the trust of significant others.

Second, during late adolescence, the maturation of cognitive control systems triggers the development of self-regulatory capacities that significantly contribute to the decline of risk-taking behaviours (Steinberg, 2008). This maturation is characterised by relevant structural changes in the adolescent brain: there is an increase of white matter in prefrontal regions of the brain,[30] enhancing the connectivity and integration of brain activity. Prefrontal regions are involved in executive functions, such as planning, problem-solving, verbal reasoning, inhibition, mental flexibility, and initiation and monitoring of actions – all of them involved in mature judgement and decision-making (Albert & Steinberg, 2011; Edwards, 2009; Klaczynsi, 2005; Luciana et al., 2009). The link between mature neurological systems and criminal activity is further suggested by evidence that offenders show poorer executive functioning than non-offenders (Cauffman, Steinberg, & Piquero, 2005).

The proliferation of white matter also has an impact on the connections between cortical and sub-cortical areas, which improve what has been called "emotional maturity": the coordination of emotional regulation and social information processing (Casey et al., 2008; Johnson, Blum, & Giedd, 2009; Monahan et al., 2009; Steinberg, 2008).

Psychosocial maturity: a bridge between brain development and decision-making

To operationalise the aforementioned changes beyond neurobiological processes, researchers have developed the concept of "psychosocial maturity" to account for the psychological and socio-emotional competences that trigger adaptive functioning and decision-making in late adolescence (Bryan-Hancock

& Casey, 2009; Cauffman & Steinberg, 2000; Galambos et al., 2005; Icenogle et al., 2019; Steinberg & Cauffman, 1996). According to Steinberg and Cauffman (1996:252), psychosocial maturity relies on three main categories of dispositions: responsibility, temperance, and perspective (see Table 1.1), which can vary across different situations. As they pointed out:

> Responsibility, temperance, and perspective are best conceived as dispositions to behave in a given way under particular conditions, rather than as fixed abilities or competences that are displayed independent of the context.

Although scarce, there is nevertheless some evidence to support that there are relevant age differences in psychosocial maturity, and that these differences start emerging in late adolescence (Bryan-Hancock & Casey, 2009; Cauffman & Steinberg, 2000; Steinberg & Cauffman, 1996; Steinberg 2008; Steinberg, Chung, & Little, 2004). Indeed, with data from the MacArthur Juvenile Capacity Study,[31] Steinberg (2008) observed that differences in psychosocial maturity did not emerge until the age of 16, and that these differences continued to develop until early adulthood. Similarly, Modecki (2008) explored age-group and gender differences in psychosocial maturity among adolescents, college students, young adults, and adult samples, finding that psychosocial maturity was significantly related to age. Moreover, using pairwise comparisons, it was shown that adolescents (ages 14–17) had lower levels of psychosocial maturity than the older age-groups.

All the preceding evidence has shown that psychosocial maturity increases with age – but are these changes involved in crime decline? Goldweber et al. (2011), in a study using prospective longitudinal data from 937 offenders aged 14–17, observed that the offenders within their sample who engaged in fewer

Table 1.1 Psychosocial maturity

	Definition	*Components*
Responsibility	The ability to take personal responsibility for one's behaviour and to resist the coercive influence of others	Personal responsibility Resistance to peer influence
Temperance	The ability to think about consequences before acting and to modulate impulsivity and aggression	Impulse control Suppression of aggression
Perspective	The ability to consider the future consequences of actions and to view one's actions from the vantage point of others	Consideration of others Future orientation

Source: Own elaboration based on Steinberg and Cauffman (1996), Monahan et al. (2009).

offences over time had greater levels of psychosocial maturity than more prolific ones. Furthermore, Modecki (2008) observed that psychosocial maturity predicted self-reported crime, as well as differentiating between low- and high-delinquency young offenders.

Cruise et al. (2008) examined the influence of psychosocial maturity on adolescent offenders' self-reported delinquent behaviour and observed that both variables were significantly correlated – although, after controlling for age, these results varied between the different components of psychosocial maturity, with temperance emerging as the most significant predictor. Similarly, Monahan et al. (2009), using data from the Pathways to Desistance Study, observed that adolescents who decreased their criminal activities across a follow-up period of three years, showed higher levels of psychosocial maturity than the ones who persisted. In this study, temperance was also the psychosocial maturity component that best distinguished between individuals who followed different criminal trajectories.

On the basis of the evidence outlined previously, it therefore seems that, when assessing the independent relations between each of the three components of psychosocial maturity and crime, increases in temperance are more related to crime decline than responsibility and perspective (though see Colwell et al., 2005). This is not surprising, since decreases in impulse control and suppression of aggression have been linked with desistance in several studies (Forrest & Hay, 2011; Forste, Clarke, & Bahr, 2011; Morizot & Le Blanc, 2007; Piquero, Moffitt, & Wright, 2007).

Improvements in moral orientation

Before starting to discuss improvements in moral orientations that may occur in late adolescence, we ought briefly to step back slightly and return to legal compliance framework of Bottoms (2002) (see the previous section). According to this framework, normative compliance – the third type of compliance – can arise from the acceptance or belief in social norms, by attachment to prosocial others or by legitimacy of legal or social authorities.

If we can assert that legal compliance increases during late adolescence, we would expect that, equally during this period, individuals also increase their capacity to (1) internalise and accept social norms, (2) start considering the norms of significant others, and/or (3) accept the legitimacy of legal institutions. We saw above how changes in the relations between individuals and significant others may be involved in desistance from crime, and I will now discuss whether changes in moral orientations that occur in late adolescence may trigger legal compliance.

Evidence suggests that the acquisition of prosocial values and the ability to exercise moral judgements is one of the key development tasks of late adolescence period (Heaven, 2001). Moreover, research in different social contexts has highlighted that one of the markers of the social maturity that characterises the transition to early adulthood is the improvement of moral reasoning and prosocial orientation (Arnett, 2004; Eisenberg et al., 2005; Mayseless & Scharf, 2003).

Although the internalisation of norms and rules is a process that starts early in life, it seems that, as adolescents age, the cognitive maturation that they acquire builds their capacity to make more sophisticated judgements – thus enabling them to make more complex decisions regarding, for example, rule breaking (Cohn et al., 2010). Indeed, during this period, perspective-taking and advances in social problem-solving skills trigger the reorganisation and advancement of moral judgements (Damon, 1977; Gibbs, 2003; Kohlberg, 1984; Palmer, 2005).

Furthermore, in the transition from adolescence to adulthood, individuals are more exposed to rules, norms, and legal controls from wider social institutions than they are during early or middle adolescence. They also, as mentioned previously, engage in more sophisticated social interactions that expose them to novel moral encounters and promote complex and abstract moral reasoning (Eisenberg et al., 2005; Hoffman, 2000). These experiences may shape their notions of morality and, in so doing, may influence law compliance (Fagan & Tyler, 2005; Piquero 2004; Tyler & Huo, 2002).

There are two main constructs that have been used to examine and explain the internalisation of norms and rules, and their impact on law compliance in criminology: moral reasoning and legal socialisation. Although these concepts are related and their integration may lead to a better understanding law compliance, they have emerged from different disciplines and have therefore commonly been studied separately (Cohn et al., 2010). Moreover, whereas the former refers to ethical judgements that govern wide aspects of individuals' lives, the latter is more oriented to perceptions and attitudes towards the legal system.

Moral reasoning has emerged from social psychology, and its roots can be found in cognitive developmental theorists – primarily in Kohlberg (1984) and Piaget (1932). In broad terms, moral reasoning refers to the individual's judgements of what is right and wrong in a wide variety of social and internal situations, ranging from one's position regarding discrimination to the decision to commit a crime (Palmer, 2005).

Despite some criticism, Kohlberg's theory of moral development (1984) is nevertheless still regarded as the strongest paradigm on moral reasoning (Killen & Smetana, 2006). It lays out three levels of moral development: pre-conventional, conventional, and post-conventional. The first level is characterised by an egocentric judgement of the morality of an action, and by its direct consequences on the individual; individuals categorised within the second level judge morality by comparing society's views and expectations; those on the third level define moral values beyond society's rules, internalising morality and judging actions according to the individual's own ethical principles.

Longitudinal studies on moral development have demonstrated that, as a result of expanding social interactions and role-taking opportunities in late adolescence, moral reasoning improves, advancing from an egoistic-instrumental orientation to an orientation characterised by mutual trust and caring (Colby & Kohlberg, 1987; Dawson, 2002; Rest et al., 1999). Moreover, it seems that, during this period, the integration of moral reasoning with identity development starts shaping individuals' decision-making and behaviour in significant ways (Labouvie-Vief, 2003; Raaijmakers, Engels, & Van Hoof, 2005).

There is also evidence suggesting that delinquents have lower levels of moral reasoning than non-delinquents (Chen & Howitt, 2007; Gregg, Gibbs, & Basinger, 1994; Palmer & Hollin, 1998; Palmer, 2005), and that these levels may differ according to gender: males have been shown to exhibit a more justice-oriented moral reasoning, and females a more care-oriented one (Gilligan & Attanucci, 1988; Palmer, 2003). Nevertheless, there has been little research to demonstrate that moral reasoning may be associated with crime decline in late adolescence.

Raaijmakers, Engels, and Van Hoof (2005) conducted a longitudinal study to investigate the developmental relation between delinquency and moral reasoning in late adolescence and young adulthood among a normative sample of Dutch youths ages from 15 to 23. They observed that moral reasoning improved with age, while delinquency declined; both variables were negatively correlated. Furthermore, Eisenberg et al. (2005) explored age-related changes in prosocial moral reasoning from middle adolescence to early adulthood. They observed an increase not only in prosocial reasoning from the ages of 15 to the early 20s, but also perspective-taking – a key capability of the conventional stage of moral reasoning.

Legal socialisation is defined as the development of standards, attitudes, and behaviours towards laws, rules, and the legal system that results from social experiences during adolescence (Fagan & Tyler, 2005; Piquero et al., 2005). Although this concept is more related to sociological perspectives, its roots can also be found in early psychological studies – particularly among those regarding the development of orientations towards the legal system (e.g. Tapp & Levine, 1977).

There is no agreement among scholars about how legal socialisation should be operationalised. Although research has included different subdomains such as moral disengagement (Fagan & Tyler, 2005), legal attitudes (Tapp & Levine, 1977), and legal reasoning (Cohn et al., 2010), it has been more concentrated in examining two specific dimensions of this construct. These attitudes towards laws and rules are defined as legal cynicism and institutional legitimacy (Fagan & Tyler, 2005; Piquero et al., 2005; Reisig et al., 2011).

Legal cynicism was introduced by Sampson and Bartusch (1998) as a measure of anomie in individuals about law, in which the rules of the dominant society are not considered binding. Although this concept represents individuals' feelings that acting outside the law is reasonable, it must not be confused with tolerance to deviance; rather, the two can coexist. By contrast, institutional legitimacy refers to the feeling of voluntary obligation to defer the law and the legal system over self-interest and personal moral values (Tyler, 2006). This sub-construct is based on the research done by Tyler (1990), which demonstrated that people's views of the legitimacy of legal authorities may shape their compliance with law.

Despite studies have been mostly carried out using community samples, the overwhelming weight of the evidence indicates that individuals with higher levels of legal socialisation (measured by the sub-constructs described previously) are more likely to comply with the law (Cohn et al., 2010; Emery, Jolley, & Wu, 2010; Finckenauer et al., 1991; Piquero et al., 2005; Reisig et al., 2011; Tyler, 2006). For example, Reisig et al. (2011) observed, using cross-sectional data from 626 students from Arizona State University, that criminal offences were significantly shaped by levels of legal cynicism and legitimacy, even when accounting for self-control measures. Furthermore, Emery, Jolley, and Wu (2010) conducted a study using longitudinal data from Chicago neighbourhoods to explore desistance from violence towards partners. Their results showed that individuals with higher levels of legal cynicism had lower desistance rates, when controlling for other relevant variables.

Fagan and Tyler (2005), with data from a community sample of 215 children and adolescents ages 10–16, explored developmental transitions of legal socialisation among children and adolescents. They observed that both levels of legal cynicism and legitimacy predicted self-reported crime. Furthermore, two studies which used a measure of legal reasoning to account for the level of legal socialisation observed that individuals with higher levels of legal reasoning were less likely to perform rule-violating behaviour (Cohn et al., 2010; Finckenauer et al., 1991).

Despite the evidence drawn from the research outlined previously, it is still not clear if the levels of legal socialisation change with age, and – more importantly – if these changes may be related to criminal decline in late adolescence. Although there have been at least two studies (Fagan & Tyler, 2005; Piquero et al., 2005) which have assessed the relation between legal socialisation and age,[32] their results do not tell us much about this issue. Indeed, although it seems that changes in legal socialisation levels would start to occur in late adolescence, those studies assessed individuals in early and middle adolescence, when there is not much change.

Young women's desistance

Research on criminological careers has shown that women desist earlier than men (Flood-Page et al., 2000; Giordano et al., 2002; Loeber, Stouthamer-Loeber, & Ahonen, 2016; McIvor, Murray, & Jamieson, 2004), and that they have much lower reoffending rates (Kruttschnitt et al., 2002; Ministry of Justice, 2011). Indeed, evidence suggests that the age-crime curve peaks earlier for females than males, and this peak tends to be higher among the latter (Elliott, 1994; Fagan & Western, 2005; Moffitt et al., 2001; Piquero, Hawkins, & Kazemian, 2012).

Nevertheless, a study conducted in the Netherlands by Block et al. (2010) showed that the peak age at termination was 41 for women and 39 for men, and that women had notably more conviction-free years than men. Furthermore, Elliot (1994), with data from the National Youth Survey, observed that the decline of the curve was steeper for females and that the gender differential became greater with time. Indeed, while at age 12 the ratio of male/female was 2; at age 21 it was 4. Similarly, Farrington (1986) also observed gender differences, with a peak of the male/female ratio of 7.5–9.5 between the ages of 16 and 22 for English offenders. Gender differences have also been observed when assessing the total length of the criminal career. Prime et al. (2001), using a cohort of British males born between 1953 and 1978, observed that while the average career length for males was 6.2 years, it was only 1.8 years for females.

Although there are no conclusive explanations for the above, one could simply argue that women desist earlier because they engage in much less serious crime than males (Loeber, Stouthamer-Loeber, & Ahonen, 2016) and violent crimes tend to peak later in life (Le Blanc & Fréchette, 1989; Sampson & Laub, 2003). Nevertheless, Barry (2012) approached the question from a different angle: using data from the Scottish Desistance Study, she observed that women experience the struggle of living a "normal" life earlier than men, having greater chances to take familial responsibilities at younger ages and thus desist from crime.

Evidence regarding the process of women's desistance has mainly emerged from four types of studies: (1) studies that have assessed the process of desistance among women, (2) studies of female crime in general, (3) studies that have explored women's reintegration process after imprisonment, and (4) studies that investigate the factors triggering desistance, and the differences as compared to samples of male offenders. The nature and aims of these studies vary significantly, ranging from small-scale qualitative studies to large-scale longitudinal research. It is therefore difficult to put them together and give them the same weight to accurately inform the theoretical discussion concerning the process of crime abandonment among women. Nevertheless, to have a general idea of the main findings of empirical research, as follows the evidence regarding the factors triggering desistance is discussed.

Relationships, responsibility, and caring roles

As with research on women's pathways into crime, several studies on desistance have pointed out the relevance of interpersonal support. Although a number of female offenders have problematic relationships with their families of origin – and have even been abused and/or neglected by them – research has found that they strongly rely on relatives as sources of emotional and economic support during their desistance and re-entry process (Giordano et al., 2007; Leverentz, 2011). Moreover, although some women want to distance themselves from these relationships, they either cannot afford the cost of this decision or are otherwise unable to follow through on the desire for distance, engaging instead in a process of re-signifying the negative feelings associated with these familial bonds (Giordano et al., 2007; Martinez & Christian, 2009).

Research has shown that family ties trigger desistance beyond marriage or intimate partner relationships (Cobbina, 2009); for several women, it is not just about being a good mother and wife, but rather it is being a good daughter or a good sister that triggers new ways of relating with relatives in a dynamic of support exchanges that confer the status of a person who has "something to give" (Leverentz, 2011; Martinez, 2009). Leverentz (2011), conducting interviews with 43 women who were involved in the criminal justice system, observed that most women defined themselves by their capacity to provide care to their families of origin, and that this had direct implications for their desistance process.

Most of these experiences occur in women's transition towards adulthood, in which offending starts to be seen as a threat against the relationships they start to develop with their families, children, and partners. Barry (2010, 2012) pointed out, with data from the Scottish Desistance Study, that care and responsibility was a new source of legitimate capital for the interviewees that supported their process of crime abandonment. She contended that capital expenditure – i.e. "giving their own capital to others or being needed by others" – was important for desistance to occur, allowing women to gain responsibility and respect (Barry, 2012:124).

Although there are some discrepancies between quantitative and qualitative studies, **motherhood** is the factor that has been most strongly associated with desistance among women offenders (Broidy & Cauffman, 2006; Fleisher & Krienert, 2004; Giordanno et al., 2011; Graham & Bowling, 1995; Kreagar, Matsueda, & Erosheva, 2010; McIvor et al., 2009; Moore & Hagedorm, 1999; Uggen & Kruttschnitt, 1998). Although there is no evidence regarding cultural differences, the conflicting results have mainly been associated with inappropriate research designs and with the fact that quantitative studies have not been capable of accurately capturing the conditions under which motherhood triggers desistance.

Qualitative studies have disentangled some of these dynamics, observing that motherhood restructures daily routines, increases the costs of crime, gives a sense of optimism and future orientation, and fosters the development of a prosocial identity (Abell, 2018; Edin & Kefalas, 2005; Fleisher & Klienart, 2004; Gålnander, 2019; Hunt, Joe-Laidler, & MacKenzie, 2005; Rumgay, 2004). Nevertheless, some research has found that the effect of motherhood on desistance tends to dissipate after childbirth (Monsbakken, Lyngstad, & Skardhamar, 2013); this is, in all likelihood, because of maternal stress triggered by economic pressures and difficulties of raising children as single mothers, or by being a mother in a constant threat of failure – especially after release from prison (Bachman et al., 2015; Brown, 2006; Brown & Bloom, 2009; Garcia-Hallett, 2018; Michalsen, 2011, 2013; Richie, 2001; Rodermond, Slotboom,

& Zoutewelle-Terovan, 2015). Moreover, desister mothers suffer from strong stigma that jeopardises their reintegration process, driven by the misconception that a young, criminalised mother lacks the capacity to properly perform the maternal role (Brown & Bloom, 2009; MacMahon, 1995; Sanders, 2007; Sharpe, 2015). The relationship between economic disadvantage, motherhood, and desistance is not straightforward, however. While Giordano et al. (2011) found that motherhood's effect on desistance was related to socio-economic status (those from highly disadvantaged backgrounds were less likely to desist), other studies have pointed out that pregnancy might have a strong transformative potential among marginalised young women (Edin & Kefalas, 2011; Kreager et al., 2010).

The acquisition of conventional relationships is commonly accompanied by the abandonment of **antisocial friends and companions**. Although evidence has suggested that girls are less susceptible to antisocial peers than boys (Mears, Ploeger, & Warr, 1998; Piquero et al., 2005), the fact that girls are more emotionally invested in friendship tends to contradict the above. Indeed, evidence suggests that girls reduce their delinquency when exposed to less delinquent friends in a way that boys do not (Haynie et al., 2014; Uggen & Kruttschnitt, 1998). Actively staying away from former friends has been highlighted as a strategy that allows women to avoid the temptations associated with an antisocial lifestyle, and it has been argued that most of these women experience periods of strong social isolation at the beginning of the desistance process (Giordano et al., 2003; McIvor, 2016; Nugent & Schinkel, 2016; Wright et al., 2013).

The role of traditional turning points

Based on research conducted with data regarding men, it has been argued that **marriage** might trigger desistance through informal social control, changing routines and social networks and enhancing commitments to conventionality (Sampson & Laub, 2003). Nevertheless, research on marriage and desistance specifically among women has found conflicting results (Rodermond et al., 2016). While some studies have found significant effects (Broidy & Cauffman, 2006; Craig & Foster, 2013; Doherty & Ensminger, 2013), others found little or none (Fleming et al., 2010; Giordano et al., 2011; Huebner, Dejong, & Cobbina, 2010; Kreager et al., 2010; Rodermond, Slotboom, & Zoutewelle-Terovan, 2015; Zoutewelle-Terovan et al., 2012). Some scholars have even observed that marriage might actually trigger persistence (De Li & MacKenzie, 2003). Moreover, most studies have found that marriage has a greater effect on men than women (Bakken, 2009; Bersani et al., 2009; De Li & MacKenzie, 2003; Doherty & Ensminger, 2013; Pelissier et al., 2003; Zoutewelle-Terovan et al., 2012). Although there is no strong empirical evidence offered in support, it has been argued that marriage does not necessarily trigger desistance among women because, while men tend to "marry up", female offenders – due to stigma – are sometimes prevented from finding a partner who operates as a pro-social influence (Giordano, 2016). Moreover, research has shown that the effect of partners' attitudes towards deviance might be stronger among women than men (Herrera, Wiersman, & Cleveland, 2010; Simons et al., 2002).

However, some research into **cohabitation and intimate partnerships** has shown that it has a stronger impact on desistance among women than men (Benda, 2005; Cobbina et al., 2012; Simons et al., 2002), but this relationship is not straightforward; for instance, it varies significantly when considering specific issues such as the quality of the relationship (though see Barr & Simons, 2015), the hierarchy of salience in the relationship and its length (Gottlieb & Sugie, 2018), the normative orientation of partners (Bui & Morash, 2010; Cobbina, 2010; Giordano, 2016; Giordano et al., 2003; Herrera, Cleveland, & Wiersma, 2010), and structural disadvantage (DiPietro, Doherty, & Bersani, 2018). Indeed, most recent research has found that romantic partnership triggered desistance among men regardless of quality, but only warm and supportive partners prompted crime abandonment among women – an effect that was aided by cognitive changes in women's views of conventional norms (Barr & Simons, 2015; Simons & Barr, 2014). This is consistent with the claim, drawn from the symbolic interaction approach, that mechanisms of informal social control support desistance but do not operate by themselves, instead catalysing identity shifts and changes in women's desirability of antisocial behaviour (Bachman et al., 2015; Giordano et al., 2002).

The fact that **employment** has stronger effects upon desistance among men than women (Benda, 2005; Cobbina et al., 2012; Simons et al., 2002) has primarily been explained by the fact that men are traditionally breadwinners, and that work is one of the foremost aspects around which they construct their identities (Verbruggen et al., 2012). Yet the decreasing differences in employment participation means the plausibility of this explanation has reduced over time; accordingly, some studies have indeed found that employment also triggers crime reduction and termination among women (Verbruggen et al., 2012). Nevertheless, the relationship between employment and desistance among women is still not clear, and it has been argued that having a job is a sufficient but not a necessary condition for desistance. It seems that – in deprived environments – women's lack of education and legitimate work experience, along with unstable jobs and earning low wages, actually transforms employment into a source of frustration and stress (Bachman et al., 2019; Brown & Bloom, 2009; Giordano et al., 2003).

Despite the strong relevance of **education** in the promotion of gender equality and female empowerment, the effect of education on desistance has been almost entirely absent in criminological research. While Huebner et al. (2010) observed that lower levels of education predicted recidivism among a large sample of women released from prison in the United States, Giordano et al. (2011) found that graduation from secondary education had no effect on desistance from crime. In a more recent study conducted by Gålnander (2019), he observed among a sample of Swedish women, that education was a way to build identity and to feel connected with mainstream society.

Identity and emotions

Women's delinquency has mainly been understood as an indication of psychological disturbance and lack of morality, and as a consequence of social rejection and isolation (Sharpe & Gelsthorpe, 2015). **Emotionality** has played a crucial role in this understanding, with scholars arguing that the gendered crime gap could be explained by the fact that females respond with more intense negative emotions to different sources of strain than males (Broidy & Agnew, 1997), reinforcing the idea of women's crime as a way of "acting out their psychological disturbances" (Sharpe & Gelsthorpe, 2015:50). Nevertheless, the role of emotions in female desistance has been hardly studied beyond the recognition by a few scholars that desistance implies a decrease in the positive emotions associated with crime and an improvement in emotional regulation (Giordano et al., 2007; Paternoster & Bushway, 2009). Furthermore, several studies have highlighted the emotional stability acquired by women who successfully began to avoid drug use and demonstrated how this was crucial in the abandonment of crime (Barry, 2012; McIvor et al., 2009; Michalsen, 2013; Rumgay, 2004; Simpson et al., 2008).

As discussed in the previous chapters, scholars exploring offenders' life narratives have pointed out that, during the transition from crime to conformity, individuals develop a more prosocial sense of self (Aresti, Eatough, & Brooks-Gordon, 2010; Christian et al., 2009; Farrall & Calverley, 2006; Giordano et al., 2002; Maruna, 2001; Paternoster & Bushway, 2009; Presser & Kurth, 2009; Vaughan, 2007). **Identity changes** have been argued to be a pivotal factor, supporting individuals in decision-making and helping them to acquire and maintain prosocial roles. While research based on men has highlighted that identity transformation is triggered by the acquisition of roles in several domains, identity reconstruction in the case of women has been primarily associated with the development of interpersonal relationships and the acquisition of conventional caring roles. Relationships that entail strong emotional attachment and a high level of reward, such as maternity, might have strong effects on identity development and thus on desistance from crime. For example, Bachman et al. (2015), using a sample of 118 women released from prison in 1990, observed that women's capacity to reclaim the maternal role after imprisonment helped them to solidify a prosocial sense of self once they had already experienced an identity transformation. Similarly, Kraeger, Matsueda, and Erosheva (2010) argued that the identity of being a good mother supported desistance because it helped women to restrain from risky activities, such as nightlife and drugs. Baskin and Sommers (1998) and Bloom and Brown (2011) confirmed the above but argued that although the maternal role constituted a conventional identity "script" that supported the desistance process among their interviewees, its effect was undermined by their sense of failure as mothers due to their previous criminal involvement. A recent study conducted by Stone et al. (2018) with women on parole in the United States showed that identity verification from parole officers and significant others helped these women to overcome the obstacles to desist from crime.

Nevertheless, other studies have highlighted the role of identity shifts beyond the acquisition of caring roles. For example, Gålnander (2019) discussed the role education to rebuild a sense of identity and Stone (2015) highlighted the role of redemptive narratives to restore moral agency.

Desistance explanations and youth crime

Desistance from crime is ultimately a process of change. As such, it is complex to explain and perhaps even impossible to cover in its full magnitude and scope – especially if is only addressed from a criminological perspective. Several scholars have made great contributions to its explanation, bringing approaches from other disciplines and incorporating most of the factors involved in the process of crime abandonment (structural, interactional, individual, moral, and cultural factors, among others). This section summarises the main explanations of crime decline available in the criminological literature.

Ontogenetic explanations about desistance

Ontogenetic approaches are based on the idea that the propensity to commit crimes is unaffected by events that occur in life, but that desistance can be explained by ageing and maturation, regardless of social factors. The decrease in offending over time is attributed to biological and maturational changes that diminish individuals' capacity and motivation to offend. Among the main ontogenetic approaches to desistance, of particular note is the General Theory of Crime of Gottfredson and Hirshi (1990), in which they argue that individuals with low self-control are likely to engage in criminal acts in a relatively stable pattern throughout their lives. According to them, desistance occurs simply "due to the inexorable ageing of the organism", and by the fact that age brings fewer opportunities to commit crime (Gottfredson & Hirshi, 1990:141). Reviews of this theory found little support, showing both that criminal pathways can display a great heterogeneity and that adult offending cannot be predicted from variables related to crime onset only (Ezell & Cohen, 2005; Kazemian, Farrington, & LeBlanc, 2009; Laub & Sampson, 2003).

Glueck and Glueck (1943), in their study Unraveling Juvenile Delinquency, also argued that desistance could not be attributed to external factors since it was the result of maturation. According to them, desistance took place when offenders "grew out of crime and settled down" (Sampson & Laub 2003:27). Contrary to Gottfredson and Hirshi (1990), these scholars did not explicitly argue that age was the direct and unique explanation of desistance, but rather they highlighted the role of maturation in terms of psychological and biological factors involved in the ageing process. Nevertheless, they did not disentangle which of these factors might be involved in maturation, or to what extend were they related to crime decline. Criticisms of this approach are mainly based on its lack of capacity to account for individuals' differences in crime decline and abandonment, thereby neglecting the role of structural and subjective factors.

Rational choice

Rational choice explanations of desistance are based on the idea that individuals stop committing crimes because they begin to accord increasingly less importance to the benefits of crime when balanced against its costs. Cusson and Pinsonnealut (1986) argued that, with age, offenders experience delayed deterrence – a process in which offenders start to consider the probabilities of being punished and increase their resistance to spend long periods of time in prison. This process is generally triggered by a shock, for instance, receiving a hard sentence or losing a friend, and it provokes an individual to reassess their life. Similarly, in his books Aging Criminals and Great Pretenders (1985 and 1996, respectively), Shover argued that older offenders have greater awareness of the costs of crime and reassess criminal behaviour accordingly, giving lesser weight to the gains and pleasures of crime. There is also a practical level, since the bodily impact of ageing means that individuals are increasingly less able to engage in the physical efforts that accompany the criminal activity.

Although it cannot be argued that rationality is completely absent from the desistance process, rational choice approaches have garnered several criticisms for neglecting the role played by several structural and internal obstacles that may hinder individuals' decision to abandon crime.

Sampson and Laub age-graded theory of informal social control

One of the main theoretical approaches explaining desistance from a sociogenic perspective was developed by Sampson and Laub (1993). Based on a reanalysis of Glueck's aforementioned study, they developed the age-graded theory of informal social control. They argued that their theory would cover two gaps in existing research on criminal careers: the relevance of social transitions in young adulthood and the relationship between socio-structural variables and social control.

Drawing upon social control theories (such as Hirshi, 1969), their approach propounds the idea that crime is the result of a weak or broken tie between the individual and society. Their model is based on the effect that social interactions with institutions of informal social control have on crime and desistance. According to these authors, desistance occurs as a result of turning points (changes in the life course) generated by life events that enhance social bonds to society.

In a later development of their theory (Sampson & Laub, 2003), using life story narratives from men who both desisted from and persisted in crime, in conjunction with trajectory analysis, the authors found that four main turning points were implicated in the desistance process: marriage, military service, correctional school, and neighbourhood change. Attachment to these institutions of informal social control was shown to improve individuals' bonds to society, as well as providing social and psychological resources that supported further life transitions.

The impact of life events on desistance has been demonstrated by other authors too. Irwin (1970), in a study combining interviews and participant observation with offenders in the United States, also found that ex-offenders needed a meaningful social group with which to share common beliefs and interests, as well as a partner and a job to "do good" and ultimately desist from crime.

Several studies have supported the above, providing evidence regarding the role of turning points in the desistance process. However, the theory has also received some criticism: notably, the argument that it has neglected the role of agency and subjective factors, portraying desistance as a passive process in which individuals have little or no participation, and social opportunities trigger changes by themselves (Vaughan, 2006).

Identity-based explanations of desistance

Sampson and Laub (2003:278) have argued that offenders desist "by default", without experiencing any identity shift or cognitive transformation. According to their age-graded theory of social control, offenders change without realising it, simply as a result of capitalising on the investment that they have made in a conventional life. Several scholars have contested the above, arguing that identity shifts play a crucial role in the desistance process, motivating and providing direction to an individual's behaviour (Paternoster & Bushway, 2009). These contrasting views are discussed next.

Bushway and Paternoster's Identity Theory of Desistance (ITD)

The main argument of the ITD, developed by Bushway and Paternoster (2012, 2013), is that changes in identity are the major initiating factor in the desistance process, allowing turning points to operate effectively. According to Bushway and Paternoster (2012, 2013), the key factor enabling identity changes within an individual is the prior existence of multiple shifting identities within that same individual: they differentiate, for instance, between the "working self" and the "possible self". The former is anchored in the present and based on current experiences, while the latter is directed towards a future of two dimensions, positive and negative. The positive dimension is related to what the individual desires to be in the future, and the negative is what they fear or do not wish to become.

The negative possible self (also called the "feared self") provides the initial motivation for identity change in desistance – yet, in the long term, it cannot sustain crime abandonment by itself. To reach desistance, it is necessary to strike a balance between "what is hoped and what is feared" (Paternoster & Bushway, 2009:1119). This changing process is gradual and incorporates a cost-benefit analysis between the working self and a more conventional identity. Motivation to change occurs when the offender attributes the cumulative failures in their life to crime, triggering a sense of dissatisfaction that is referred to by the authors as the "crystallization of discontent".

Additionally, there are two subsequent changes that ensure and assist identity change: first, a change in preferences must occur, involving modifications of both views and orientations; second, a change in social networks must take place. Paternoster and Bushway (2009) argue that changes towards a more conventional social network are intentional and lend support to the development of a prosocial identity by providing sources of social capital.

Although ITD has generated a relevant contribution, bringing the role of identity in the desistance process into the mainstream, it has received several criticisms. Perhaps its main shortcoming, though, is its strong reliance on the rational choice approach, seeking to portray identity shifts as a decision rather than as an ongoing interactional process. Moreover, the attempts to operationalise and measure identity shifts through quantitative means have limited their scope: relevant aspects of the process through which individuals develop their identities are foregone, as are the ways in which these identities orient individuals' behaviours.

The narrative of identity

Maruna (1999:8) was one of the first scholars to introduce the narrative approach, which refers to "an individual's internalized, evolving, and integrative story of the self", to explain identity changes involved in the desistance process. Based on results from the Liverpool Desistance Study, Maruna (2001) observed that ex-offenders desisting from crime built a coherent narrative to explain and justify their change. This narrative or "redemption script" has a logical structure that connects past and present experiences and involves incremental and gradual shifts rather than a complete, rapid, and unexpected change. The narratives of the desisters he interviewed were characterised by three main issues.

First, ex-offenders' narratives make explicit who they think they really are – the so-called real me (Maruna, 2001:88) – providing a framework for their choices and behaviours. These narratives also need support at a societal level, a process – drawn by Maruna (2001) from the symbolic interactionist approach – called the "looking glass" process (see Cooley, 1902). With this external support given to an individual by people who believe in their worth and capacity to change, stigmatised individuals are provided with the initial impulse for a transition to occur (Maruna, 2004).

Second, Maruna (2001) observed that desisters were more optimistic than persisters, and that they had the perception of being in control of their own destinies. In addition, they also demonstrated the ability to take something good from a negative situation; in other words, they believed that "one's mistake can make one a stronger person" (Maruna, 2001:99).

Finally, desisters seem to look for a purpose by realising that things apart from crime are important in their lives. One way to instil this sense of purpose is by mentoring new generations to keep them away from crime, helping them to transform their antisocial story into a "moral tale" (Maruna, 2001:105) and give something back to the subsequent generations – this thereby leads them to experience a kind of redemption narrative that allows them to move forward and leave crime behind.

Vaughan's internal conversation

Vaughan (2006) developed a similar explanation of identity based on narrative theory. He argued that desisters fashion a narrative identity through an "internal moral conversation" (2006:390), incorporating disclaimers against past actions and a compromise with a future self.

This involves several steps: the first is discernment, referring to a willingness to consider a different and new lifestyle; the second is deliberation, including a cost-benefit analysis of the current self and the desired future self, similar to that outlined above by Bushway and Paternoster (2012); the third stage is dedication, which indicates the process through which the conversion occurs. This final stage is gradual, rooted an interaction between social and internal controls. In this new position, the individual gains self-esteem and respect, and their behaviour falls in line with their new self.

Despite the pivotal role that identity plays in desistance explanations, there are no agreements regarding the scope and timing of these changes. Moreover, it is not clear how they interact with other factors involved in the desistance process. While some scholars argue that shifts towards desistance will not take place until a new, conventional and non-offending identity replaces the former one (Giordano et al., 2002; Harris, 2009; Paternoster & Bushway, 2009; Vaughan, 2007), others suggest that individuals do not necessarily slough off or deny their pasts, but fashion a new, non-offender self that incorporates their former identity – in other words, a reconstructive process (Aresti, Fatough, & Brooks-Gordon, 2010; Gadd & Farrall, 2004; Hundleby, Gfellner, & Racine, 2007; Le Bel et al., 2008; Maruna, 2001; Maruna & Roy, 2007; Opsal, 2011).

Integrated theories

Although drawing from different approaches, and with an emphasis on diverse factors, integrated theories explain desistance as the interaction between structural, agentic, and subjective processes. In the words of Weaver (2016:22), "desistance essentially occurs as the outcome of an individual to alter their socio–structural context, and in so doing acquiring new behaviours and new pro-social roles, or vice-versa, variously resulting in associated shifts in the individual's personal and social identify". I will now address three of the main integrated theories that hold relevance for the present research.

Giordano's Theory of Cognitive Transformation

Giordano, Cernkovich, and Rudolph (2002), using data from the Ohio Longitudinal Study, developed the Theory of Cognitive Transformation. This theory emerges as a challenge to social control and social learning approaches, which, in their emphasis on the role of external factors, neglect any internal changes that might be involved in the desistance process. According to Giordano (2014), cognitive transformations are an integral part of desistance since they can help pinpoint why some individuals exposed to turning points fail to benefit from them, and why others, who lack sources of informal social control, are successful in their attempts to desist from crime.

Drawing upon Symbolic Interactionism theories, Giordano (2014) developed four types of cognitive transformations that might be involved in the process of moving away from crime: openness to change, openness to hooks for change, identity transformations, and changes in the meaning/desirability of the criminal behaviour.

"Openness to change" refers to the process through which individuals are willing to undertake a new pattern of behaviour; this change thereby enables individuals to become more receptive to particular catalysts or opportunities (i.e. a prosocial partner, a conventional job), termed by the authors as "hooks for change". The mere exposure to hooks for change does not, however, guarantee cognitive changes and agentic moves towards desistance; indeed, they vary in their transformative potential. Successful hooks for change are those that provide opportunities for prosocial identity development and connection with conformist others in prosocial settings.

Identity transformations occur when individuals begin to fashion a replacement sense of self which provides organisation and coherence to one's cognitions and actions. The new identity orients decision-making towards prosocial actions, inaugurating a newly negative consideration of the meaning and desirability of criminal behaviour. This theory stands in contrast to social control assumptions that individuals' motivations to commit crimes are invariant throughout life.

Although Giordano, Cernkovich, and Rudolph (2002) described a sequential order to these processes in their original formulation of the theory, they subsequently revised their conclusions to argue that "the idea of a series of steps is itself not all that helpful or accurate as description of what occurs" (Giordano, 2014:15). Accordingly, the four elements highlighted by the Theory of Cognitive Transformations might be better understood as mutually reinforcing aspects of the desistance process.

Heuristic and interactive model of the early stages of desistance

Bottoms and Shapland (2016), with data from the Sheffield Desistance Study, developed a model to explain the early stages of the desistance process. Drawing upon the social control approach and Giordano's Cognitive Transformation Theory, their model presents a complex process in which previous criminal habits and history are bound together with new social opportunities within a demanding social context that does not offer many opportunities for change.

Agency, self-perception, and self-efficacy are key issues within the model, triggering early intentions to desist. According to Bottoms and Shapland (2011), desistance involves a process of active maturation in which individuals start considering their goals and ethical norms through reflection on what sort of person they should be. This kind of ethical reflection described in Virtue Ethics Theory stresses that individuals approach moral dilemmas not simply by considering the moral rule itself, but by their own dispositions and beliefs as embedded in a certain context. This kind of reflection might be a crucial part of the process of moving away from crime, supporting identity changes which, after the individual has encountered several reinforcements of their new way of life, are consolidated at the end of the desistance process.

Within this model, desistance is a gradual process wherein each step towards change is influenced by the individual's dispositions and the available social capital – or, in other words, hooks for change. This process entails several obstacles, most of which are not easily overcome. Nevertheless, the authors argue that this does not imply that a complete regression towards crime will take place, since many individuals resume their efforts to desist afterwards.

Accordingly, "desistance is the process of learning to live a non-criminal life when one has been leading a largely criminal life" (Bottoms & Shapland, 2014:7). This means that, when desisting from crime, individuals have to change their routine, lifestyles, and friends – as well as more generally resisting the inevitable temptations that they will encounter during their attempt to abandon a life of crime. Drawing on Kennett (2001), these scholars argue that offenders adopt tactics of diachronic self-control through which they purposefully engage with or avoid certain situations that might lead them to failure in their attempts to change. As Bottoms and Shapland (2011:274) pointed out:

> Desisters are not only trying to combat habits or patterns of offending behaviour, or resisting opportunities they perceive (though entirely law-abiding people would not perceive them). They have also to think through the possible pattern of their day and how to ensure that they are not tempted beyond their ability to resist.

The heuristic and interactive model of the early stages of desistance is one the most comprehensive approaches to explain desistance, though there is still a substantial shortcoming in the lack of evidence as to whether these processes are applicable to advanced stages of desistance as well.

Farrall's structural- and individual-level processes of desistance

Farrall et al. (2014) developed an approach to explain the process of crime abandonment that results from the interaction between individual choices and social forces, giving special weight to the fact that individual agency is embedded within specific social contexts that affect it in several ways. They strongly emphasise the situational context in which individuals act, separating desistance into two levels: the structural and the individual.

This model has strong similarities to that of Bottoms and Shapland (2011), but also includes a greater exploration of the emotional aspects of desistance – an issue that had previously only been explored by Giordano et al. (2007). According to Farrall and Calverley (2006), desistance progresses through different stages that may be characterised by diverse emotional states. At the beginning of the process, guilt, shame, and regret are common emotions relating to the individuals' previous lives and to crime relapses. Anxiety is quite common among individuals at this phase as well, rooted in an uncertainty regarding their future lives. As individuals move along the path to crime abandonment, positive emotions start progressively to emerge – particularly hope – which are crucial to trigger engagement with the process of personal change that desistance requires.

Farrall et al. (2014) have also contributed to the understanding of the spatial dynamics of desistance. They argue that these dynamics operate on two main levels: moves within towns and cities and moves between towns and cities. The former is more common among non-drug users and is related to shifts in time-space routines, while the latter is more frequently observable among users. Interestingly, these scholars challenge the casual relationship between relocation and desistance – or, in Maruna's words, the "geographic cure" (2001:153–154) – that has been articulated elsewhere (e.g. Kirk, 2009; Piquero, Farrington, & Blumstein, 2007). They argue that changes in spatial dynamics are a reflection of a wish to change, of a desire for "being in normal places" that they can legitimately inhabit and in which they feel they have the right to belong (Farrall et al., 2014:186). Places and routines are therefore shown to have specific meanings that allow or hinder certain social interactions, in turn shaping individuals' sense of self.

Final comments

Change is an individual process involving subjective experiences that are extremely difficult to investigate empirically. Trying to limit explanations of desistance only to what we can directly verify through the traditional criminological methods therefore risks blocking theoretical advances. In that sense, flexibility and openness are needed to develop explanations of desistance that not only serve as theoretical advances but can informing correctional practice as well.

Moreover, it must be understood that explanations of desistance do not need to elucidate the whole process and account for the experiences of every individual, cultural setting and society; indeed, such a pursuit (drawn from modernist ideals in criminology) would be mistaken (Daly, 2010; Garland, 2002). Exploring desistance in specific contexts, and most importantly within certain types of crimes, comes with an expectation of difference: as Giordano (2016:22) argued, the notion of a "generality of deviance" might be actively unhelpful. It stands to reason that the process of crime abandonment among individuals who are, for example, exiting property crimes will differ from that of those who are abandoning the perpetration of domestic violence.

Some approaches, such as the one developed by Maruna (2001), do much to explain the role played by subjective and interactional factors, while others, such as Farrall et al. (2014), have made significant contributions to explaining the spatial dynamics involved in the process of crime abandonment. Indeed, it is perhaps the very absence of an ambition to explain the whole process, and to develop a theory that can be generalised to every single case, that renders these explanations of such great use to the project of understanding desistance from crime.

Integrative theories advanced by Bottoms and Shapland (2011) and Giordano (2016) offer broader explanations of desistance that account for a more diverse set of factors, and that accurately try to explain the dynamics of the process. These scholars have developed their theories through prospective studies, constantly reviewing their previous arguments demonstrating flexibility regarding the temporal order of the events they try to explain. Therefore, they have avoided getting trapped within the limits of what they are not able to explain or empirically confirm.

In that sense, it can be argued that diverse explanations of desistance might be needed to understand properly the different experiences of individuals when leaving crime behind. The focus merely on causal factors and their chronology might hinder the understanding of a process in which several factors interact within diverse social contexts that impose specific obstacles which are experienced and interpreted subjectively by each individual. This is not to say that the search for causal mechanisms is irrelevant, but rather to point out that the understanding of the desistance process should not be limited to it. As Hollway and Jefferson (2000:127) noted:

> We are all more or less irrational subjects. The point is to explain the relationship between the rational and irrational in human behaviour; not to stop when we have reached the limits of the rational.

Notes

1 The Seattle Social Development Project is a prospective longitudinal survey of 808 youths drawn from the population (1,053) of fifth-grade students attending 18 elementary schools in high-crime neighbourhoods of Seattle in the autumn of 1985.
2 The Youth Development Study is a longitudinal survey of 1,000 students who attended Saint Paul, Minnesota, public schools in the 1980s.
3 Behavioural desistance in this study was composed by measures of self-reported crime and also measures of other kinds of antisocial self-reported activities that are not illegal.
4 The Sheffield Pathways out of Crime Study is a longitudinal study, which examines desistance among a sample of 113 young adult recidivist offenders.
5 Farrall's (2002:65) operationalization of desistance and persistence included five categories: no offending, showing signs of desistance, continued offending (trivial), continued offending (non-trivial), continued offending (escalating).
6 The RYDS is a longitudinal study of 1,000 urban adolescents that examines the development of delinquency and drug use, guided by interactional and social network theories (Krohn, 1986; Thornberry, 1987, respectively).
7 Glueck and Glueck conducted a longitudinal study that followed, for a period of 50 years, 510 juvenile offenders who had been diverted to a correctional school in Massachusetts.
8 Disruptive behaviour was defined by measures of attention deficit, hyperactivity symptoms and unaccountability.
9 The Cambridge Study in delinquent development is a prospective longitudinal survey that examines the development of offending and antisocial behaviour among 411 London males, mostly born in 1953. The Montreal Two Samples Longitudinal Study is a longitudinal study that includes two samples of 470 delinquent and non-delinquent Caucasian French-speaking individuals, first recruited in the mid-1970s at ages 12–16.
10 Displacement also needs to be differentiated from heterotypic continuity, a concept of developmental psychopathology that has been used in criminal career research. Heterotypic continuity describes an underlying developmental process which continues over time, but can change in the form of its manifestation. In other words, it refers to the sequencing of different conducts with similar underlying functions (Shaw & Gross, 2008). The development of childhood aggression or oppositional behaviour into antisocial or criminal activity during adolescence and adulthood would be a prime example of this process.
11 Drug dealing is among the crimes with the highest likelihood of persistence from adolescence to adulthood (Rosenfeld, White, & Esbensen, 2012; White, Loeber, & Farrington, 2008).

12 The Scottish Desistance Study was conducted in Scotland between 2000 and 2001 using a sample of 20 young males and 20 young female offenders aged 18–33 years old.
13 Kohlberg's (1984) theory of moral development differentiates between three levels of moral development: pre-conventional, conventional, and post-conventional. The first level is characterised by an egocentric judgment of the morality of an action by its direct consequences on the individual; on the second level, individuals judge morality by comparing society's views and expectations; on the third level, individuals define moral values beyond society's rules, relying upon their own internal ethical principles.
14 Bottoms' (2002) Legal Compliance Framework differentiates between four different types of legal compliance: the first type, termed "instrumental/prudential", the individual's conformity is motivated by rational self-interests; the second, situational, is based on physical or societal constraints; the third is "normative", and can arise from the acceptance or belief in social norms, through attachment to pro-social others, or through legitimacy of legal or social authorities; finally, "habitual" compliance is more automatic and is based on life habits and routines.
15 See also Tyler (2006) for a discussion of legal compliance.
16 See Rumgay (2004). According to Rumgay (2004), identities that may present themselves as available during the process of leaving crime behind provide a "script" by which to enact a conventional, prosocial social role.
17 The Oxford Recidivism Study was a two-year longitudinal study that followed a cohort of 130 male property offenders in their progression from prison to the community.
18 Cohort effects constitute any effect associated with being a member of a group born at roughly the same time and bonded by common life experiences; age effects are the consequences of growing older; and period effects are the consequences of influences that vary through time. Although period effects are a constant in cross-sectional curves, they can be influenced by ageing or cohort effects. Moreover, they could also be biased by particular events that occur in a certain year (Farrington, 1986).
19 LCA is a subset of structural equation modelling, used to find groups or subtypes of cases in multivariate categorical data.
20 The National Youth Survey is a longitudinal study based at the University of Colorado that began in 1976. At that time, 1,725 adolescents between the ages of 11 and 17 years old – as well as one of their parents – were interviewed.
21 The Rutgers Health and Human Development Project is a prospective, longitudinal study of the emergence of alcohol and other drug-use behaviours in interaction with the individual's physical, psychological, and social development from adolescence into adulthood.
22 See the next section for further development of the age-graded theory of informal social control.
23 "Job quality" is defined as the non-economic aspects of jobs, such as the nature and content of the work performed, working-time arrangements and workplace relationships. It also includes adequate earning and labour security.
24 The National Supported Work Demonstration Project was a randomly controlled trial that assigned ex-offenders, ex-addicts, and juveniles to employment and control groups across 15 sites in the United States.

25 The Peterborough Adolescent and Young Adult Development Study (PADS+) is an ongoing longitudinal study of a cohort of 716 randomly selected boys and girls from the UK city of Peterborough who turned 12 in 2003.
26 The Teesside Studies of Youth Transition and Social Exclusion are a range of qualitative studies of youth transitions in contexts of multiple deprivation that were undertaken in the poorest towns of England between the 1990s and early 2000s.
27 The OLS is a three-wave panel study of adolescents, surveyed in 1982 when they resided in state-level juvenile correctional institutions.
28 The DESDRUG study was a research conducted in Belgium with desisting and recovering offenders.
29 The inmates had two previous convictions for felony and were on average 27 years old at the first wave of the study in 1978.
30 White matter volume is a measure of myelin, a material that forms a layer around the axon of a neuron and allows nerve impulses to travel quicker, improving the integration of brain activity (Paus et al., 2001).
31 The MacArthur Juvenile Capacity Study was conducted in the United States, and examined age differences in those cognitive and psychosocial capacities that are relevant to juveniles' criminal blameworthiness. For this research, data from 935 males and females aged 10–30 was analysed.
32 Piquero et al. (2005) explored the developmental transition of legal socialisation using longitudinal data; meanwhile, Fagan and Tyler (2005) examined the relation of legal socialisations using cross-sectional data.

References

Abeling-Judge, D. (2020). Social bonding experiences facilitating desistance in adolescence. Crime & Delinquency, 7(2): 287–315.

Abell, L. (2018). Exploring the transition to parenthood as a pathway to desistance. *Journal of Developmental and Life-Course Criminology*, 4(4): 395–426.

Agnew, R. (2003). An integrated theory of the adolescent peak in offending. *Youth & Society*, 34(3): 263–299.

Albert, D. and Steinberg, L. (2011). Judgment and decision making in adolescence. *Journal of Research on Adolescence*, 21(1): 211–224.

Albertson, K., Phillips, J., Fowler, A., & Collinson, B. (2020). Who owns desistance? A triad of agency enabling social structures in the desistance process. *Theoretical Criminology* 1–20.

Anderson, A. and Hughes, L. (2009). Exposure to situations conducive to delinquent behavior: The effects of time use, income, and transportation. *Journal of Research in Crime and Delinquency*, 46: 5–34.

Apel, R., and Horney, J. (2017). How and why does work matter? Employment conditions, routine activities, and crime among adult male offenders. *Criminology*, 55(2): 307–343.

Aresti, A., Eatough, V. and Brooks-Gordon, B. (2010). Doing time after time: An interpretative phenomenological analysis of reformed ex-prisoners' experiences of self-change, identity and career opportunities. *Psychology Crime and Law*, 16(3): 169–190.

Arnett, J. J. (2004). *Emerging Adulthood: The Winding Road from the Late Teens through the Tweties*. New York, NY: Oxford University Press.

Aronson, E. (1968). 'Dissonance theory: Progress and problems'. In: Abelson, R. P., Aronson, E., McGuire, W. J., Newcomb, T. M., Rosenberg M. J. and Tannenbaum P. H. (eds.) *Theories of Cognitive Consistency: A Sourcebook*. Chicago, IL: Rand McNally, pp. 5–27.

Ayers, C., Williams, J., Hawkings, J. D., Peterson, P., Catalano, R. and Abbot, R. (1999). Assessing correlates of onset, escalation, deescalation, and desistance of delinquent behavior. *Time*, 15(3): 277–306.

Bachman, R., Kerrison, E. M., Paternoster, R., Smith, L. and O'Connell, D. (2015). The complex relationship between motherhood and desistance. *Women and Criminal Justice*, 26(3): 212–231.

Bachman, R., Rodriguez, S., Kerrison, E. M., & Leon, C. (2019). The recursive relationship between substance abuse, prostitution, and incarceration: Voices from a long-term cohort of women. *Victims and Offenders*, 14(5): 587–605.

Bakken, N. W. (2009). *Making it on the Outside: Gender Differences in the Desistance Process among Drug Involved Offenders*. PhD thesis, USA: University of Delaware.

Barnett, A., Blumstein, A. and Farrington, D. P. (1989). A prospective test of a criminal career model. *Criminology*, 27(2): 373–387.

Barr, A. B. and Simons, R. L. (2015). Different dimensions, different mechanisms? Distinguishing relationship status and quality effects on desistance. *Journal of Family Psychology*, 29(3): 1–11.

Barry, M. (2006). *Youth Offending in Transition: The Search for Social Recognition*. London: Routledge.

Barry, M. (2010). Youth transitions: From offending to desistance. *Journal of Youth Studies*, 13(1): 121–136.

Barry, M. (2012). 'Young woman in transition: From offending to desistance'. In: Losel, F., Bottoms, A. and Farrington, D. P. (eds.) *Lost in Transition: Young Adult Offenders in the Criminal Justice System*. Cullompton: Willan Publishing, pp. 113–127.

Baskin, D. R. and Sommers, I. B. (1998). *Casualties of community disorder: women's careers in violent crime*. New York: Routledge.

Basto-Pereira, M., and Farrington, D. P. (2020). Lifelong conviction pathways and self-reported offending: Towards a deeper comprehension of criminal career development. *The British Journal of Criminology*, 60(2): 285–302.

Beaver, K. M., Wright, J. P., DeLisi, M. and Vaughan, M. G. (2008). Desistance from delinquency: The marriage effect revisited and extended. *Social Science Research*, 37: 736–752.

Beelmann, A. and Lösel, F. (2006). Child social skills training in developmental crime prevention: Effects on antisocial behavior and social competence. *Psicothema*, 18(3): 603–610.

Benda, B. B. (2005). Gender differences in life-course theory of recidivism: A survival analysis. *International Journal of Offender Therapy and Comparative Criminology*, 49(3): 325–342.

Berndt, T. J. (1979). Developmental changes in conformity to peers and parents. *Developmental Psychology*, 15(6): 608–616.

Berntsen, D. and Rubin, D. (2004). Cultural life scripts structure recall from autobiographical memory. *Memory & Cognition*, 32(3): 427–442.

Bersani, B. E., Laub, J. H. and Nieuwbeerta, P. (2009). Marriage and desistance from crime in the Netherlands: Do gender and socio-historical context matter?. *Journal of Quantitative Criminology*, 25: 3–34.

Bloom, B. & Brown, M. (2011). 'Incarcerated women: Motherhood on the margins'. In J. Lawston & A. Lucas (eds.). *Razor Wire Women: Prisoners, Activists, Scholars and Artists*. Albany, NY: State University of New York Press, pp. 51–66.

Block, C. R., Blokland, A., van der Werff, C., van Os, R. and Nieuwbeerta, P. (2010). Long-terms patterns of offending in women. *Feminist Criminology*, 5(1): 73–107.

Blokland, A. and Nieuwbeerta, P. (2005). The effects of life circumstance on longitudinal trajectories of offending. *Criminology*, 43(4): 1203–1240.

Blumstein, A. and Cohen, J. (1987). Characterizing criminal careers. *Science*, 237: 985–991.

Blumstein, A., Cohen, J., Roth, J. A. and Visher, C. A. (1986). *Criminal Careers and 'Career Criminals'*. Washington, DC: National Academy Press.

Boonstoppel, S. (2019). "It's not about me no more": Fatherhood and mechanisms of desistance among at-risk men. *Journal of Developmental and Life-Course Criminology*, 5(3): 335–365.

Bottoms, A. (2002). 'Morality, crime, compliance and public policy'. In: Bottoms, A. and Tonry, M. (eds.) *Ideology, Crime and Criminal Justice*. Portland, United States: Willan Publishing, pp. 20–51.

Bottoms, A. (2014). 'Desistance from Crime'. In: Ashmore, Z. and Shuker, R. (eds.) *Forensic Practice in the Community*. London: Routledge, pp. 251–273.

Bottoms, A. and Shapland, J. (2011). 'Steps towards desistance among male young adult recidivists'. In: Farrall, S., Hough, M., Maruna, S. and Sparks, R. (eds.) *Escape Routes: Contemporary Perspectives on Life after Punishment*. Oxon: Routledge, pp. 43–80.

Bottoms, A. and Shapland, J. (2014). Can persistent offenders acquire virtue?. *Studies in Christian Ethics*, 27(3): 318–333.

Bottoms, A. and Shapland, J. (2016). 'Learning to desist early adulthood: the Sheffield Desistance Study'. In: Shapland, J., Farrall, S. and Bottoms, A. (eds.) *Global perspective on desistance: reviewing what we know, looking to the future*. London: Routledge, pp. 99–125.

Bottoms, A., Shapland, J., Costello, A., Holmes, D. and Muir, G. (2004). Towards desistance: Theoretical underpinnings for an empirical study. *The Howard Journal*, 43(4): 368–387.

Bouffard, L. A. and Laub, J. H. (2004). 'Jail or the army: Does military service facilitate desistance from crime?'. In: Maruna, S and Immarigeon, R (eds.) *After Crime and Punishment: Pathways to Offender Reintegration*. Cullompton: Willan Publishing, pp. 129–151.

Bowles, R. A. and Pradiptyo, R. (2005). *Young Adults in the Criminal Justice System: Cost and Benefit Considerations*. Unpublished report of study commissioned by Barrow Cadbury Trust.

Brame, R. et al. (2004). Criminal careers of serious delinquents in two cities. *Youth Violence and Juvenile Justice*, 2(3): 256–272.

Bramlett, M. D. and Mosher, W. D. (2002). 'Cohabitation, Marriage, Divorce and Re-Marriage in the United States'. *Vital Health Statistcs. Series 23, Data from the National Survey Family Growth*, 23(1): pp. 1–93.

Broidy, L. M. and Agnew, R. (1997). Gender and crime: A general strain theory perspective. *Journal Research in Crime and Delinquency*, 34: 275–306.

Broidy, L. M. and Cauffman, E. (2006). *Understanding the Female Offender (NJRS 216615)*. Washington, DC: U.S. Department of Justice, Office of Justice Programs, National Institute of Justice.

Brown, B. B. (2004). 'Adolescent's relationship with peers'. In: Lerner, R. M. and Steinberg, L. (eds.) *Handbook of adolescent psychology*. Hoboken: John Wiley, pp. 363–394.
Brown, M. (2006). Gender, ethnicity, and offending over the life course: Women's pathways to prison in the Aloha State. *Critical Criminology*, 14(2): 137–158.
Brown, M. and Bloom, B. (2009). Reentry and renegotiating motherhood: Maternal identity and success on parole. *Crime & Delinquency*, 55(2): 313–336.
Bryan-Hancock, C. and Casey, S. (2009). Psychological maturity of at-risk juveniles, young adults and adults: Implications for the justice system. *Psychiatry, Psychology and Law*, 17(1): 57–69.
Bryman, A. (2004). *Social Research Methods* (2nd ed.). Oxford: Oxford University Press.
Bryne, C, and Trew, K. (2008). Pathways through crime: The development of crime and desistance in the accounts of men and women offenders. *The Howard Journal of Criminal Justice*, 47(3): 238–258.
Bui, H. and Morash, M. (2010). The impact of network relationships, prison experiences, and internal transformation on women's success after prison release. *Journal of Offenders Rehabilitation*, 49(1): 1–22.
Burnett, R. (2004). 'To re-offend or not re-offend? The ambivalence of convicted property offenders'. In: Maruna, S and Immarigeon, R. (eds.) *After Crime and Punishment: Pathways to Offender Reintegration*. Cullompton: Willan Publishing, pp. 152–180.
Burt, K. B., and Masten, A. S. (2010). 'Development in the transition to adulthood: Vulnerabilities and opportunities'. In: Grant, J. E. and Potenza, M. N. (eds.) *Young Adult Mental Health*. New York, NY: Oxford University Press, pp. 5–18.
Bushway, S. D., Shawn D., Piquero, A., Broidy, L. Cauffman, E. and Mazerolle, P. (2001). An empirical framework for studying desistance as a process. *Criminology*, 39(2): 491–516.
Bushway, S. D., Thornberry, T. P. and Krohn, M. D. (2003). Desistance as a developmental process: A comparison of static and dynamic approaches. *Journal of Quantitative Criminology*, 19(2): 129–153.
Bushway, S. D. and Paternoster, R. (2012). 'Understanding desistance: Theory testing with formal empirical models'. In: MacDonald, J. (ed.) *Measuring Crime and Criminality: Advances in Criminological Theory* (Vol. 7). New Brunswick, NJ: Transaction Publishers, pp. 299–334.
Bushway, S. D. and Paternoster, R. (2013). 'Desistance from crime: A review and ideas for moving forward'. In: Gibson, C. L. and Krohn, M. D. (eds.) *Handbook of Life-Course Criminology*. New York, NY: Springer, pp. 213–231.
Cannon, M. D., and Wilson, B. K. (2005). *2001 recidivism study*. Pine Bluff: Arkansas Department of Corrections.
Capaldi, D. M., Kim, H. K. and Owen, L. D. (2008). Romantic partners' influence on men's likelihood of arrest in early adulthood. *Criminology*, 46(2): 267–299.
Carlsson, C. (2013). 'Masculinities, persistence, and desistance'. *Criminology*, 51(3): 661–693.
Carlsson, C. (2016). 'Human agency, criminal careers, and desistance'. In: Shapland, J., Farrall S. and Bottoms, T. (eds.) *Global Perspectives on Desistance*. Abingdon: Routledge, pp. 28–49.
Casey, B., Getz, S. and Galvan, A. (2008). The adolescent brain. *Developmental Review*, 28(1): 62–77.
Cauffman, E. and Steinberg, L. (2000). '(Im)maturity of judgment in adolescence: why adolescents may be less culpable than adults'. *Behavioral Science & the Law*, 18(6): 741–60.

Cauffman, E., Steinberg, L. and Piquero, A. R. (2005). Psychological, neuropsychological and physiological correlates of serious antisocial behavior in adolescence: The role of self-control. *Criminology*, 43(1): 133–176.

Cauffman, E., Shulman, E. P., Steinberg, L., Claus, E., Banich, M. T., Graham, S. and Woolard, J. (2010). Age differences in affective decision making as indexed by performance on the Iowa Gambling Task. *Developmental Psychology*, 46(1): 193–207.

Christian, J., Veysey, B., Herrschaft, B. and Tubman-Carbone, H. (2009). 'Moments of transformations: Formerly incarcerated individuals' narratives of change'. In: Veysey, B., Christian J. and Martinez D. J. (eds.) *How Offenders Transform Their Lives*. Cullompton: Willan Publishing, pp:12–29.

Cline, H. F. (1980). 'Criminal behavior over the life span.' In: Brim, O. G. and Kagan, J. (eds.) *Constancy and Change in Human Development*. Cambridge, MA: Harvard University Press.

Cobbina, J. (2009). 'From prison to home: Women's pathways in and out of crime'. Paper presented at the annual meeting of the ASC Annual Meeting, *St. Louis, Missouri, St. Louis Adam's Mark*.

Cobbina, J. (2010). Reintegration success and failure: Factors impacting reintegration among incarcerated and formerly incarcerated women. *Journal of Offenders Rehabilitation*, 49(3): 210–232.

Cobbina, J., Huebner, B. and Berg, M. (2012). Men, women, and postrelease offending: An examination of the nature of the link between relational ties and recidivism. *Crime and Delinquency*, 58: 331–361.

Codd, H. (2020). Prisons, older people, and age-friendly cities and communities: Towards an inclusive approach. *International Journal of Environmental Research and Public Health*, 17(24): 1–15.

Cohn, E. S., Bucolo, D., Rebellon, C. J. and Van Gundy, K. (2010). An integrated model of legal and moral reasoning and rule-violating behavior: The role of legal attitudes. *Law and Human Behavior*, 34(4): 295–309.

Colby, A. and Kohlberg, L. (1987). *The Measurement of Moral Judgment (Vol. 1). Theoretical Foundations and Research Validations; (Vol. 2) Standart Issue Scoring Manual*. New York, NY: Cambridge University Press.

Coleman, C. and Vander Laenen, F. (2017). 'The desistance process of offenders who misuse drugs'. In: Hart, E. L. and van Ginneken, E. (eds.) *New Perspectives on Desistance. Theoretical and Empirical Developments*. London: Palgrave Macmillan, pp. 61–84.

Colwell, L. H., Cruise, K. R., Guy, L. S. and McCoy, W. K. (2005). The influence of psychosocial maturity on male juvenile offenders' comprehension and understanding of the Miranda warning. *The Journal of the American Academy of Psychiatry and the Law*, 33(4): 444–454.

Cooley, C. H. (1902). *Human Nature and the Social Order*. Cornell: Cornell University Library Print.

Copp, J. E., Giordano, P. C., Longmore, M. A., & Manning, W. D. (2019). Desistance from crime during the transition to adulthood: The influence of parents, peers, and shifts in identity. *Journal of Research in Crime and Delinquency*, 57(3): 294–332.

Craig, J. and Foster, H. (2013). Desistance in the transition to adulthood: The roles of marriage, military, and gender. *Deviant Behavior*, 34(3): 208–223.

Crone, E., Bunge, S., Latenstein, H. and van der Molen, M. (2005). Characterization of children's decision making: Sensitivity to punishment frequency, not task complexity. *Child Neruropsychology*, 11(3): 245–263.

Cross, S. E. and Gore, J. S. (2005). 'Cultural models of the self'. In: Leary, M. R. and Tangney, J. P. (eds.) *Handbook of Self and Identity*. London: Guilford Press, pp. 536–564.
Cruise, K., Fernandez, K., McCoy, W. K., Guy, L. S., Colwell, L. H. and Douglas, T. R. (2008). The influence of psychosocial maturity on adolescent offenders delinquent behavior. *Youth Violence and Juvenile Justice*, 6(2): 178–194.
Cusson, M., and Pinsonneault, P. (1986). 'The decisión to give up crime'. In: Cornish D. and Clarke R. (eds.) *The Reasoning Criminal: Rational Choice Perspectives on Offending*. New York, NY: Springer-Verlag, pp. 72–82.
Daly, K. (2010). 'Feminist perspectives in criminology: a review with Gen Y in mind'. In E. McLaughlin and T. Newburn (eds.) *The Handbook of Criminological Theory*. London: Sage, pp. 225–246.
Damon, W. (1977). *The Social World of the Child*. San Francisco, CA: Jossey-Bass.
Dawson, T. L. (2002). New tools, new insights: Kohlberg's moral judgement stages revisited. *International Journal of Behavioral Development*, 26(2): 154–166.
De Li, S. and MacKenzie, D. L. (2003). The gendered effects of adult social bonds on the criminal activities of probationers. *Criminal Justice Review*, 28(2): 278–298.
DiPietro, S. M., Doherty, E. E., & Bersani, B. E. (2018). Understanding the role of marriage in black women's offending over the life course. *Journal of Developmental and Life-Course Criminology*, *4*(2): 162–187.
Doherty, E. E. and Ensminger, M. E. (2013). Marriage and offending among a cohort of disadvantaged African Americans. *The Journal of Research in Crime and Delinquency*, 50(1): 104–131.
Doherty, E. E. and Bersani, B. E. (2018). Mapping the age of official desistance for adult offenders: Implications for research and policy. *Journal of Developmental and Life-Course Criminology*, 4(4): 516–551.
Donovan, J. E., Jessor, R. and Costa, F. M. (1991). Adolescent health behavior and conventionality-unconventionality: An extension of problem-behavior therapy. *Health Psychology*, 10(1): 52–61.
Ebaugh, H. R. (1988). *Becoming an EX*. Chicago, IL: University of Chicago Press.
Edin, K. & Kefalas, M. J. (2005) *Promises I can keep: Why poor women put motherhood before marriage*. Berkeley, CA: University of California Press.
Edin, K. and Kefalas, M. (2011). *Promises I Can Keep: Why Poor Women Put Motherhood before Marriage*. Berkeley, CA: University of California Press.
Edwards, T. M. (2009). Capacity and the adolescent brain. *Psychiatry, Psychology and Law*, 16(3): 427–434.
Eisenberg, N., Cumberland, A., Guthrie, I., Murphy, B. C. and Shepard, S. A. (2005). Age changes in prosocial responding and moral reasoning in adolescence and early adulthood. *Journal of Research on Adolescence: The Official Journal of the Society for Research on Adolescence*, 15(3): 235–260.
Elliot, D. (1994). Serious and violent offenders: Onset, development course, and termination—The American society of criminology 1993 presidential address. *Criminology*, 32: 1–21.
Elliot, D. S., Huizinga, D. and Menard, S. (1989). *Research in Criminology. Multiple Problem Youth: Delinquency, Substance Use, and Mental Health Problems*. New York, NY: Springer.
Emery, C. R., Jolley, J. M. and Wu, S. (2010). Desistance from intimate partner violence: The role of legal cynicism, collective efficacy, and social disorganization in Chicago neighborhoods. *American Journal of Community Psychology*, 48(3–4): 373–383.

Erickson, K. G., Crosnoe, R. and Dornbusch, S. M. (2000). A social process model of adolescent deviance: Combining social control and differential association perspectives. *Journal of Youth and Adolescence*, 29(4): 395–425.

Ezell, M. E. and Cohen, L. E. (2005). *Desisting from Crime: Continuity and Change in Long-Term Crime Patterns of Serious Chronic Offenders*. New York, NY: Oxford University Press.

Fabio, A., Tu, L., Loeber, R. and Cohen, J. (2011). Neighborhood socioeconomic disadvantage and the shape of the age-crime curve. *American Journal of Public Health*, 101: S325–S332.

Facio, A. and Micocci, F. (2003). Emerging adulthood in Argentina. *New Directions for Child and Adolescent Development*, 100: 21–31.

Fagan, A. (1989). The social organization of drug use and drug dealing among urban gangs. *Criminology*, 27(4): 633–670.

Fagan, A. and Tyler, T. (2005). Legal socialization of children and adolescents. *Social Justice Research*, 18(3): 217–241.

Fagan, A. and Western, J. (2005). Escalation and deceleration of offending behaviours from adolescence to early adulthood. *Australian and New Zealand Journal of Criminology*, 38(1): 59–76.

Farrall, S. (2002). *Rethinking What Works with Offenders: Probation, Social Context and Desistance from Crime*. Willan: Cullompton.

Farrall, S. (2010). European criminal careers research: An introduction to the special issue. *European Journal of Criminology*, 7(6): 419–423.

Farrall, S. and Bowling, B. (1999). 'Structuration, human development and desistance from crime'. *The British Journal of Criminology*, 39(2): pp. 253–268.

Farrall, S. and Calverley, A. (2006). *Understanding Desistance from Crime: Theoretical Directions in Resettlement and Rehabilitation*. Maidenhead: Open University Press.

Farrall S., Hunter B., Sharpe G. and Calverley, A. (2014) *Criminal Careers in Transition: The Social Context of Desistance from Crime*. Oxford: Oxford University Press.

Farrington, D. P. (1986). Age and crime. *Crime and Justice*, 7: 189–250.

Farrington, D. P. (1989). Early predictors of adolescent aggression and adult violence. *Violence and Victims*, 4(2): 79–100.

Farrington, D. P. (2007). Advancing knowledge about desistance. *Journal of Contemporary Criminal Justice*, 23(1): 125–134.

Farrington, D. P. (2019). The duration of criminal careers: How many offenders do not desist up to age 61?. *Journal of Developmental and Life-Course Criminology*, 5(1): 4–21.

Farrington, D. P. et al. (2003). Predictive, concurrent, prospective and retrospective validity of self-reported delinquency. *Criminal Behaviour and Mental Health*, 13(3): 179–197.

Farrington, D. P. and Hawkins, J. D. (1991). Predicting participation, early onset, and later persistence in officially recorded offending. *Criminal Behaviour and Mental Health*, 1: 1–33.

Farrington, D. P. and Welsh, B. C. (2007). *Saving Children from a Life of Crime: Early Risk Factors and Effective Interventions*. Oxford: Oxford University Press.

Farrington, D. P. & West, D. J. (1995). 'Effects of marriage, separation and children on offending by adult males'. In: Blau, Z. S., & Hagan J., (eds.) *Current perspectives on aging and the life cycle: Vol. 4. Delinquency and disrepute in the life course*. Greenwich, CT: JAI Press, pp. 249–281.

Farrington, D. P., Barnett, A. and Blumstein, A. (2020). The meaning of "intermittency" in criminal careers. *Journal of Developmental and Life-Course Criminology*, 6(4): 524–528.

Farrington, D. P., Loeber, R. and Jolliffe, D. (2008). 'The age-crime curve in reported offending'. In: Loeber, D. P., Farrington, D. P., Stouthamer-Loeber, M. and White, H. R. (eds.) *Violence and Serious Theft: Development and Prediction from Childhood to Adulthood*. New York, NY: Routledge.

Farrington, D. P., Auty, K. M., Coid, J. W., & Turner, R. E. (2013). Self-reported and official offending from age 10 to age 56. *European Journal on Criminal Policy and Research*, 19(2): 135–151.

Farrington, D. P., Ttofi, M. M., Crago, R. V. and Coid, J. W. (2014). Prevalence, frequency, onset, desistance and criminal career duration in self-reports compared with official records. *Criminal Behaviour and Mental Health*, 24(4): 241–253.

Finckenauer, J. O., Tapp, J. and Yakovlev, A. M. (1991). *American and Soviet Youth: A Comparative Study of Legal Socialization*. New Brunswick, NJ: Transaction.

Fleisher, M. S. and Krienert, J. L. (2004). Life-course events, social networks, and the emergence of violence among female gang members. *Journal of Community Psychology*, 32(5): 607–622.

Fleming, C. B., White, H. R., Oesterle, S, Haggerty, K. P. and Catalano, R. F. (2010). Romantic relationship status changes and substance use among 18- to 20-year-olds. *Journal of Studies on Alcohol and Drug*, 71: 847–856.

Flood-Page, C., Campbell, S., Harrington, V. and Miller, J. (2000). 'Youth crime: Findings from the 1998/99 youth lifestyles survey'. In: *Home Office Research Study 209*. Home. Office: London. Available from: https://www.oijj.org/sites/default/files/documentos/documental_548_en.pdf

Forrest, W. and Hay, C. (2011). Life-course transitions, self-control and desistance from crime. *Criminology and Criminal Justice*, 11(5): 487–513.

Forrest, W. (2014). Cohabitation, relationship quality, and desistance from crime. *Journal of Marriage and Family*, 76(3): 539–556.

Forste, R., Clarke, L. and Bahr, S. (2011). Staying out of trouble: Intentions of young male offenders. *International Journal of Offenders Therapy and Comparative Criminology*, 55(3): 430–444.

Fowers, B. J. (2006). 'Psychotherapy, character, and the good life'. In: Slife, B. D. and Richardson, F. C. (eds.) *Critical Thinking about Psychology: Hidden Assumptions and Plausible Alternatives*. Washington, DC: American Psychological Association, pp. 39–60.

Gadd, D. and Farrall, S. (2004). Criminal careers, desistance and subjectivity: Interpreting men's narratives of change. *Theoretical Criminology*, 8(2): 123–156.

Galambos, N. L., Turner, P. K. and Titon-Weave, L. C. (2005). Chronological and subjective age in emerging adulthood the crossover effect. *Journal of Adolescent Research*, 20(5): 538–556.

Gålnander, R. (2019). Desistance from crime—To what? Exploring future aspirations and their implications for processes of desistance. *Feminist Criminology*, 15(3): 255–277.

Ganem, N. M. and Agnew, R. (2007). Parenthood and adult criminal offending: The importance of relationship quality. *Journal of Criminal Justice*, 35(6): 630–643.

Garcia-Hallett, J. (2018). Maternal identities and narratives of motherhood: A qualitative exploration of women's pathways into and out of offending. *Feminist Criminology*, 14(2): 214–240.

Gardner, M. and Steinberg, L. (2005). Peer influence on risk taking, risk preference, and risky decision making in adolescence and adulthood: An experimental study. *Developmental Psychology*, 41(4): 625–635.
Garland, D. (2002). *The Culture of Control. Crime and Social Order in Contemporary Society*. Chicago, IL: University of Chicago Press.
Gibbons, D. C. (1965). *Changing the Lawbreaker*. Englewood Cliffs: Prentice-Hall.
Gibbs, J. C. (2003). *Moral Development and Reality: Beyond the Theories of Kohlberg and Hoffman*. Thousand Oaks, CA: Sage Publications.
Giddens, A. (1991). *Modernity and Self-Identity. Self and Society in the Late Modern Age*. Stanford, CA: Stanford University Press.
Gilligan, C. and Attanucci, J. (1988). Two moral orientations: Gender differences and similarities. *Merrill-Palmer Quarterly*, 34(3): 223–237.
Giordano, P. C. (2014). 'Gender, crime, and desistance: Toward a theory of cognitive transformation.' In John A. Humphrey and Peter Cordella (eds.), *Effective Interventions in the Lives of Criminal Offenders*. New York, NY: Springer, pp. 41–62.
Giordano, P. C. (2016). 'Mechanism underlying the desistance process: Reflections on a theory of cognitive transformation'. In: Shapland, J., Farrall S. and Bottoms T. (eds.) *Global Perspectives on Desistance*. Abingdon: Routledge, pp. 11–27.
Giordano, P. C., Cernkovich, S. A. and Holland, D. D. (2003). Changes in friendship relations over the life course: Implications for desistance from crime. *Criminology*, 41(2): 293.
Giordano, P., Cernkovich, S. and Rudolph, J. (2002). Gender, crime, and desistance: Toward a theory of cognitive transformation. *American Journal of Sociology*, 107(4): 990–1064.
Giordano, P. C., Longmore, M.A., Schroeder, R. D. and Seffrin, P. M. (2008). A life-course perspective on spirituality and desistance from crime. *Criminology*, 46(1): 99–132.
Giordano, P. C., Schroeder, R. D. and Cernkovic, S. A. (2007). Emotions and crime over the life course: A neo-median perspective on criminal community and change. *American Journal of Sociology*, 112(6): 1603–1661.
Giordano, P. C., Seffrin, P. M., Manning, W. D. and Longmore, M. A. (2011). Parenthood and crime: The role of wantedness, relationships with partners, and ses. *Journal of Criminal Justice*, 39(5): 405–416.
Glaser, D. (1969). Introduction. *Journal of Research in Crime and Delinquency*, 6(2): 109.
Glueck, S. and Glueck, E. (1943). *Criminal Career in Retrospect*. New York, NY: The Commonwealth Fund.
Goffman, E. (1963). *Stigma: Notes on the Management of Spoiled Identity*. Hoboken, NJ: Prentice-Hall.
Goldweber, A., Dmitrieva, J., Cauffman, E., Piquero, A. and Steinberg, L. (2011). The development of criminal style in adolescence and young adulthood: Separating the lemmings from the loners. *Journal of Youth and Adolescence*, 40(3): 332–346.
Gottfredson, M., and Hirshi, T. (1983). Age and the explanation of crime. *The American Journal of Sociology*, 3: 552–584.
Gottfredson, M., and Hirshi, T. (1990). *A General Theory of Crime*. Stanford, CA: Stanford University Press.
Gottlieb, A. and Sugie, N. F. (2018). Marriage, cohabitation, and crime: Differentiating associations by partnership stage. *Justice Quarterly*, 36(3): 503–531.
Gove, W. (1985). 'The effect of age and gender on deviant behavior: A biopsychosocial perspective'. In: Rossi, A. S. (ed.) *Gender and the Life Course*. New York, NY: Aldine, pp. 115–144.

Graber, J. A., Brooks-Gunn, J. and Galen, B. R. (1998). 'Betwixt and between: Sexuality in the context of adolescent transitions'. In: Jessor, R. (eds.) *New perspectives on adolescent risk behavior.* New York: Cambridge University, pp. 270–316.
Graham, J. and Bowling, B. (1995). *Young People and Crime.* Home Office Research Study N° 145. London: Home Office.
Greenberg, J. and Pyszczynski, T. (1985). Compensatory self-inflation: A response to the threat to self-regard of public failure. *Journal of Personality and Social Psychology,* 49(1): 273–280.
Gregg, V., Gibbs, J. C. and Basinger, K. S. (1994). Patterns of developmental delay in moral judgment by male and female delinquents. *Merrill-Palmer Quarterly,* 40(4): 538–553.
Gross, N.C., Mason, W.S., & Mceachern, A.W. (1958). Explorations in role analysis: Studies of the school superintendency role. *American Sociological Review, 23,* 463.
Hagan, J. (1998). 'Life course capitalization and adolescent behavioral development'. In: Jessor R. (ed.) *New Perspectives on Adolescent Risk Behavior.* New York, NY: Cambridge University Press, pp. 499–517.
Harris, J. R. (2009). *The Nurture Assumption: Why Children Turn Out the Way They Do.* New York, NY: Free Press.
Hay, C. and Forrest, W. (2008). Self-control theory and the concept of opportunity: The case for a more systematic union. *Criminology,* 46(4): 1039–1072.
Haynie, D. (2002). Friendship networks and delinquency: The relative nature of peer delinquency. *Journal of Quantitative Criminology,* 18(2): 99–134.
Haynie, D., Doogan, N. and Soller, B. (2014). Gender, friendship networks, and delinquency: A dynamic network approach. *Criminology,* 52(4): 688–722.
Healy, D. (2010). *The Dynamics of Desistance: Charting Pathways through Change.* Portland, OR: Willan Publishing.
Healy, D. (2013). Changing fate? Agency and the desistance process. *Theoretical Criminology,* 17(4): 557–574.
Healy, D. (2014). Becoming a desister: Exploring the role of agency, coping and imagination in the construction of a new self. *British Journal of Criminology,* 54(5): 873–891.
Heaven, P. (2001). *The Social Psychology of Adolescence.* London: Palgrave Macmillan.
Herrera, V., Wiersma, J. D. and Cleaveland, H. (2010). Romantic partners' contribution to the continuity of male and female delinquent and violent behavior. *Journal of Research on Adolescence,* 21(3): 608–618.
Hill, T. W. (1971). 'From hell-raiser to family man'. In: Spradley, J. P. and McCurdy, D. W. (eds.) *Conformity and Conflict: Reading in Cultural Anthropology.* Boston, MA: Little, Brown, pp. 186–200.
Hirshi, T. (1969). *Causes of delinquency.* Berkley: University of California Press.
Hoffmann, M. L. (2000). *Empathy and Moral Development: Implications for Caring and Justice.* New York, NY: Cambridge University Press.
Hollway, W. and Jefferson, T. (2000). *Doing Qualitative Research Differently.* London: SAGE Publications.
Hopkins, R. (2009). *An Introduction to Criminological Theory.* Devon: Willan Publishing.
Horney, J. D., Osgood, W. and Marshall, I. (1995). Criminal careers in the short-term: Intra-individual variability in crime and its relation to local life circumstances. *American Sociological Review,* 60: 655–673.
Horney, J. D., Tolan, P. and Weisburd, D. (2012). 'Contextual influence'. In: Loeber, R. and Farrington, D. P. (eds.) *From Juvenile Delinquency to Adult Crime: Criminal Careers, Justice Policy and Prevention.* Oxford: Oxford University Press, pp. 86–117.

Huebner, B., Dejong, C. and Cobbina, J. (2010). Women coming home: Long-term patterns of recidivism. *Justice Quarterly*, 27(2): 225–254.
Hundleby, J. D., Gfellner, B. M. and Racine, D. (2007). Desistance and identity change among aboriginal females. *Identity*, 7(3): 225–253.
Hunt, B. and Farrall, S. (2015). Space, place and desistance from drug use. *Oñati Socio-Legal Series*, 5(3): 954–968.
Hunt, G., Joe-Laidler, K. and MacKenzie, K. (2005). Moving into motherhood: Gang girls and controlled risk. *Youth & Society*, 36(3): 333–373.
Icenogle, G., Steinberg, L., Duell, N., Chein, J., Chang, L., Chaudhary, N., Di Giunta, L., Dodge, K. A., Fanti, K. A., Lansford, J. E., Oburu, P., Pastorelli, C., Skinner, A. T., Sorbring, E., Tapanya, S., Uribe Tirado, L. M., Alampay, L. P., Al-Hassan, S. M., Takash, H. and Bacchini, D. (2019). Adolescents' cognitive capacity reaches adult levels prior to their psychosocial maturity: Evidence for a "maturity gap" in a multinational, cross-sectional sample. *Law and Human Behavior*, 43(1): 69–85.
Irwin, J. (1970). *The Felon*. Englewood Cliffs, NJ: Prentice-Hall.
Johnson, S., Blum, R. and Giedd, J. (2009). Adolescent maturity and the brain: The promise and pitfalls of neuroscience research in adolescent health policy. *The Journal of Adolescent Health: Official Publication of the Society for Adolescent Medicine*, 45(3): 216–221.
Johnson, W. L. and Giordano, P. C. (2020). The role of marriage and military service on reoffending: Race, "the respectability package," and the desistance process. *Armed Forces & Society*, 47(1): 106–125.
Kazemian, L. (2007). Desistance from crime: Theoretical, empirical, methodological, and policy considerations. *Journal of Contemporary Criminal Justice*, 23(1): 5–27.
Kazemian, L., Farrington, D. P. and Le Blanc, M. (2009). Can we make accurate long-term predictions about patterns of de-escalation in offending behavior? *Journal of Youth and Adolescence*, 38(3): 384–400.
Kazemian, L. and Le Blanc, M. (2004). Exploring patterns of perpetration of crime across the life course offense and offender-based viewpoints. *Journal of Contemporary Criminal Justice*, 20(4): 393–415.
Kemper, T. D. (1966). Self-conceptions and the expectations of significant others. *The Sociological Quarterly*, 7(3): 323–344.
Kennedy, S. and Bumpass, L. L. (2008). 'Cohabitation and children's living arrangements: New estimates from the United States'. *Demographic Research*, 19(47): 1663–1692.
Kennet, J. (2001). *Agency and responsibility: A common-sense moral psychology*. Oxford/New York: Clarendon Press/Oxford University Press.
Killen, M. and Smetana, J. G. (eds.) (2006). *Handbook of Moral Development*. Mahwah, NJ: Lawrence Erlbaum Associates Publishers.
King, R. D. (2013). Assisted desistance and experience of probation supervision. *Probation Journal*, 60(2): 136–151.
King, S. (2014). *Desistance Transitions and the Impact of Probation*. London: Routledge.
King, R. D., Massoglia, M. and Macmillan, R. (2007). The context of marriage and crime: Gender, the propensity to marry, and offending in early adulthood. *Criminology*, 45(1): 33–65.
Kirk, D. S. (2009). A natural experiment on residential change and recidivism: Lessons from Hurricane Katrina. *American Sociology Review*, 74(3): 484–505.
Klacynski, P. A. (2005). 'Metacognition and cognitive variability: A dual-process model of decision making and its development'. In: Jacobs, J. E. and Klacynski, P. A.

(eds.) *The Development of Judgment and Decision Making in Children and Adolescents.* London: Publisher, pp. 39–76.

Kohlberg, L. (1984). *The Psychology of Moral Development.* New York, NY: Harper & Row.

Kreagar, D. A., Matsueda, R. L. and Erosheva, E. A. (2010). Motherhood and criminal desistance in disadvantaged neighborhoods. *Criminology*, 48(1): 221–258.

Krohn, M. D. (1986). The web of conformity: A network approach to the explanation of delinquent behavior. *Social Problems*, 33(6): S81–S93.

Kruttschnitt, C., Ferrano, K. and Garter, R. (2002). Women's involvement in serious interpersonal violence. *Aggression and Violent Behavior*, 7(6): 529–565.

Labouvie-Vief, G. (2003). Dynamic integration: Affect, cognition, and the self in adulthood. *Current Directions in Psychological Science*, 12(6): 201–206.

Langan, P. and Farrington, D. P. (1983). Two-track or one-track justice? Some evidence from an English longitudinal. *Journal of Criminal Law and Criminology*, 74: 519–546.

Larson, M., Sweeten, G. and Piquero, A. R. (2016). With or without you? Contextualizing the impact of romantic relationship breakup on crime among serious adolescent offenders. *Journal of Youth and Adolescence*, 45(1): 54–72.

Laub, J. H. and Sampsons, R. J. (2001). Understanding desistance from crime. *Crime and Justice*, 28: 1–69.

Laub, J. H., Sampsons, R. J. and Sweeten, G. A. (2006). 'Assessing Sampson and Laub's life-course theory of crime'. In: Cullen, F. T., Wright, J. P. and Blevins, K. R. (eds.) *Advances in Criminology Theory (Vol 15) Taking Stock: The Status of Criminological Theory.* Piscataway, NY: Transaction Publishers, pp. 313–333.

Le Blanc, M. and Fréchette, M. (1989). *Male Criminal Activity from Childhood to Youth: Multilevel and Developmental Perspectives.* New York, NY: Springer-Verlag.

Le Blanc, M., Côté, G. and Loeber, R. (1991). Temporal paths in delinquency: Stability, regression, and progression analyzed with panel data from an adolescent and a delinquent male sample. *Canadian Journal of Criminology*, 33(1): 23–44.

Le Blanc, M. L. (2002). The offending cycle, escalation and de-escalation in delinquent behavior: A challenge for criminology. *International Journal of Comparative and Applied Criminal Justice*, 26(1): 37–41.

Le Blanc, M. (2011). Escalation and de-escalation in delinquent behaviour: A challenge for criminology. *International Journal of Comparative and Applied Criminal Justice*, 26(1): 53–83.

LeBel, T. P., Burnett, R., Maruna, S. and Bushway, S. (2008). The 'chicken and egg' of subjective and social factors in desistance from crime. *European Journal of Criminology*, 5(2): 131–159.

Lee, W., Moon, J. and Garcia, V. (2020). The pathways to desistance: A longitudinal study of juvenile delinquency. *Deviant Behavior*, 41(1): 87–102.

Leibrich, J. (1992). 'Against the odds: Community based care for psychiatric disabilities in Britain and New Zealand'. In: Close, P. (ed.) *The State and Caring.* London: Palgrave Macmillan, pp. 214–231.

Leibrich, J. (1993). *Straight to the Point, Angels on Giving up Crime.* Dunedin: University Otago Press.

Leverentz, A. (2011). Being a good daughter and sister: Families of origin in the reentry of African American female ex-prisoners. *Feminist Criminology*, 6(4): 239–267.

Lindegaard, M. and Jacques, S. (2014). Agency as a cause of crime. *Deviant Behavior*, 35(2): 85–100.

Loeber, R. and Farrington, D. P. (2012). *From Juvenile Delinquency to Adult Crime: Criminal Careers, Justice Policy and Prevention.* Oxford: Oxford University Press.
Loeber, R. and Le Blanc, M. (1990). Towards a developmental criminology. *Crime and Justice*, 12: 375–473.
Loeber, R. and Le Blanc, M. (1998). Developmental criminology updated. *Crie and Justice*, 23: 115–198.
Loeber, R., Stouthamer-Loeber, M, Van Kammen, W. and Farrington. D. P. (1991). Initiation, escalation, and desistance in juvenile offending and their correlates. *Journal of Criminal Law and Criminology*, 82: 36–82.
Loeber, R. and Le Blanc, M. (1998). Developmental criminology updated. *Crime and Justice*, 23: 115–198.
Loeber, R., Farrington, D. P., Stouthamer-Loeber, M. and Raskin White, H. (2008). *Violence and Serious Theft: Development and Prediction from Childhood to Adulthood.* New York, NY: Routledge.
Loeber, R., Farrington, D. P., Hipwell, A. E., Stepp, S. D., Pardini, D. and Ahonen, L. (2015). Constancy and change in the prevalence and frequency of offending when based on longitudinal self-reports or official records: Comparisons by gender, race, and crime type. *Journal of Developmental and Life-Course Criminology*, 1(2): 150–168.
Loeber, R., Stouthamer-Loeber, M. and Ahonen, L. (2016). 'Key behavioral aspects of desistance from conduct problems and delinquency'. In: Shapland, J., Farrall, S. and Bottoms, T. (eds.) *Global Perspectives on Desistance.* Abingdon: Routledge, pp. 85–98.
Loughran, T. A., Piquero, A. R., Fagan, J. and Mulvey, E. P. (2012). Differential deterrence: Studying heterogeneity and changes in perceptual deterrence among serious youthful offenders. *Crime & Delinquency*, 58(1): 3–27.
Luciana M, Collins P. F., Olson E. A. and Schissel A. M. (2009). Tower of London performance in healthy adolescents: The development of planning skills and associations with self-reported inattention and impulsivity. *Developmental Neuropsychology*, 34: 461–475.
Lynn, K. (2008). Addressing gaps in the maturity of judgment literature: Age differences and delinquency. *Law and Human Behavior*, 32(1): 78–91.
MacDonald, R. and Shildrick, T. (2007). Street corner society: Leisure careers, youth (sub)culture and social exclusion. *Leisure Studies*, 26(3): 339–355.
MacMahon, M. (1995). *Engendering Motherhood: Identity and Self-Transformation in Women's Lives.* New York, NY: Guilford Press.
Maimon, D. and Browning, C. R. (2010). Unstructured socializing, collective efficacy, and violent behavior among urban youth. *Criminology*, 48(2): 443–474.
Maloney, K. P., Moller, L. F. and van den Bergh, B. J. (2009). Women in prison: The central issues of gender characteristics and trauma history. *Public Health*, 123(6): 426–430.
Martinez, D. J. (2009). 'Former prisoners, their family members, and the transformative potential of support'. In: Veysey, B. M., Christian, J. and Martinez, D. J. (eds.) *How Offenders Transform Their Lives.* London: Willian Press, pp. 56–64.
Martinez, D. J. and Christian, J. (2009). The familial relationships of former prisoners. Examining the link between residence and informal support mechanisms. *Journal of Contemporary Ethnography*, 38(2): 201–224.
Maruna, S. (1999). Desistance and development: The psychosocial process of going straight. *British Society of Criminology Conference Selected Proceedings*, 2: 1–25.
Maruna, S. (2001). *Making Good: How Ex-Convicts Reform and Rebuild Their Lives.* Washington, DC: American Psychological Association.

Maruna, S. (2004). Desistance from crime and explanatory style: A new direction in the psychology of reform. *Journal of Contemporary Criminal Justice*, 20(2): 184–200.

Maruna, S. and Farrall, S. (2004). Desistance from crime: A theoretical reformulation. *Kôlner Zeytschrift fûr Soziologie und Sozialpsychologie*, 43: 171–194.

Maruna, S. and Roy, K. (2007). Amputation or reconstruction? Notes on the concept of "knifing off" and desistance from crime. *Journal of Contemporary Criminal Justice*, 23(1): 104–124.

Maruna, S., LeBel, T., Naples, M. and Mitchell, N. (2009). 'Looking-glass identity transformation: Pygmalion and Golem in the rehabilitation process'. In: Veysey, B., Christian, J. and Martinez, D. J. (eds.) *How Offenders Transform Their Lives*. Cullompton: Willan Publishing, pp. 30–55.

Massoglia, M. (2006). Desistance or displacement? The changing patterns of offending from adolescence to young adulthood. *Journal of Quantitative Criminology*, 22(3): 215–239.

Massoglia, M. and Uggen, C. (2007). Subjective desistance and the transition to adulthood. *Journal of Contemporary Criminal Justice*, 23(1): 90–103.

Matsueda, R. L. and Heimer, K. (2004). 'A symbolic interactionist theory of role-transitions, role-commitments, and delinquency'. In: Thornberry, T. P. (ed.) *Advances in Criminological Theory: Developmental Theories of Crime and Delinquency* (Vol. 7). New Brunswick, NJ: Transaction Publishers, pp. 163–213.

Matza, D. (1964). *Delinquency and Drift*. New York, NY: Routledge.

Mayseless, O. and Scharf, M. (2003). What does it mean to be an adult? The Israeli experience. *New Directions for Child and Adolescent Development*, 2003(100): 5–20.

Mazerolle, P., Brame, R., Paternoster, R., Piquero, A. and Dean, C. (2000). Onset age, persistence, and offending versatility: Comparisons across gender. *Criminology*, 38: 1143–1172.

Mazerolle, P. and McPhedran, S. (2019). 'Specialization and versatility in offending'. In: Farrington, D. P., Kazemian, L. and Piquero, A. R. (eds.) *The Oxford Handbook of Developmental and Life-Course Criminology*. New York: Oxford University Press, pp. 49–69.

McCuish, E., Lussier, P., & Rocque, M. (2020). Maturation beyond age: Interrelationships among psychosocial, adult role, and identity maturation and their implications for desistance from crime. *Journal of Youth and Adolescence*, 49(2), 479–493.

McIvor, G., Murray, C. and Jamieson, J. (2004). 'Desistance from crime: Is it different for woman and girls?'. In: Maruna S. and Immarigeon R. (eds.) *After Crime and Punishment: Pathways to Offender Reintegration*. Cullompton: Willan Publishing, pp. 181–197.

McIvor, G., Trotter, C. and Sheehan, R. (2009). Women, resettlement and desistance. *Probation Journal*, 56(4): 347–361.

McIvor, G. (2016). 'Offending and desistance among young women'. In: Kruttschnitt, C. and Bijleveld, C. (eds.) *Lives of Incarcerated Women: An International Perspective. Routledge Frontiers of Criminal Justice, 28*. New York, NY: Routledge, pp. 159–175.

McNeill, F. (2004). Desistance, rehabilitation and correctionalism: Developments and prospects in Scotland. *The Howard Journal of Criminal Justice*, 43(4): 420–436.

McNeill, F. (2016). The fuel in the tank or the hole in the boat? Can sanctions support desistance? In: Shapland, S. F. and Bottoms, T. (eds.) *Global Perspectives on Desistance*. Abingdon: Routledge, pp. 265–281.

Mears, D. P., Ploeger, M. and Warr, M. (1998). Explaining the gender gap in delinquency: Peer influence and moral evaluations of behavior. *Journal of Research in Crime and Delinquency*, 35(3): 251–266.

Meier, A. and Allen, G. (2009). Romantic relationships from adolescence to young adulthood: Evidence from the National Longitudinal Study of Adolescent Health. *The Sociological Quarterly*, 50(2): 308–335.

Meisenhelder, T. (1977). An exploratory study of exiting from criminal careers. *Criminology*, 15: 319–334.

Merton, R. (1957). *Social Theory and Social Structure*. New York, NY: Free Press.

Michalsen, V. (2011). Mothering as a life course transition: Do women go straight for their children? *Journal of Offenders Rehabilitation*, 50(6): 349–366.

Michalsen, V. (2013). A cell of one's own? Incarceration and other turning points in women's journeys to desistance. *International Journal of Offender Therapy and Comparative Criminology*, 63(6): 940–959.

Mijares, J. C. (1997). Early drug use and quits and discharges among adolescent males. *The Journal of Socio-Economics*, 26(4): 439–458.

Miller, J. (2012). Individual offending, routine activities, and activity settings: Revisiting the routine activity theory of general deviance. *Journal of Research in Crime and Delinquency*, 50(3): 390–416.

Ministry of Justice (2011). Re-offending of juveniles: results from the 2009 cohort England and Wales. Ministry of Justice Statistic Bulletin. Available from: www.justice.gov.uk/downloads/publications/statistics-and-data/mojstats/juvenile-reoffending-statistics-09.pdf (Accessed 9 August 2011).

Miranda, A. and Corcoran, C. (2000). Comparison of perpetration characteristics between male juvenile and adult sexual offenders: Preliminary results. *Sexual Abuse: A Journal of Research and Treatment*, 12(3): 179–188.

Modecki, K. (2008). Addressing gaps in the maturity of judgment literature: Age differences and delinquency. *Law and Human Behavior*, 32(1): 78–91.

Moffitt, T. E. (1993). Adolescence-limited and life course persistent antisocial behaviour: A developmental taxonomy. *Psychological Review*, 100: 674–701.

Moffit, T. E. et al. (2001). *Sex Difference in Antisocial Behaviour. Conduct Disorder, Delinquency, and Violence in the Dunedin Longitudinal Study*. Cambridge: Cambridge University Press.

Moloney, M., MacKenzie, K., Hunt, G. and Joe-Laider, K. (2009). The path and promise of fatherhood for gang members. *The British Journal of Criminology*, 49(3): 305–325.

Monahan, K. C., Cauffman, E. and Steinberg, L. (2009). Affiliation with antisocial peers, susceptibility to peer influence, and antisocial behavior during the transition to adulthood. *Developmental Psychology*, 45(6): 1520–1530.

Monsbakker, C., Lyngstad, T. and Skardhamar, T. (2013). Crime and the transition to parenthood the role of sex and relationship context. *British Journal of Criminology*, 53(1): 129–148.

Moore, J. W. and Hagedorn, J. M. (1999). 'What happens to girl in the gang?'. In: Chesney-Lind, M. and Hagedorn, J. M. (eds.) *Female Groups in America*. Chicago, IL: Lake View Press, pp. 177–186.

Morizot, J. and Le Blanc, M. (2007). Behavioral, self, and social control predictors of desistance from crime: A test of launch and contemporaneous effect models. *Journal of Contemporary Criminal Justice*, 23(1): 50–71.

Mulvey, E. P., Steinberg, L., Fagan, J., Cauffman, E., Piquero, A. R. and Chassin, L. (2004). Theory and research on desistance from antisocial activity among serious adolescent offenders. *Youth Violence and Juvenile Justice*, 2(3): 1–24.
Mulvey, E. P., Steinberg, L., Piquero, A. R., Besana, M., Fagan, J., Schubert, C. and Cauffman, E. (2010). Trajectories of desistance and continuity in antisocial behavior following court adjudication among serious adolescent offenders. *Development and Psychopathology*, 22(2): 453.
Murray, C. (2009). Typologies of young resisters and desisters. *Youth Justice*, 9(2): 115–129.
Na, C., Paternoster, R. and Bachman, R. (2015). Within-individual change in arrests in a sample of serious offenders: The role of identity. *Journal of Developmental and Life-Course Criminology*, 1(4): 385–410.
Nagin, D. S. and Land, K. C. (1993). Age, criminal careers, and population heterogeneity: Specification and estimation of a nonparametric, mixed Poisson model. *Criminology*, 31(3): 327–362.
Nagin, D. S., Farrington, D. P. and Moffit, T. E. (1995). Life-course trajectories of different types of offenders. *Criminology*, 33: 111–139.
Nguyen, H. and Loughran, T. A. (2018). On the measurement and identification of turning points in criminology. *Annual Review of Criminology*, 1: 335–358.
Nguyen, H., Kamada, T. and Ramakers, A. (2020). On the margins: Considering the relationship between informal work and reoffending. *Justice Quarterly*, 1–28.
Nieuwbeerta, P., Nagin, D. and Blokland, A. (2009). Assessing the impact of first-time imprisonment on offenders' subsequent criminal career development: A matched samples comparison. *Journal of Quantitative Criminology*, 25: 227–257.
Nugent, B. and Schinkel, M. (2016). The pains of desistance. *Criminology and Criminal Justice*, 16(5): 568–584.
Opsal, T. D. (2011). Women disrupting a marginalized identity: Subverting the parolee identity through narrative. *Journal of Contemporary Ethnography*, 40(2): 135–167.
Osgood, D. and Anderson, A. (2004). Unstructured socializing and rates of delinquency. *Criminology*, 42(3): 519–550.
Palmer, E. (2003). An overview of the relationship between moral reasoning and offending. *Australian Psychologist*, 38: 165–174.
Palmer, E. (2005). 'The relationship between moral reasoning and aggression, and the implications for practice'. *Psychology, Crime and Law*, 11(4): pp. 353–361.
Palmer, E. and Hollin, C. (1998). A comparison of patterns of moral development in young offenders and non-offenders. *Legal and Criminological Psychology*, 3: 225–235.
Paternoster, R. (1989). Decisions to participate in and desist from four types of common delinquency: Deterrence and the rational choice perspective. *Law & Society Review*, 23(1): 7–40.
Paternoster, R. and Bushway, S. D. (2009). Desistance and the "feared self": Toward an identity theory of criminal desistance. *Journal of Criminal Law and Criminology*, 99(4): 1109–1156.
Paternoster, R., Bachman, R., Kerrison, E. and O'Connell, D. J. (2016). Desistance from crime and identity. An empirical test with survival time. *Criminal Justice and Behavior*, 43(9): 1204–1224.
Paus, T., Collins, D. L., Evans, A. C., Leonard, G., Pike, B. and Zijdenbos, A. (2001). Maturation of white matter in the human brain: a review of magnetic resonance studies. *Brain Research Bulletin*, 54(4): pp. 255–266.

Pellissier, B. M., Camp, S. D., Gaes, G. G., Saylor, W. G. and Rhodes, W. (2003). Gender differences in outcomes from prison-based residential treatment. *Journal of Substance Abuse Treatment*, 24(2): 149–160.

Piaget, J. (1932). *The Moral Judgment of the Chile.* Glencoe, IL: Free Press.

Piquero, A. (2004). 'The intermittency of criminal careers'. In: Maruna S. and Immarigeon R. (eds.) *After Crime and Punishment: Pathways to Offender Reintegration.* Cullompton: Willan Publishing, pp. 102–125.

Piquero, A. (2011). Invited address: James Joyce, Alice in Wonderland, The Rolling Stones, and criminal careers. *Journal of Youth and Adolescence*, 40(7): 761–775.

Piquero, A., Farrington, D. P. and Blumstein, A. (2003). The Criminal Career Paradigm. *Crime and Justice*, 30: 359–506.

Piquero, A., Farrington, D. P. and Blumstein, A. (2007). *Key Issues in Criminal Career Research: New Analyses of the Cambridge Study in Delinquent Development.* Cambridge: Cambridge University Press.

Piquero, A., Hawkins, J. D. and Kazemian, L. (2012). 'Criminal career patterns'. In: Loeber, R. and Farrington, D. P. (eds.) *From Juvenile Delinquency to Adult Crime: Criminal Careers, Justice Policy and Prevention.* New York, NY: Oxford University Press, pp. 14–46.

Piquero, A., Moffitt, T. and Wright, B. (2007). Self-control and criminal career dimensions. *Journal of Contemporary Criminal Justice*, 23(1): 72–89.

Piquero, A., Paternoster, R., Mazerolle, P., Brame, R. and Dean, C. (1999). Onset age and offense specialization. *Journal of Research in Crime and Delinquency* 36: 275–299.

Presser, L. (2008). *Been a Heavy Life: Stories of Violent Men.* Urbana, IL: University of Illinois Press, pp. 72–86.

Presser, L. and Kurth, S. (2009). 'I got a quick tongue': Negotiating ex-convict identity in mixed company'. In: Veysey, B., Christian, J. and Martinez, D. J. (eds.) *How Offenders Transform Their Lives.* Cullompton: Willan Publishing.

Prime, J., White, S., Liriano, S. and Patel, K. (2001). *Criminal Careers of Those Born between 1953 and 1978.* Great Britain, Home Office, Research, Development and Statistics Directorate.

Prior, D. et al. (2011). *Maturity, Young Adults and Criminal Justice: A Literature Review.* Birmingham: University of Birmingham.

Prochaska, J. O., Norcross, J. C. and DiClemente, C. C. (1994). *Changing for Good.* New York, NY: William Morrow and Company. Inc./Avon Books.

Quetelet, A. (1984). *Research on the Propensity for Crime at Different Ages.* Cincinnati, OH: Anderson Publishing Company.

Raajimakers, Q., Engels, R. and Van Hoof, A. (2005). Delinquency and moral reasoning in adolescence and young adulthood. *International Journal of Behavioral Development*, 29(3): 247–258.

Reisig, S., Wolfe, S. and Holtfreter, K. (2011). Legal cynicism, legitimacy, and criminal offending: The nonconfounding effect of low self-control. *Criminal Justice and Behavior*, 38(12): 1265–1279.

Rest, J. R., Bebeau, M. J., Narvaez, D. and Thoma, S. (1999). Postconventional moral thinking: A neo-Kohlbergian approach. *Journal of Moral Education*, 29(4): 381–395.

Reyna, V. and Rivers, S. (2008). Current theories of risk and rational decision making. *Development Review*, 28(1): 1–11.

Richie, B. E. (2001). Challenges incarcerated women face as they return to their communities: Findings from life history interviews. *Crime & Delinquency*, 47: 368–389.

Robins, L. N. (1966). *Deviant Children Grown Up: A Sociological and Psychiatric Study of Sociopathic Personality*. Baltimore: William and Wilkins.

Rocque, M. (2015). The lost concept: The (re) emerging link between maturation and desistance from crime. *Criminology and Criminal Justice*, 15(3): 340–360.

Rocque, M., Posick, C. and White, H. (2015). Growing up is hard to do: An empirical evaluation of maturation and desistance. *Journal of Developmental and Life Course Criminology*, 1(4): 350–384.

Rocque, M. (2017). *Desistance from Crime. New Advances in Theory and Research*. New York, NY: Palgrave Macmillan.

Rodermond, E., Kruttschnitt, C., Slotboom, A.-M. and Bijleveld, C. C. (2016). Female desistance: A review of the literature. *European Journal of Criminology*, 13(1): 3–28.

Rodermond, E., Slotboom, A. and Zoutewelle-Terovan, M. (2015). 'Women's re-incarceration: the influence of marriage and children'. In: Kruttschnitt, C. and Bijleveld, C. (eds.) *Lives of Incarcerated Women: An international perspective*. New York: Routledge, pp. 142–158.

Rosenfeld, R., White, H. and Esbensen, F. (2012). 'Special categories of serious and violent offenders: Drug dealers, gang members, homicide offenders, and sex offenders. In: Loeber, R. and Farrington, D. P. (eds.) *From juvenile delinquency to adult crime: Criminal careers, justice policy, and prevention*. New York: Oxford University Press, pp. 118–149.

Rumgay, J. (2004). Scripts for safer survival: Pathways out of female crime. *The Howard Journal of Criminal Justice*, 43(3): 405–419.

Sampson, R. J. and Bartusch, D. (1998). Legal cynicism and (subcultural?) tolerance of deviance: The neighborhood context of racial differences. *Law and Society Review*, 32: 777–804.

Sampson R. J. and Laub J. H. (1993) *Crime in the Making: Pathways and Turning Points through Life*. Cambridge, MA: Harvard University Press.

Sampson, R. J. and Laub, J. H. (2003). Life-course desisters? Trajectories of crime among delinquent boys followed to age 70. *Criminology*, 41(3): 555–592.

Sampson, R. J., Laub, J. H. and Wimer, C. (2006). Does marriage reduce crime? A counterfactual approach to within-individual causal effects. *Criminology*, 44(3): 465–508.

Sanders, T. (2007). Becoming an ex-sex worker a deviant career. *Feminist Criminology*, 2(1): 74–95.

Savolainen, J. (2009). Work, family and criminal desistance: Adult social bonds in a Nordic welfare state. *British Journal of Criminology*, 49(3): 285–304.

Schinkel, M. (2019). Rethinking turning points: Trajectories of parenthood and desistance. *Journal of Developmental and Life-Course Criminology*, 5(3): 366–386.

Schroeder, R. D., Girodano, P. C. and Cernkovich, S. A. (2007). Drug use and desistance processes. *Criminology: An Interdisciplinary Journal*, 45(1): 191–222.

Schroeder, R. D. and Frana, J. F. (2009). Spirituality and religion, emotional coping, and criminal desistance: A qualitative study of men undergoing change. *Sociological Spectrum*, 29(6): 718–741.

Sharpe, G. (2015). Precarious identities: 'Young' motherhood, desistance and stigma. *Criminology and Criminal Justice*, 15(4): 407–422.

Sharpe, G. and Gelsthorpe, L. (2015). 'Women and sentencing: Challenges and choices' In: Roberts, J.V. (ed.) *Exploring Sentencing Practice in England and Wales*. London: Palgrave Macmillan, pp. 118–136.

Shaw, D. S. and Gross, H. (2008) 'What we have learned about early childhood and the development of delinquency'. In: Liberman, A. (eds.) *The long view of crime: A synthesis of longitudinal research*. New York: Springer, pp. 79–127.

Short, J. and Nye, F. (1957). Reported behavior as a criterion of deviant behaviour. *Social Problems* 5: 207–213.

Shover, N. (1996). *Great pretenders: Pursuits and careers of persistent thieves*. Boulder, CO: Westview Press.

Shover, N. and Thompson, C. Y. (1992). Age, differential expectations, and crime desistance. *Criminology*, 30(1): 89–104.

Shover, N. (2004). 'Foreword'. In: Maruna S. and Immarigeon R. (eds.) *After Crime and Punishment: Pathways to Offender Reintegration*. New York, NY: Willan Publishing, pp. vii–xii.

Siennick, S. E. and Osgood, D.W. (2008). 'A review of research on the impact on crime of transitions to adult roles'. In: Liberman, A. (ed.) *The Long View of Crime: A Synthesis of Longitudinal Research*. New York, NY: Springer, pp. 161–187.

Simons, R. L. and Barr, A. B. (2014). Shifting perspectives: Cognitive changes mediate the impact of romantic relationships on desistance from crime. *Justice Quarterly*, 31(5): 793–821.

Simons, R. L, Stewart, E., Gordon, L. C., Conger, R. D. and Enlder, G. H. J. (2002). A test of life-course explanations for stability and change in antisocial behavior from adolescence to young adulthood. *Criminology*, 40: 401–143.

Simpson, S. S., Yahner, J. L., & Dugan, L. (2008). Understanding women's pathways to jail: Analysing the lives of incarcerated women. *Australian and New Zealand Journal of Criminology*, 41(1): 84–108.

Skardhammar, T. and Lyngstad, T. H. (2009). *Family formation, fatherhood and crime. An invitation to a broader perspective on crime and family transitions*. Discussion Papers 579. Statistics Norway, Research Department.

Soothill, K., Francis, B. and Fligestone, R. (2002). *Patterns of Offending Behaviour: A New Approach (Full Report)*. London: Home Office.

Soothill, K., Fitzpatrick, C. and Francis, B. (2009). *Understanding Criminal Careers*. New York: Routledge.

Staff, J., Schulenberg, J., Maslowsky, J., Bachman, J., O'Malley, P., Maggs, J. and Johnston, L. (2010). Substance use changes and social role transitions: Proximal developmental effects on ongoing trajectories from late adolescence through early adulthood. *Development and Psychopathology*, 22: 917–932.

Steinberg, L. (2008). A social neuroscience perspective on adolescent risk-taking. *Developmental Review*, 28(1): 78–106.

Steinberg, L. and Cauffman, E. (1996). Maturity of judgment in adolescence: Psychosocial factors in adolescent decision-making. *Lay and Human Behavior*, 20: 249–272.

Steinberg, L., Chung, H. and Little, M. (2004). Reentry of young offenders from justice system: A developmental perspective. *Youth Violence and Juvenile Justice*, 2(1): 2.

Steinberg, L. and Mohana, K. C. (2007). Age differences in resistance to peer influence. *Development Psychology*, 43(6): 1531–1543.

Steinberg, L. and Silverberg, S. B. (1986). The vicissitudes of autonomy in early adolescence. *Child Development*, 57(4): 841–851.

Stets, J. and Burke, P. (2005). New directions in identity control theory. *Advances in Group Processes*, 22: 43–64.

Stone, R. (2015). Desistance and identity repair: Redemption narratives as resistance to stigma. *British Journal of Criminology*, 56(5): 956–975.

Stone, R., Morash, M., Goodson, M., Smith, S. and Cobbina, J. (2018). Women on parole, identity processes, and primary desistance. *Feminist Criminology*, 13(4): 382–403.

Stouthamer-Loeber, M. A. G. D. A., Wei, E., Loeber, R. and Masten, A. S. (2004). Desistance from persistent serious delinquency in the transition to adulthood. *Development and Psychopathology*, 16(4): 897–918.

Sullivan, C. J., & Piquero, A. R. (2016). The criminal career concept: Past, present, and future. *Journal of Research in Crime and Delinquency*, 53(3): 420–442.

Swann, W. B. (1990). 'To be adored or to be known: The interplay of self-enhancement and self-verification'. In: Higgins, E.T. and Sorrentino, R. M. (eds.) *Handbook of Motivation and Cognition: Foundations of Social Behavior*. New York, NY: The Guilford Press, pp. 408–448.

Tapp, J. and Levine, F. (eds.) (1977). *Law, Justice and the Individual in Society: Psychological and Legal Issues*. New York, NY: Holt, Rinehart & Winston.

Theobald, D. and Farrington, D. P. (2009). Effects of getting married on offending: Results from a prospective longitudinal survey of males. *European Journal of Criminology*, 6(6): 496–516.

Theobald, D. and Farrington, D. P. (2010). Why do the crime-reducing effects of marriage vary with age?. *The British Journal of Criminology*, 51(1): 136–158.

Theobald, D., Farrington, D. P., and Piquero, A. R. (2015). Does the birth of a first child reduce the father's offending? *Australian & New Zealand Journal of Criminology*, 2015, 48(1): 3–23.

Thornberry, T. P. (1987). Toward an interactional theory of deliquency. *Criminology*, 25: 863–891.

Thornberry, T. P. and Krohn, M. D. (1997). 'Peer, drug use, and delinquency'. In: Stoff, D. M., Breiling, J. and Maser J. D. (eds.) *Handbook of Antisocial Behavior*. Hoboken, NJ: John Wiley, pp. 218–233.

Thornton, D. and Reid, R. L. (1982). Moral reasoning and type of criminal offence. *British Journal of Social Psychology*, 21(3): 231–238.

Tripodi, S. J., Kim, J. S. and Bender, K. (2010). Is employment associated with reduced recidivism?: The complex relationship between employment and crime. *International Journal of Offender Therapy and Comparative Criminology*, 54(5): 706–720.

Turanovic, J. J. (2019). Victimization and desistance from crime. *Journal of Developmental and Life-Course Criminology*, 5(1), 86–106.

Turner, V. (1967). *Betwixt-and-Between: The Liminal Period in Rites de Passage. In The Forest of Symbols: Aspects of Ndembu Ritual*. New York, NY: Cornell University Press.

Tyler, T. R. (1990). *Why People Obey the Law*. New Haven: Yale University Press.

Tyler, T. R. (2006). *Why People Obey the Law*. New Jersey: Princeton University Press.

Tyler, T. R. and Huo, Y. J. (2002). *Trust in the Law: Encouraging Public Cooperation with the Police and the Courts*. New York, NY: Russell Sage Foundation.

Uggen, C. (1999). Ex-offenders and the conformist alternative: A job quality model of work and crime. *Social Problems*, 46(1): 127–151.

Uggen, C. (2000). Work as a turning point in the life course of criminals: A duration model of age, employment, and recidivism. *American Sociological Review*, 65(4): pp. 529–546.

Uggen, C. and Kruttschnitt, C. (1998). 'Crime in the breaking: Gender differences in desistance'. *Law & Society Review*, 32(2): pp. 339–366.

Uggen, C., Manza, J. and Behrens, A. (2004). 'Less than the average citizen: Stigma, role transition, and the civic reintegration of convicted felons: Pathways to offender reintegration'. In: Maruna, S. and Immarigeon, R. (eds.) *After Crime and Punishment: Pathways to Offender Reintegration*. Cullompton: Willian Publishing, pp. 258–290.

Uggen, C., and Staff, J. (2001). Work as a turning point for criminal offenders. *Corrections Management Quarterly*, 5(4): 1–16.

Van Der Put & C.E., Dekovic, M. (2011). Changes in risk factors during adolescence: implications for risk assessment. *Criminal Justice and Behavior*, 38(3): 248–262.

Van Gennep, A. (1960). *The Rites of Passage*. Chicago, IL: University of Chicago Press.

Vaughan, B. (2006). The internal narrative of desistance. *The British Journal of Criminology*, 47(3): 390–404.

Vaughan, B. (2007). Editor's note. *Community College Review*, 34(3): 165.

Verbruggen, J., Blokland, A. A. J., & Van Der Geest, V. R. (2012). Effects of employment and unemployment on serious offending in a high-risk sample of men and women from ages 18 to 32 in the Netherlands. *British Journal of Criminology*, 52(5): 845–869.

Veysey, B. M., Martinez, D. J. and Christian, J. (2009). *How Offenders Transform Their Lives*. New York, NY: Routledge.

Visher, C., Winterfield, L. and Coggeshall, M. (2005). Ex-offender employment programs and recidivism: A meta-analysis. *Journal of Experimental Criminology*, 1(3): 295–315.

Warr, M. (1998). Life-course transitions and desistance from crime. *Criminology*, 36(2): 183–216.

Warr, M. (2002). *Companions in Crime. The Social Aspects of Criminal Conduct*. Edinburgh: Cambridge University Press.

Weaver, B. (2016). *Offending and Desistance: The Importance of Social Relations*. London: Routledge.

Weaver, B. and McNeil, F. (2015). Lifelines: Desistance, social relations, and reciprocity. *Criminal Justice Behavior*, 42(1): 95–107.

West, D. J. (1963). *The Habitual Prisoner: An Enquiry by the Cambridge Institute of Criminology. Cambridge Studies in Criminology* (Vol. 19). New York, NY: Macmillan.

Wikström, P.-O. H. (2004). 'Crime as alternative. Towards a cross-level situational action theory of crime causation'. In: McCord, J. (ed.) *Beyond Empiricism: Institutions and Intentions in the Study of Crime*. New Brunswick, NJ: Transaction, pp. 1–37.

Wikström, P-O. H., Mann, R. and Hardie, B. (2018). Young people's differential vulnerability to criminogenic exposure: Bridging the gap between people- and place-oriented approaches in the study of crime causation. *European Journal of Criminology*, 15(1): 10–31.

Wright, J. P. and Cullen, F. T. (2004). Employment, peers, and life-course transitions. *Justice Quarterly*, 21(1): 183–205.

Wright, E., DeHart, D., Koons-Witt, B., and Crittenden, C. (2013). 'Buffers' against crime? Exploring the roles and limitations of positive relationships among women in prison. *Punishment and Society* 15: 71–95.

Wyse, J. J., Harding, D. J. and Morenoff, J. D. (2014). Romantic relationships and criminal desistance: Pathways and processes. *Sociological Forum*, 29(2): 365–385.

Yamaguchi, K. and Kandel, D. B. (1985). Dynamic relationships between premarital cohabitation and illicit drug use: An event-history analysis of role selection and role socialization. *American Sociological Review*, 50(4): 530–546.

Young, J. (2007). *The Vertigo of Late Modernity*. London: Sage.

Zoutewelle-Terovan, M., van der Geest, V., Liefbroer, A. and Biljeveld, C. (2012). Criminality and family formation: Effects of marriage and parenthood on criminal behavior for men and woman. *Crime & Delinquency*, 60(8): 1209–1234.
Zoutewelle-Terovan, M., van der Geest, V., Liefbroer, A. and Biljeveld, C. (2014). Criminality and family formation: Effects of marriage and parenthood on criminal behavior for men and women. *Crime & Delinquency*, 60(8): 1209–1234.

Chapter 2

Researching transitions

During the design, implementation, and analysis phases of the present research, several methodological decisions were made; the rationale underpinning them is described here. First, I wanted to immerse myself deeply in the environments, routines, and cultures that provided the context for the life stories of young offenders. I therefore decided to embark personally on a primary data collection effort. This process was substantially enriched not only by the time I spent collecting the data directly, but also by the time I spent in the participants' own neighbourhoods, waiting for them in probation centres and listening to the informal conversations they had with each other, or talking with their families when trying to locate them. All these experiences allowed me to gain a first-hand understanding of cultural meanings and resonances that were of strong relevance when interpreting the results.

Second, I decided only to include young people who were serving community sanctions to observe the desistance process and the obstacles they face in their lived experience; in the first wave of the study, therefore, young people who were serving prison sentences were excluded. As a result, the present cohort of respondents has an unavoidable bias, in that it is composed of less serious offenders than the ones who were imprisoned. Despite this, however, the young people in the study were by no means first time offenders: they all had a relevant criminal history and several previous convictions. The study included young offenders aged between 16 and 20 years – the period of late adolescence in which crime peaks, and after which it begins to decline. This choice stemmed from the desire to investigate the first stages of the desistance process and to bring new evidence to light regarding desistance during late adolescence. In the case of women, since the number of young female offenders who were serving community sentences in Santiago in 2012 was very small (they represent 8% of adolescent offenders in Chile), it was decided not to include them in the panel, and to investigate their desistance process through in-depth interviews.

Third, the use of mixed methods was a key decision for the study. As noted in the introduction of the book, there is lack of large-scale quantitative

DOI: 10.4324/9781003160809-3

criminological research in Latin America, developing a panel study with juvenile offenders was therefore essential not only for academic purposes, but more importantly as a means of informing public policy decisions. In Chile, there are many myths about juvenile delinquency that pervade the popular imagination, leading to the promotion of harsher sentences and even political campaigns to lower the age of criminal responsibility. Having data on the trajectories of adolescent offenders is key to demonstrating that delinquency is not chronic, and that young people who commit crimes are not the "evil children" that many citizens seem to believe they are.

Nevertheless, quantitative methods have some limitations – especially when addressing phenomenological aspects linked to desistance, such as identities, emotions, tensions, and symbols that arise throughout the process of leaving crime behind (Presser, 2010); this research, therefore, strongly emphasises the information drawn from qualitative sources. Indeed, besides providing crucial data in and of themselves, the in-depth interviews contributed to a far deeper understanding of several aspects revealed in the questionnaires; they offered windows into social and cultural meanings which otherwise would have been impossible to interpret correctly (Patton, 2002). As Young (2011:82) pointed out, "Correlation alone cannot assure causality, it is only the narratives which link factors to outcomes that can do this".

Fourth, to allow the desistance process to be investigated without falling foul of the bias that may result from the recapitulation of past events, a prospective longitudinal questionnaire over one year was used. Due to practical exigencies, it was not possible to conduct in-depth interviews prospectively – an unfortunate limitation of the study, since it would have been particularly interesting to re-interview the qualitative sample one year after the first interview. Nevertheless, since the aim of the present research is to explore the process of crime abandonment, it was of lesser importance to focus on juveniles who had already desisted from crime (something which is in any case impossible to determine); instead, the task was to observe the changing process and, in Maruna's words, to note how they were actually changing "right before my eyes as I interviewed them" (2001:38).

Finally, the sources of information of the present study were the narratives of the young people themselves. Again, the practicalities of this study mean that it was not possible to interview significant others, probation officers, or peers. Given that the process of moving away from crime is so strongly anchored in the so-called "looking-glass self-concept" (Maruna, 2001), this is undoubtedly an important limitation of the study that must be accounted for and corrected in future waves.

The Trajectories Study

The research was exploratory in nature and combined quantitative and qualitative methods. As outlined in the introduction, the general aim of this research was to explore the transition from crime to conformity among a sample of Chilean juvenile offenders, and to identify theoretical, policy, and practice implications from the findings. For these purposes, the research is divided in three specific objectives: (1) to explore the process of moving away from crime, its obstacles and challenges; (2) to investigate the factors that may be involved in the transition from crime to conformity among a sample of male young offenders; and (3) to explore the gender particularities of the process of moving away from crime among a sample of young female offenders. As it will be shown next, each of these aims uses different data sources to be explored. Table 2.1 presents them in detail. The analyses presented in the next chapters draw from three data sources:

- A two-wave prospective questionnaire (panel), administered over one year to a sample of 334 late-adolescent offenders (males, aged 16–20) who were sentenced to probation and semi-prison[1] in 2012 in Santiago, Chile;
- 35 in-depth interviews conducted with a sub-sample of individuals from the panel in the first wave of interviews; and
- 30 retrospective semi-structured interviews conducted during the first wave of the study with a sample of juvenile female offenders (aged 16–20) who were sentenced to probation or semi-prison in 2012 in Santiago, Chile.

Table 2.1 Aims, research questions, and sources of information

Aim	*Research questions*	*Sources of information*
To explore the process of moving away from crime, its obstacles and challenges	Who desists and who persists? How do the participants experience the process and failed process of moving away from crime?	Two waves of prospective questionnaires with a sample of 334 young male offenders 35 in-depth interviews with young male offenders
To investigate the factors that may be involved in the transition from crime to conformity among a sample of male young offenders	Which factors increase the probability of desistance? Do these factors change when different explanatory models and operationalisations of desistance are used?	Two waves of prospective questionnaires with a sample of 334 young male offenders 35 in-depth interviews with young male offenders
To explore the gender particularities of the desistance process among a sample of young female offenders	How does gender shape, limit, and structure women's process of moving away from crime?	30 in-depth interviews with young female offenders

Prospective questionnaire

It is important to mention that the quantitative data used for the present research comes from a larger study, whose objectives are broader than the research of the processes of crime abandonment. The data comes from the Trajectories Study, a longitudinal research project (based at the Centre of Studies on Justice and Society of the Pontificia Universidad Católica de Chile) that explores the criminal and life trajectories within a sample panel of young male and female offenders in Chile. Three waves of questionnaires have been completed since it began in 2012. As part of this research centre, I actively participated in this study as a researcher: together with my colleagues, I designed the questionnaires, participated in its application, and was part of all the relevant methodological decisions during the fieldwork. It is, however, a data set designed to satisfy a number of different research interests; as a result, it includes data not only relating to desistance, but also to drug use and mental health (among other things). Our work was supported by nine other interviewers – a group comprised of advanced students of sociology and psychology, trained by myself and my research colleagues for the application of the questionnaires.

Although the study has three waves of data, the third was not complete at the time of writing; my analyses therefore only use data from the first and the second waves. The first wave took place between August 2012 and January 2013, and the second wave between November and April 2013; each wave consisted of one questionnaire.

First wave of surveys

The study intended to include all the male young offenders (ages 16–20) who were serving a community sentence or a semi-prison sentence between August 2012 and January 2013 in Santiago, the capital city of Chile.[2] For these purposes, we signed an agreement with the Chilean Youth Justice Board and they gave us access to their data sets. These data contained the socio-demographic information of the young offenders, as well as the name of the probation and semi-prison centres in which they were serving their sentences. Therefore, the first step was to contact the centres and to coordinate visits to arrange the interviews.

At that time, there were a total of 26 centres in Santiago; we visited all of them. During those visits, we met with the centres' directors and probation officers, and arranged the dates on which we were going to interview the juveniles. We discussed with them the ethical issues involved in the study (see next) and agreed that every juvenile who was going to participate had to be contacted first by his probation officer, who would then tell him about the study and ensure his willingness to participate. In the case of the probation centres, since these juveniles did not spend the whole day there, the probation officer helped us to arrange a specific date and time for the interviews. Juveniles in semi-prison centres only stay there during the evening and night, so we visited those centres over the course of several evenings.

The questionnaire was administered by a team of researchers (including myself) and other trained interviewers, and each lasted for an average of 40–60 minutes. Every participant signed an informed consent form and got a leaflet about the study which contained contact details of the team in case any doubts or questions arose. A total of 57% of the juveniles who were serving a community sentence in Santiago during the fieldwork period were interviewed (613 of a possible 1069); of the remainder, 15% did not want to participate and 28% were not found in the centres (despite their names appearing on the lists provided by the Youth Justice Board). A bias analysis using the data provided by the Youth Justice Board was conducted (ISUC, 2013) due to non-response in the sample. Although this analysis has several limitations,[3] it was possible to determine that there was a bias of 7% which mainly refers to the fact that the study sample was composed by younger offenders, with lower consumption of drugs and a lower proportion of young people convicted for theft than the reference population (the 1069 young people who were on the official lists). Nevertheless, no bias was found regarding the amount of previous convictions.

The questionnaire used for the first wave was focused on several areas (see Table 2.2). A life calendar (Roberts & Horney, 2010) was used to collect retrospective information regarding life trajectories from the age of 4 in the areas of living arrangements, drug use, criminal behaviour, school attendance, and occupation. The questionnaire also included a section for them to fill in their contact details for the second wave, such as addresses, phone numbers, and Facebook profile name.

The quality of the information collected was assessed through a supervision process, in which an aleatory sample of questionnaires was cross-checked with official data. Before applying the questionnaire, a pilot stage was undertaken in which it was discussed with a group of seven young offenders (who did not subsequently participate in the full study) and a group of three probation officers. All their suggestions were incorporated, with several changes being made to word choices and idiomata; this ensured that the questions would make sense to the participants, and that the flow of the questionnaire would not produce unintended resistance or emotional disturbance.

Second wave of surveys

For the second wave, the questionnaire was adapted to collect data on relevant events that occurred between the first and the second waves; new measures were also included (see Table 2.2). The life calendar designed for the second wave questionnaire used months instead of years as the unit of information, allowing for greater detail in assessing participants' lifestyle and activities. The process started in September 2013, the point at which we made contact with the probation and semi-prison centres to update the contact information that

Table 2.2 Areas assessed in the first and second waves' questionnaires

Area	*Sub-area*	*Wave 1*	*Wave 2*
Living arrangements	Household structure	✓	✓
	Household income	✓	✓
	If he lived in a foster house	✓	✓
	If he lived on the street	✓	✓
Family	Family structure	✓	✓
	Crime in the family	✓	✓
	Abuse or neglect	✓	✓
	Stressful family circumstances	✓	✓
	Parents or main caregiver education	✓	
	Parents occupation	✓	
	Familial bonds	✓	
Education	Educational trajectory	✓	✓
	Educational current enrolment	✓	✓
	Academic performance	✓	
Romantic relationships	Romantic relation trajectories	✓	✓
	If he lives with a partner	✓	✓
	Current partnership		✓
	Type of relationship (girlfriend/ boyfriend, espouse, partner, fiancé)		✓
	Length of relationship		✓
	Quality of relationship		✓
Children	Number of children (if any)	✓	✓
	If he lives with his child/children	✓	✓
	Closeness with children		✓
Crime[1]	Age of onset	✓	✓
	Reasons (desistance/persistence)	✓	✓
	Frequency	✓	✓
	Perceptions of the harm caused[2]		✓
Criminal justice system	Trajectory of arrest	✓	✓
	Trajectory of convictions	✓	✓
	Current convictions	✓	✓
Occupation	Occupational trajectory	✓	✓
	Currently occupation (formal/ informal/full time/ part time)		✓
	Job quality		✓
	Income		✓
Leisure activities	Types of activities		✓
	Frequency		✓
Drug use (per type of drug)	Age of onset	✓	✓
	Current use	✓	✓
	Frequency	✓	✓
	Relationship with crime	✓	✓
	If he has been under treatment	✓	✓
Peers	Antisocial peers	✓	✓
	Peer's influence	✓	✓
	Peer's pressure	✓	✓
	Involvement in gangs	✓	✓

Table 2.2 Cont.

Area	*Sub-area*	*Wave 1*	*Wave 2*
Individual characteristics	Antisocial identity	✓	✓
	Legal cynicism		✓
	Consideration for others		✓
	Self-efficacy		✓
	Future aspirations		✓
Desistance/ Persistence	Future aspirations regarding crime		✓
	Perceptions of control on crime		✓
	Intentions to continue		✓
	Ambivalence		✓
Social environment	Social disorganisation		✓
	Collective efficacy		✓
Mental health	Mental health assessment tool	✓	

Notes:
[1] Questions were asked for each declared crime committed from a list of 28 offences.
[2] This was asked for a list of 11 offences.

we had from the participants. We also ascertained at this stage whether they still were serving the same sentences as in the first wave, if they were serving a sentence in a different centre, or if they were in prison. For this reason, we also cross-checked their IDs with data from the adult prison system. After gathering all the necessary information, young people were surveyed in the same order as in the first wave, to ensure that the full year had elapsed between the two waves.

To promote participation in this second wave, we gave each participant two tickets for the cinema and reimbursed transportation costs for those interviews which did not take place in the participant's house. Most of the interviews took place in the probation centres, prison and semi-prison centres, and some in interviewees' houses. For this stage, we reinforced the supervision of the interviewers, cross-checking 30% of the surveys conducted by each of them against other sources of information (i.e. data provided by the centres, data from the previous wave, and data obtained by calling some interviewees directly by telephone). We managed to apply the questionnaire to 60% of the juveniles who were surveyed in the first wave (368 of a possible 613). A bias analysis due to non-contact in the second wave showed that the juveniles who were re-interviewed were less involved in drugs and had attended more years of school than those who did not participate. Regarding their criminal history, only the years of involvement in crime differed – those who were not surveyed showed longer criminal careers – demonstrating that the ones who participated in both waves of the study were most probably less exposed to vulnerabilities and were also less involved in crime. This is a limitation of the study that is discussed in Chapter 6.

The participants

In total, the analysis considered 334 juveniles of the final sample (the ones who completed both waves of questionnaires). Thirty four juveniles were excluded because of their age (they were younger than 16 or older than 21),[4] or because their questionnaires contained missing data. Here, some characteristics of the participants are presented regarding their life trajectories and lifestyles, with a special emphasis on the observation period (i.e. the year between the two waves of surveys). As mentioned earlier, the juveniles who participated in the first wave of the study (2012) were serving a community sentence. At the time of the second wave, 55% were serving the same sentence, 12% were serving a new one,[5] and 33% had finished serving their sentence. Their mean age at that time was 18, with 37% of participants above this age.

Regarding their living arrangements and their families of origin, over 80% of the interviewees lived with their mothers between the ages of 6 and 14. At the age of 15, 7% of them started living with their partners – a percentage that grew to 12% by the age of 18. Only 9% of the participants had a child. Between the first and second waves, 25% lived with a partner and 19% did not have a partner during that period. During that interim year, 35% of the participants lived either sporadically with at least one of his parents or not at all. If we compare participants with the general Chilean population aged 16–21 (INJUV, 2018), we can observe that a higher proportion of these juveniles were parents (9% versus 2.7%) and lived with their partners (25% versus 14%) and a smaller proportion lived with at least one of their parents (65% versus 71%). The above could indicate a faster transition towards adulthood among participants, than the general population. Some of their family members were involved in crime during that year, with 20% of the participants having at least one relative who was arrested, in jail, or involved in delinquency; 11% said that this relative was a sibling.

Between the ages of 6 and 13, more than 90% of the participants were enrolled in school – a percentage that does not differ much from the general Chilean population of the same age (92%) (Mineduc, 2017). Nevertheless, school enrolment started to decrease from the age of 13, at which point some participants started to work (see Figure 2.1). At the age of 17, only 50% of the participants were enrolled in school, a much lower proportion than the general Chilean population of the same age, which was 73% (Mineduc, 2017). During the year between the two waves, 50% of participants declared that they had attended school, and 48% had a full-time job. Nevertheless, when assessing the time period during which they were involved with any of those activities, it was observed that 43% of them were not involved at all for a period of at least seven months.

Regarding drug use, the average age of onset was 13 for marijuana, 14 for pasta base de cocaína (PBC),[6] and 14 for cocaine. In terms of the addictive potential of the drugs the participants used, they followed an increasing pattern: they

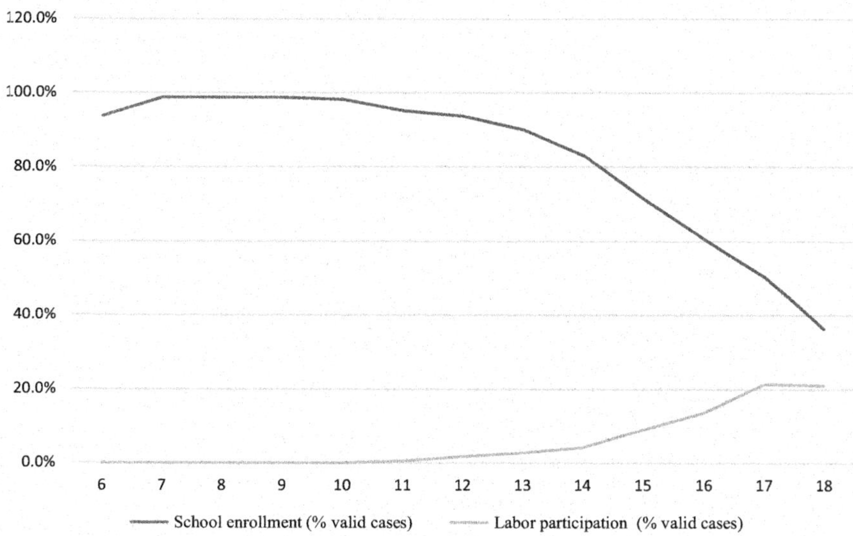

Figure 2.1 School enrolment and labour participation by age.

started using marijuana, followed by cocaine and pasta base (see Figure 2.2). Between the two waves, 76% used marijuana, 30% cocaine, and 4% pasta base. This is quite high if we compare them with the same age-range from across general Chilean population in the same year: this showed a drug use prevalence of 32% for marijuana, 2% for cocaine, and 0.4% for pasta base (Senda, 2015). 13% declared that they had attended drug treatment during that year.

The average age of crime onset was 12, reaching a peak at the age of 15; 78% of participants committed crimes at that age. Crime started to decline thereafter, with only 35% of participants declaring that they committed a crime at 18. At the time of the first wave, the participants had on average two previous convictions. If we analyse their criminal trajectories by type of crime, it is possible to observe that thefts started earlier in life, peaking at the age of 14 and declining afterwards; robbery started later in life, however, peaking at the age of 16 and dramatically decreasing from the age of 17 onwards (see Figure 2.3). It is interesting to note that the participants followed a pattern of escalation until the age of 17, after which crime started to decline.

In terms of criminal versatility, it is possible to observe that the number of different types of crime committed by participants decreased with age, with 19% of them committing three or more types of crimes at the age of 16, and only 4% showing the same pattern of versatility at the age of 18.

Finally, in terms of poverty and vulnerability, 40% of the participants lived in a household, with a total income below the Chilean poverty line (500 USD per month for an average-size household). This proportion is much higher than

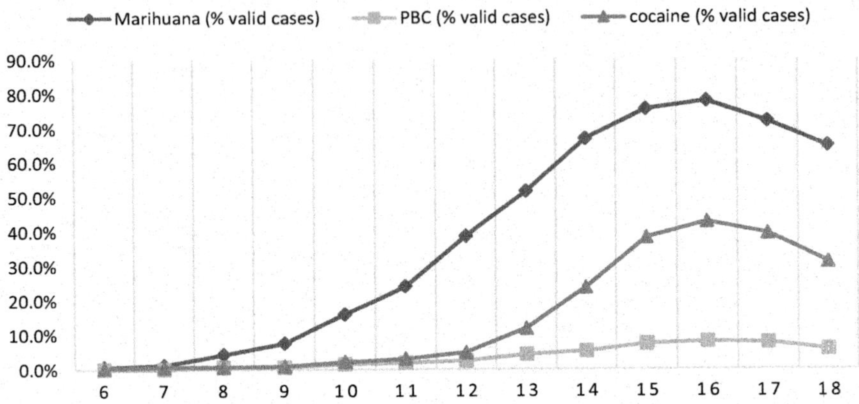

Figure 2.2 Drug use by age.

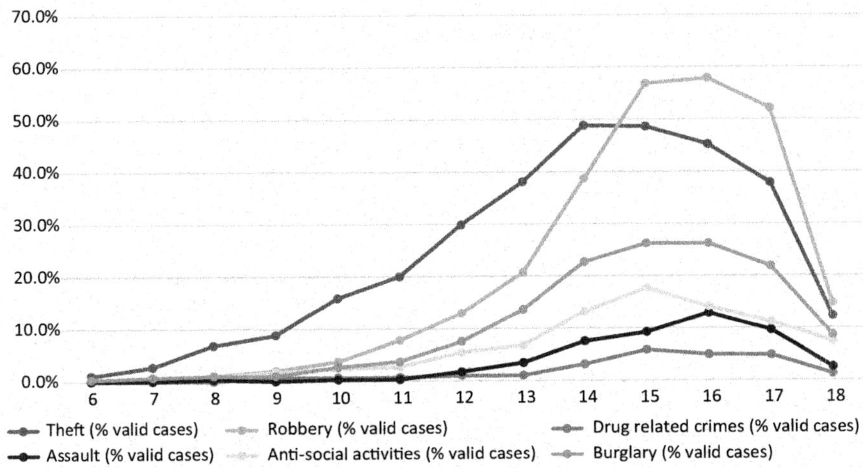

Figure 2.3 Types of crimes committed by age.

the general Chilean population. In the same year, only 8% of the total Chilean population were living under the poverty line (Cepal, 2016). Moreover, most of the participants lived in neighbourhoods with high occurrence of criminal activities. 78% noted that drug traffic was frequent or very frequent in their neighbourhoods, while 58% said the same of fights between gangs.

Overall, it can be argued from the data described above that the interviewees were characterised by strong vulnerabilities which started early in life. Around the age of 12, several started risky behaviours such as drug use and crime, and school enrolment started to decrease significantly from the age of 13. Over 80% of the interviewees lived with their mothers at home between the ages of 6 and 14. Nevertheless, their households and social environments were not free of crime: 20% of the participants had at least one relative who was arrested, in jail, or involved in delinquency during the year previous the second wave, and there was a high prevalence of criminal activity in their neighbourhoods. In the following chapters, these issues will be discussed further while also addressing the ways in which they interact with the process of crime abandonment.

In-depth interviews conducted with young male offenders

Participants were asked after completing the questionnaire whether they were available to be re-contacted for an in-depth interview; only 22% indicated that they were, and a sub-sample was created from a random selection of 35 juveniles from probation centres in the five Santiago counties with the highest proportion of participants. This diverse geographic spread avoided any bias that could occur by only interviewing young people from one neighbourhood. These young people of the sub-sample were re-contacted by the probation officers to schedule the interviews, which lasted one hour on average and took place in a private space within the probation centres. I personally conducted all the interviews, and they were recorded with the approval of the participants. Although the interviews were discursive, allowing the natural flow of conversation to dictate structure, an outline of issues to address during the interviews was used as a memory aid.

Speaking with young male offenders

During the interviews, it was essential to ensure a climate of trust and confidentiality that enabled the young interviewees to speak openly. For these purposes, special effort was made to avoid confrontation, show empathy, listen actively, and maintain a high awareness of resistance. The interviews began with an open question: "I would like you to tell me about yourself – about your life, your interests, your family; anything you want to share with me so I can get to know you". This open question was intended to make clear that there were no set expectations regarding the interview, and that I had a genuine interest in knowing about their lives. I also encouraged them to reflect on how they came to be the people they were today, focusing on key events and social actors. These questions, in most cases, led them to start talking about their childhood or their past. Without me imposing a structure, stories naturally tended to follow a relatively chronological order (i.e. a biographical orientation).

The connection with their childhood paved the way towards sentiments of vulnerability (most of them had experienced a difficult childhood marked by poverty and parental neglect), and this allowed them to break down some barriers derived from the normative masculine imperative to present themselves as strong and resolute. However, at other moments within these narratives, masculinity was asserted strongly – particularly when participants referred to their criminal behaviour. This was evident both in those who persisted and those who had been out of crime for a long time. On the other hand, masculinity was also evident when participants referred to their positive changes – their process of maturation and current stability; in these moments, they demonstrated pride in their ability to take charge of their own lives and destiny.

The young men interviewed

Since the participants in the in-depth interviews also participated in the survey, they share the characteristics described earlier. Specifically, they were between 16 and 20 years old, with an average age of 18. Twenty individuals had abandoned crime for a period of at least one year and 15 were still committing crimes. Nevertheless, nine of the ones who persisted with crime had demonstrated a decrease in the seriousness and/or frequency of the criminal offences they committed. The desisters were working, studying, or searching for an occupation, and – although some of their jobs were informal and sporadic – half of them were engaged in formal and full-time jobs. Some of the persisters also combined their criminal activities with some sporadic informal jobs.

In terms of family circumstances, 3 had children and 1 was expecting a baby; 24 were living with their parents or relatives, 8 with friends or sporadically with their families, and 5 with their partners. Thirty of them reported marijuana use and 8 used cocaine sporadically; the rest either had been or were under drug treatment at the time (the one exception was a participant who had converted to a religion which prohibits drug use). Fifteen of them reported previous drug addiction that was overcome in some cases with treatment provided at the probation centres.

All of them started crime early in life and explained their criminal behaviour as a means of gaining money, popularity, and excitement. Several revealed how, with time, their criminal behaviour started to become more structured and specialised. Their strongest affective ties were with women – whether mothers or partners – who exerted an important influence over their lives and were sometimes even connected with the desistance process. At the age 18, several started to assume the breadwinner role and to feel the obligation to become a "man of good". While for some these expectations prompted the process of leaving crime behind, for others it was experienced as pressure which was strongly resisted. Nevertheless, almost all of them aspired to leave crime behind at some point in the future.

In-depth interviews conducted with young female offenders

As mentioned previously, the aim of the in-depth interviews with young female offenders was to explore how gender shapes, limits, and structures women's pathways out of crime. For this purpose, 30 retrospective semi-structured interviews were conducted during the first wave of the study with a sample of young female offenders (aged 16–20) who were sentenced to probation or semi-prison in 2012 in Santiago, Chile. These interviews were conducted between November 2012 and February 2013 in the probation and semi-prison centres and lasted approximately one hour. They explored the experiences, norms, identities, institutions, and relations involved in the process of crime abandonment – whether successful or not.

The focus was on capturing these women's experiences in such a way as to move beyond traditional explanations of desistance and to uncover any structural constraints that might be part of the process (Gelsthorpe, 2007). There were no selection criteria for participants: all the young women who were serving a sentence at the six centres visited during the process of data collection (a total of 46 women) were invited to participate,[7] and the final sample comprised those who were willing to be interviewed.

Speaking with women

Establishing a way to approach these women was a great challenge. I intended to minimise the hierarchies between myself and the participants as much as possible, recognising their subjectivity and following a flexible approach, and constantly reflecting on my own assumptions about them that could bias or otherwise negatively impact the interviews (Gelsthorpe, 2007; Mason & Stubb, 2010).

Presentation was crucial not only to promote an open conversation, but also to tackle some of the prejudices or preconceived ideas that the interviewees may have had about me and/or the study that could have triggered resistance during the interviews. The first step I took was always to declare my ignorance and the possible bias in my own knowledge regarding the dynamics behind desistance and persistence from crime, acknowledging that it was mainly based on theoretical accounts and previous research (whether my own or that of others). In that sense, I assumed the role – highlighted by Leverentz – of the "socially acceptable incompetent, or someone who needed to be taught about their experiences and the realities of their lives" (2011:247).

Next, I explained how their own stories, perspectives, and explanations would help me to understand a process of which I had no direct experience – not only because of my lack of involvement with crime, but also because of my social position. They were aware of the social distance between us, and we openly discussed this during the interviews. They made considerable effort to accurately explain the experiences they thought I would not have understood.

Interestingly, the fact that I was pregnant during the interviews helped somewhat to dissolve the implicit social boundaries between us. Almost all the interviewees asked me about my pregnancy, and several – without my asking for it – offered some advice on how to avoid morning sickness and deliver a healthy baby. My own pregnancy evidenced the fact that, beyond social hierarchies, we were ultimately all women affected by similar fears and expectations regarding maternity issues.

The interviews took place in the probation or semi-prison centres where they spent considerable time. Whenever I went there to conduct interviews, I remained for the whole day to be adaptable and not interfere with their activities; I wanted to affirm that I was available whenever they found a time to talk with me. It also helped that I engaged in informal conversations in the garden and was flexible when they had to cancel our appointments. I adapted to each centre's routine, taking part in it as much as I could during my visits (i.e. having lunch with participants and staff) to become a known and trusted presence.

The young women interviewed

Unlike most research on women's desistance (with Barry, 2012 as a notable exception), this sample was mostly composed of young women who had committed serious offences. Only three women had been convicted for minor crimes such as theft or drug-related offences; the rest had been involved in robberies and burglaries, with one interviewee declaring that they had committed two homicides. On average, they had been involved in crime for a period of five years. The mean age of crime onset was 12 years of age, with none of them having started committing crimes after the age of 14. On average, they had two previous convictions, and seven of them had served sentences in prison.

This background information is extremely important if we consider that several research studies on female offenders have been oriented towards those convicted of minor offences or other misbehaviour that does not constitute crime in some jurisdictions and countries, such as prostitution, drug use, and running away from home. This has meant a paucity of young women in studies of the traditionally male area of serious delinquency (see Chesney-Lind & Pasko, 2004).

Another departure from former research is that although several women from the sample had previous stories of child abuse and neglect, they did not provide a straightforward correlation of motives for committing crime with the street, battered, harmed, or drug-addicted women described in several previous studies (Daly, 1992, 1994; Richie, 1996; Simpson, Yahnur, & Dugan, 2008). In the case of these women, their criminal behaviour was more related to a desire to access money and material goods, gain independence, and respect, find excitement, and give a sense of purpose to their daily lives; it was rarely a response to a history of harm, violence, and drug abuse (Kruttschnitt & Carbone-Lopez, 2006; Morrisey, 2003). This is not to say that vulnerability and trauma was not associated with their criminal paths at all, but simply to argue that – perhaps because of the nature of the crimes they committed – the reasons behind them differ from those that can be found behind prostitution or drug misuse.

The interviewees were between the ages of 16 and 20 at the time of the interview, and the average age was 18 years old. Of these women, 11 were serving their sentences in semi-prison centres and were thus living there; the rest were on probation, and half of them were living with their parents while the other half were living with their partners. Their narratives were characterised by stories and circumstances of extreme vulnerability in terms of poverty, deprivation, and neglect. One-third had abandoned their homes during childhood or adolescence around the age of 14 (mostly because they were kicked out), which was found to be associated with both the acquisition of some economic independence through crime and with the establishment of intimate relationships with partners (with whom they began cohabiting). Indeed, as mentioned before, despite their young age, almost half of them (13 in total) declared that they had lived with their partners.

Two-thirds grew up in families in which at least one member was involved in crime and served a prison sentence; some even had both parents in prison for almost their whole childhood. Prison visits and police stop-and-searches both on the street and in their own houses were part of their daily lives. All of them had either a direct or vicarious experience of imprisonment that shaped their socialisation process, making them perceive prison as a normal part of life, and a central institution in their social landscapes:

Javiera: My mum left prison two years ago – she was there for five years the last time. And my dad went to prison when I was one year old for ten years. I met him there.

Interviewer (I): How was that for you?

Javiera: I missed them, and it was hard at school with all the children knowing that.

I: Were you ashamed?

Javiera: No, why would I be? Everyone can go to prison. I felt bad, because no one took care of me, and I saw the other girls with their mothers.

(Javiera, persister, age 16)

Of the group, 18 of them were mothers, 11 were in an intimate relationship with the father of their children, 13 of them declared that they stopped committing crimes because of their children, and the rest were still engaged in crime but committing less severe offences than before. More than half of them (17) completed only primary education, and just 2 were pursuing further education. Although most of them were not studying at the time they were interviewed, only 11 declared they had worked – and, of these jobs, half were informal or sporadic. This is not surprising if we consider Chilean macro-level data, which show that only 30% of the women from the lowest income quintile work. This number is even strikingly lower if we consider young women between the ages of 15 and 19: only 10.9% of them participate in the labour force (Observatorio Social, 2017).

All of them had used marijuana at least once in their lives, and 5 had undergone drug treatment; 20 were using marijuana, and 9 using cocaine or crack sporadically. Although the prevalence of drug use was quite high compared with the general population (Senda, 2015), only four interviewees mentioned that their drug use was problematic and related to their criminal activity.

Analysis and integration

As noted at the beginning of this chapter, the quantitative data sources were used to explore the first and second aims of this study. First, the questionnaires from both waves were reviewed, and a data set was created which contained the data for each participant (whose anonymity was ensured by the assignment of an identification number). Second, this data set was supplemented with official criminal data provided by the National Office of the Defence Attorney, which detailed arrests and convictions between both waves of questionnaires. Finally, the key variables used in the analysis for the present study were created. A detailed description of both the creation of key variables, the analysis itself and its robustness is offered in Chapters 3 and 4, respectively.

The analysis of the interviews followed a reflective and bottom-up approach that departed from a focus on the interviewees' narratives, which were augmented by my fieldwork notes. The data were organised in codes that identified the main ideas and themes. A narrative approach was followed, with a focus on the lives of the participants as told in their own terms as a life story. This approach not only considers what the interviewees say, but also – more importantly – how and why they say it, and what they feel and experience (Gibbs, 2007). As Presser (2010) has argued, narrative analysis is of great utility when conducting research with offenders, since it allows for the emergence of ethical and moral aspects of life.

The coding process focused first on descriptively interrogating the participants' accounts of their life events: I assessed – among other things – what happened, when and where it happened, the context and circumstances under which it happened, and who was involved. After that, I followed an interpretative approach focusing on the meanings, contexts, constraints, emotional reactions, and social interactions. Finally, I compared different cases, searching for common issues and differences. I analysed those commonalities and differences, giving special consideration to age, criminal involvement, gender, and desister/persister categories.

To correctly interpret the way in which the participants experienced their life events, I placed particular focus on the feelings, symbols, and perceptions of social contexts, metaphors, excuses, resistances, and inconsistencies – as well as what was negated, hidden, or otherwise not said (Gibbs, 2007). For that purpose, although the interviews were transcribed, I listened to them again and noted anything that was not evident in the transcribed text. My fieldwork notes were of great help, since they recorded relevant insights from the interviewing process and the interactions between participants and myself.

A special emphasis was placed upon social practices relating to gender and class, which were linked afterwards with the process of crime abandonment (Daly, 2010). To assess how these identities influenced the participant's narratives, I reflected during analysis upon the degree of control that they had on their stories, highlighting narratives which were a clear reflection of structural constraints (Gibbs, 2007).

As a validation strategy of the data collected, three workshops were conducted with a total of 30 probation officers, each lasting two hours. Two workshops were focused on discussing the research findings, and another on how the findings could be translated into practice. I presented the findings and my ideas regarding their practical implications and we discussed these issues openly as a group. The aim was to discover whether the findings were consistent with the reality they observed in their daily work with young offenders, and to critically interrogate the research findings from the perspective of a "real" expert. Notes were taken from these encounters that helped me to review my findings, and – where appropriate – to reinterpret or adjust them.

This type of validation strategy seemed to be of far greater use than an intercoder strategy, in which two or more independent coders agree on the coding of the content of interest with an application of the same coding scheme (Lavrakas, 2008). The colleagues and research assistants who would have been able to participate in such a strategy, however, share several similarities with me in terms of academic background and social position. Therefore, the opinion of professionals who knew the participants better than us offered a greater contribution to the improvement of the research findings.

Finally, it has to be mentioned that a better strategy of validation would have been discussing the research findings with the participants themselves. However, considering the demanding nature of the research itself (two waves of questionnaires, interviews, and several instances of contact in between the waves to ensure up-to-date contact information), it was decided not to pursue such a strategy.

A concurrent strategy of integration was used, in which quantitative and qualitative data collection and analysis were conducted separately yet concurrently. The findings were integrated during the interpretation phase of the study, and both sources of information mutually informed further analysis. Consistent with Burt (2015), three simultaneous and non-exclusive stages were developed to integrate the different sources of data: triangulation (convergence or corroboration), complementarity (clarifying results from one method with the results of the other), and development (using results from one method to develop or inform the other). Besides the above, findings are presented in a structure in which insights drawn from quantitative data precede those from qualitative sources. This is due to the fact that quantitative data show a more general picture of the issues examined, while qualitative data shows for a deeper analysis and interpretation.

Desistance and persistence operationalisation: who desists and who persists?

In Chapter 1, I have discussed how some current definitions of desistance in the field of criminology have been limited by three main issues: first, the belief that desistance is an overnight change; second, the idea that desistance necessarily implies a clean cut with criminal activity; and third, the notion that a radical internal transformation towards conformity is a sine qua non condition for desisting from crime. Nevertheless, perhaps the main and crucial limitation for operationalising desistance is that, with the methods available to researchers, it is impossible to determine whether someone has definitively abandoned crime for good. Therefore, in strict terms, research on desistance has been characterised by the illusion that crime-free gaps indicate desistance from crime (Droppelmann, 2017).

There are different ways to determine if crime cessation is taking place in an individual's life, relying on official data (arrests or convictions), or on self-reported crime. One can also consider only the absence of criminal offences, or the individual's own perceptions of themselves as offenders or non-offenders, described by Maruna and Farrall (2004) as "secondary desistance", implying the transition from non-offending behaviour to self-identification as a non-offender. To assess crime cessation in the second wave, I have classified the individuals

Table 2.3 Desistance and persistence rates in the second wave

Categories	*Operationalisation*	*Desistance – 2nd wave (%)*	*Persistence – 2nd wave (%)*
1. Behavioural desistance	Reports no crime in the last year, checked against official records	41	59
2. Intentional desistance	Positive response to "I have abandoned crime completely in the last year"	65	35
3. Identity desistance	Negative response to "I see myself as a delinquent"	79	21
4. Behavioural, intentional and identity desistance	Positive response to "I have abandoned crime completely in the last year", no crime reported in the last year, and negative answer to "I see myself as a delinquent"	33	67

N = 341

from the study as desisters or persisters on the basis of self-reported data from the second wave questionnaire, checked against official records (Table 2.3).

As it can be seen, desistance rates vary considerably when different measures are used. The rate of identity desistance (individuals who don't see themselves as offenders) is considerably higher than that of behavioural desistance. Since the latter was assessed as a period of at least one year without any self-reported and official criminal offences, this difference could be due to individuals who had stopped committing crimes for a period shorter than one year. If so, contrary to the belief that self-identification as a non-offender is something that happens gradually and incrementally after crime cessation, it is possible to argue that secondary desistance occurred relatively quickly for these individuals (at least in a period shorter than one year without any criminal offence). It could also be the case that identity changes occurred simultaneously with behavioural changes, and that they are – as Giordano (2016:15) has observed – "mutually reinforcing facets of the change process". Or it could simply be, as several scholars have noted, because these individuals maintained a non-offender identity alongside their criminal behaviour (see Gibbons, 1965; Healy, 2010; Irwin, 1970; Murray, 2009; Presser, 2008).

It is also interesting to note that when a stricter operationalisation of desistance was used – one that amalgamated behavioural, intentional, and identity measures – the desistance rate decreased further than when only behavioural changes were taken into account. This supports the contention that desistance might include dimensions that are beyond the binary crime or no-crime classification (Droppelmann, 2017).

Although these operationalisations are informative and show differences in the desistance and persistence rates, some of them were problematic when conducting inferential statistical analysis. This is the case of "identity desistance", which is constructed with a negative response to the statement "I see myself as a delinquent". Given that a non-delinquent identity is a relevant factor associated with desistance, it was preferred to use this measure as an independent variable (than using it as a dependent variable) when conducting logistic regression to explore the factors associated with desistance in Chapter 4.

The operationalisation of desistance as a process (including changes in seriousness, frequency, and versatility of criminal behaviour) was also a challenge. The data set did not contain information to construct a measure of changes in versatility and the observation period (one year only) was too short to properly assess those changes, which are generally seen within longer observational periods. Seriousness and frequency were not assessed as continuous variables, they were assessed in the questionnaire in a way that only allowed to construct categorical variables (maintain, increase, or decrease), presenting problems when conducting inferential analysis due to the sample size. Therefore, it was decided in Chapter 3, to present some descriptive statistics regarding the changes in seriousness and frequency and to combine them with qualitative data to explore the process of moving away from crime beyond the operationalisation of desistance as a crime-free gap only.

Considering the above limitations, in Chapter 4, which quantitatively (using inferential statistics) and qualitatively explores the factors that increase the probability of desistance, it was decided to operationalise desistance as a crime-free gap. As mentioned earlier, in strict terms, the study of desistance would need to follow individuals until their death to establish whether or not they had truly stopped committing crimes. Since this is not feasible, most studies have operationalised desistance as the presence of a certain period of time without any criminal offence. The data collected in the present study did allow to consider a one-year crime-free gap only. Although this measure has several limitations, such as the short observation period and the fact that it captures the absence or presence of crime only, it allowed me to conduct several useful analyses that were crucial to properly explore the process of moving away from crime. It is important to mention, that to avoid possible bias due to desirability in self-reports, self-reported crime was complemented with official data obtained from the National Defence Attorney Office.

In the case of Chapter 5, which explores how gender shapes, limits, and structures women's pathways out of crime, desistance was explored qualitatively and it was operationalised as one-year crime-free gap to be consistent with the previous chapters. Nevertheless, changes in seriousness and frequency were also explored to properly account for the process of staying away from crime.

Therefore, considering all the above limitations and methodological decisions, when using the terms desistance and persistence across this book, I am most precisely referring to a period in which interviewees *stayed away from crime* or *continue committing crimes*, respectively. If desistance would stop, would last for another period or for a lifetime is a question that remains unanswered. Moreover, if we consider the age of the participants (16–21), it is very likely that the period in which they stayed away from the crime is reflecting temporary desistance, early states of desistance or simple zig-zag periods within their criminal career, and therefore the concept of liminality (the space between crime and conformity) becomes of primary importance in the present study.

Notes

1 Semi-prison is a type of sanction in which youth offenders spend the night in custody, and leave the youth training centre to work or study under close supervision during the day. It is an intermediate sanction that stands between probation and custody.

2 Although the age of criminal responsibility is between the ages of 14 and 18, several juvenile offenders over 18 years of age remain in the Youth Justice System because they were sentenced as youngsters and it is not mandatory to divert them to the adult system.

3 During the fieldwork, it was noted that official data from the Youth Justice Board lacked quality and was not up-to-date; this analysis must be interpreted with caution as a result. The data were used despite this, since they provided the only available population parameter.
4 The decision of excluding participants younger than 16 and older than 21 was made because the study was oriented towards examining the desistance process among late-adolescent offenders.
5 55% of them were serving a prison sentence (21 out of 38).
6 Pasta base de cocaína, also known as cocaine paste, is a type of drug derived from coca leaf which bears similarities to crack. It is relatively inexpensive and is widely used by low-income populations in South America.
7 In Santiago, there are 26 probation centres for juvenile offenders and one semi-prison for female juvenile offenders.

References

Barry, M. (2012). 'Young woman in transition: From offending to desistance'. In: Losel, F., Bottoms, A. and Farrington, D. P. (eds.) *Lost in Transition: Young Adult Offenders in the Criminal Justice System*. Cullompton: Willan Publishing, pp. 113–127.

Burt, J. (2015). Following the mixed methods trail: Some travel advice. *British Journal of General Practice*, 65(634): 264–265.

Cepal. (2016). Estudio económico de América Latina y el Caribe. Available from: www.cepal.org/es/publicaciones/40326-estudio-economico-america-latina-caribe-2016-la-agenda-2030-desarrollo.

Chesney-Lind, M. and Pasko, L. (2004). *The Female Offenders: Girls, Women, and Crime*. London: Sage.

Daly, K. (1992). Women's pathways to felony court: Feminist theories of lawbreaking and problems of representation. *Southern California Review of Law and Women's Studies*, 2: 11–52.

Daly, K. (1994). *Gender, Crime and Punishment*. New Haven: Yale University Press.

Daly, K. (2010). 'Feminist perspectives in criminology: a review with Gen Y in mind'. In E. McLaughlin and T. Newburn (eds.) *The Handbook of Criminological Theory*. London: SAGE, pp. 225–246.

Droppelmann, C. (2017). Leaving behind the deviant other in desistance-persistence explanations. In: E Hart and E. Van Ginneken (Eds.), *New Perspectives on Desistance*. London: Palgrave Macmillan, pp. 213–240.

Gelsthorpe, L. (2007). The Jack-Roller: Telling a story? *Theoretical Criminology*, 11(4): 515–542.

Gibbs, G. R. (2007). *Analyzing Qualitative Data*. London: Sage.

Gibbons, D. C. (1965). *Changing the Lawbraker*. Englewood Cliffs: Prentice-Hall.

Giordano, P. (2016). 'Mechanism underlying the desistance process: reflections on a theory of Cognitive Transformation'. In J. Shapland, S. Farrall and T. Bottoms (eds.) *Global Perspectives on Desistance*. Abingdon: Routledge, pp. 11–27.

Healy, D. (2010). *The dynamics of desistance: Charting pathways through change*. USA: Willan Publishing.

INJUV. (2018). Novena Encuesta Nacional de Juventud. Available from: www.injuv.gob.cl/9encuestanacionaldejuventud.

ISUC (2013). Trayectorias de jóvenes infractores de ley. Investigaciones sobre población adolescente. Available from: file:///Users/catalina/Downloads/_Informe%20 Trayectorias%20FSCM%20(4).pdf

Kruttschnitt, C. and Carbone-Lopez, K. (2006). Moving beyond the stereotypes: Women's subjective accounts of their violent crime. *Criminology: An Interdisciplinary Journal*, 44(2): 321–351.

Lavrakas, P. J. (2008). *Encyclopedia of survey research methods*. Thousand Oaks, CA: Sage.

Leverentz, A. (2011). Being a good daughter and sister: Families of origin in the reentry of African American female ex-prisoners. *Feminist Criminology*, 6(4): 239–267.

Maruna, S. (2001). *Making Good: How Ex-Convicts Reform and Rebuild Their Lives*. Washington, DC: American Psychological Association.

Maruna, S. and Farrall, S. (2004). Desistance from crime: A theoretical reformulation. *Kôlner Zeytschrift fûr Soziologie und Sozialpsychologie*, 43: 171–194.

Mason, G. and Stubbs, J. (2010). 'Feminist approaches to criminological research'. In: Gadd, D., Karstedt, S. and Messner, S. (eds.) *Criminological Research Methods*. London: Sage, pp. 486–499.

Mineduc. (2017). Revisión de las políticas educativas en Chile. Available from: https://centroestudios.mineduc.cl/wp-content/uploads/sites/100/2017/06/CBR_Mineduc-WEB.pdf.

Morrissey, B. (2003). *When Women Kill*. London and New York, NY: Routledge.

Murray, C. (2009). 'Typologies of Young Resisters and Desisters'. *Youth Justice*, 9(2), pp. 115–129.

Observatorio Social (2017). Encuesta de caracterización socioeconómica nacional. Available from: http://observatorio.ministeriodesarrollosocial.gob.cl/encuesta-casen-2017.

Patton, M. Q. (2002). *Utilization-Focused Evaluation*. California: Sage Publication.

Presser, L. (2008). *Been a Heavy Life: Stories of Violent Men*. Urbana: University of Illinios Press.

Presser, L. (2010). Collecting and analyzing the stories of offenders. *Journal of Criminal Justice Education*, 21(4): 431–446.

Richie, B. (1996). *Compelled to Crime: The Gender Entrapment of Battered Black Women*. New York, NY: Routledge.

Roberts, J. and Horney, J. (2010). 'The life event calendar method in criminology research'. In: Piquero, A. and Weisburd, D. L. (eds.) *Handbook of Quantitative Criminology*. New York, NY: Springer, pp. 289–312.

Senda. (2015). Décimo Primer Estudio de drogas en población escolar. Available from: www.senda.gob.cl/observatorio/estudios/enpe-2015/.

Simpsons, S., Yahner, J. and Dugan, L. (2008). Understanding women's pathways to jail: Analysing the lives of incarcerated women. *Australian and New Zealand Journal of Criminology*, 41(1): 84–108.

Young, J. (2011). *The Criminological Imagination*. Cambridge: Polity Press.

Chapter 3

The process and failed process of moving away from crime

> *Ontological insecurity gives rise to a desire for clear-cut delineations, and for othering: it generates a binary of those in society and those without it, which is seen to correspond to the normal, on the one side, and the deviant and criminal on the other*
>
> (Young, 2011:64)

As discussed in Chapter 1, desisters and persisters do not fall into discrete categories. Glaser (1969) argued that, although it can be easier to divide offenders into those who ultimately succeed or fail in their intention to abandon crime, this division erases the great variation that can be observed in offenders' efforts in *acting* on that intention. Therefore, it can be argued, that some current definitions of desistance and persistence in the field of criminology have been limited by three main issues: first, the belief that desistance is an overnight change; second, the notion that a radical internal transformation towards conformity is a *sine qua non* condition for desisting from crime, implying clean-cut with criminal activity; and third, the idea that persisters are individuals who identify themselves with antisocial values and aspirations, and who are strongly involved in a delinquent culture.

This chapter explores this complexity, shading light on the process and failed process of crime abandonment among the young male offenders of the study. It aims to answer the first two questions of the present research: who desists and who persists? and how do the participants experience the process and failed process of moving away from crime? First, operationalisations of desistance as a continuous variable are explored, showing that desistance and persistence categories are far from absolute and are rather two ends of a continuum that individuals can move along fluidly. Second, the way in which participants experience desistance and persistence processes is discussed to illustrate how transversal issues appeared as impacting this process among young male offenders, affecting them bilaterally, capable of both pulling them away from crime and pushing them back towards it. Finally, the conclusion summarises the main findings and limitations, opening the way to the theoretical and practical implications that are presented in Chapter 6.

DOI: 10.4324/9781003160809-4

As mentioned in Chapter 2, the data used for the analyses later come from the prospective questionnaire, conducted in two waves over one year, which was administered to a sample of 334 late-adolescent offenders (males aged 16–20) who were sentenced to probation in 2012 in Santiago. In addition, 35 in-depth interviews were conducted with a subsample of individuals from the panel in the first wave of interviews.

Assessing desistance and persistence from crime: beyond an overnight change

As explained in Chapter 2, in order to assess crime cessation in the second wave, I have classified the individuals from the study as desisters or persisters on the basis of self-reported data checked against official records, observing that 41% reported no crime in the last year, while 59% persisted in crime in the same period. When comparing these rates with those reported in the first wave of interviews, it is possible to observe that 34% (n=114) of the individuals from the sample changed category between waves, challenging the dichotomous argument and upholding instead the understanding of desistance and persistence as existing on a continuum along which individuals may move (in either direction) over time. Indeed, 40% of the participants who were categorised as desisters in the first wave resumed crime in the second wave, and 31% who were categorised as persisters declared no crime in the same period.

As pointed out by Loeber and Le Blanc (1990:407), "Desistance refers to the process that leads to cessation of crime, either entirely or in part". Indeed, many offenders do not reach a zero crime point in their lives, and they continue to be engaged in different sorts of antisocial activities (Healy, 2010; Sampson & Laub, 2003). Even those who do stop committing crimes may never reach a lifestyle of absolute conformity or achieve a deep and radical internal transformation.

Whilst most of the literature about criminal trajectories considers intermittency, there has been no in-depth study into the fact that desistance can include partial change. Instead, desistance has primarily been described in dichotomous terms as either the absence or the presence of criminal activities in an individual's life. We can therefore see that, although several definitions of desistance put the emphasis on the maintenance process of a crime-free life rather than the termination point, it still describes desistance in absolute terms. According to these descriptions, an individual can be an offender or a non-offender, but there is no definition of a "halfway" criminal – or, using Healy's (2010:102) phrasing, of individuals "who exist in the liminal place betwixt and between crime and convention". In order to assess desistance as a continuous variable, reductions in frequency and seriousness of crime must first be explored.

Deceleration can be understood as "a slowing down in the frequency of offending" (Loeber & Le Blanc, 1990:382). In order to assess changes in crime frequency, participants were asked (in both waves) how often they had committed crimes in the last year (Droppelmann, 2017). This question was

Table 3.1 Changes in frequency matrix

First wave	*Second wave*				
	Never	*Only once*	*A few times*	*Several times*	*A lot of times*
Only once	Desistance	Maintain	Increase	Increase	Increase
A few times	Desistance	Decrease	Maintain	Increase	Increase
Several times	Desistance	Decrease	Decrease	Maintain	Increase
A lot of times	Desistance	Decrease	Decrease	Decrease	Maintain

provided for each category of criminal offence that they reported. The answer categories given were as follows: "never", "only once", "a few times", "several times", and "a lot of times". A matrix was created to calculate changes in crime frequency from one wave to the other (see Table 3.1).

Only 8% of the individuals who were criminally active in the first wave increased, while 28% maintained the frequency of their criminal behaviour. A total of 31% stopped committing crimes completely, and 33% decreased the frequency of their offences. Out of second-wave participants who persisted in crime, 36% continued committing crimes less often than in the first wave.

Another way to assess desistance as a continuous variable is to explore de-escalation. Unfortunately, not many studies contain the specific data regarding the nature of the offences committed by individuals which would have enabled scholars to assess de-escalation. As a result of that absence, research has instead been more oriented towards the study of deceleration (Kazemian, Farrington, & Le Blanc, 2009; Le Blanc, 2002; Loeber & Le Blanc, 1990; Piquero, Hawkins, & Kazemian, 2012). De-escalation has primarily been defined as the decreasing severity of crime when two consecutive time periods of observation are compared (Loeber, Stouthamer-Loeber, & Ahonen, 2016). Mainly, scholars of criminology have used the seriousness rating score developed by Wolfgang et al. (1985) that divides offences into three levels of seriousness: minor, moderate, and serious.[1] As I have argued in a former article (Droppelmann, 2017), the main disadvantages of Wolfgang's classification are that it puts offences of a dissimilar nature in the same category, does not necessarily match with the level of seriousness that the criminal offences have been assigned by the criminal justice system, and does not consider the perceptions of the individuals who commit the crime.

In order to address these limitations (Droppelmann, 2017), I have constructed a measure of seriousness in which a score (1, 2, or 3) was assigned to each criminal offence from the list of all the offences included in the questionnaire, according to the seriousness in terms of the applicable conviction and the individual's perception regarding the harm that the offences generate in society. The final score was obtained by creating an average from both scores (see Table 3.2).

In the first wave, each individual received a score (1, 2, or 3) according to the most serious criminal behaviour that they declared having committed in the

Table 3.2 Seriousness measure

	Level 1	*Level 2*	*Level 3*
Applicable conviction according to the Chilean Criminal Code	Diversion	Prison sentence for a maximum of 3 years	Prison sentence for a maximum of 5 years
How much harm (specific offence) generated to society[1]	None	Some	A lot

Note:
[1] This question was included in the questionnaire.

last year; the same procedure was used for the second. It can be observed, that 31% of the individuals who were criminally active in the first wave (persisters, first wave) stopped committing crimes by the second wave. Additionally, while 39% of the individuals maintained the seriousness of their offences between the two waves, 28% decreased it and only 2% showed an increase.

Regarding the individuals who were categorised as persisters in the second wave (independently of whether they were desisters or persisters in the first wave), 43% of them continued offending or resumed crime in a less serious category than before.[2] It should be mentioned that, in the first wave, 94% of the individuals of the sample who were active in crime (persisters) were classified in the most serious category of offending (Level 3). Thus, the low number of individuals who increased the seriousness of their offences (only 3%) is partially explained by the fact that only 6% of the individuals had the possibility of escalating to a more serious level in the second wave. Regarding those who decreased the seriousness of their offences, it is worth pointing out that just over half (51%) of them did so at a level of minor offences, such as thefts, misdemeanours, vandalism, and threats. Finally, it was also observed that 12% of the individuals who persisted started taking part in antisocial behaviours that they had not previously been involved with – a phenomenon known in the research of criminal careers as "displacement". Interestingly, 68% of these behaviours were minor offences as well.

Although the downward changes in crime patterns discussed in this section might not be a consequence of a definite decision to leave crime behind, they must be considered not only when researching desistance but also when promoting it through correctional practices. As will be discussed later, partial changes towards conformity might represent the experience of several young offenders who exist in liminality.

Desistance

The beginnings: crime avoidance, lifestyle, and meanings

As can be observed in the former analysis of changes in the severity and frequency of crime, a large section of the study's participants were not involved in a radical process of crime abandonment, but they were nevertheless experiencing various qualitative changes. The triggers of those changes have not been seriously considered in the study of desistance (with certain notable exceptions discussed in Chapter 1), since the desistance paradigm remains quite in thrall to the idea that desistance is an overnight change triggered mainly by opportunities for change or turning points that appear in individuals' lives.

Most participants in the present study did not, for example, immediately begin to search for a job, a partner, or a new place to live when trying to leave crime behind. Indeed, several interviewees (desisters and persisters) rather argued that, in periods during which they were criminally prolific, they reached a tipping point at which they recognised they were risking too much, since they were under high surveillance by the police. When they reached this point, they used strategies such as decreasing the seriousness or frequency of their offences in order to fall off the police's radar for a while (Droppelmann, 2017). Desisting from crime in the long term was not their conscious purpose in this endeavour, yet the tactic(s) they employed triggered several unintended processes that – in some cases – opened the way for crime abandonment.

Moreover, since crime was an exciting activity that most of them enjoyed and was strongly embedded in their lives, they knew that abandoning it had several costs beyond purely economic constraints. Accordingly, aware of the temptation they were going to encounter, several interviewees simply began avoiding certain types of people, places, and situations that either triggered crime or were related to it. In several cases, the process of crime abandonment in fact started as a strategy of crime *avoidance* and was even triggered by the impetus to continue offending without being caught or despised by significant others.

Avoidance is a clever strategy to begin with,[3] since it does not necessarily imply complete crime cessation and thus allows individuals to manage their ambivalent desires to desist (Droppelmann, 2017). It is not as radical as saying "never again" but instead is about trying to resist the temptations of crime until a point is reached at which a non-criminal life starts to be habitual. As one interviewee pointed out,

Alvaro: I never said, "Okay, now I will change." I never proposed such a thing to myself. I just said to myself, "I hope everything turns out for the best and I hope that I will have the strength to avoid crime." It was difficult, because there were lots of temptations. Sometimes you are just walking in the street and you see a lady leaving her bag unattended and you say, "Fuck, it's so easy, no-one will see me ..." I was so afraid of being tempted.

Interviewer: How did you manage temptations?

Alvaro: I just started going out less and spending more time at home. I started to do more stuff at home, with the family – a quieter life, you know? Then I just got used to it and crime stopped attracting me as much as before.

(Alvaro, desister, age 22)

This process of acquiring dispositions without a rational decision to do so, but rather as the result of the experiences of everyday life, is precisely what

Bourdieu (1990:53) describes as "habitus'". In his words, habitus is composed of "principles which generate and organise practices and representations that can be objectively adapted to their outcomes without presupposing a conscious aiming at ends or an express mastery of the operations necessary in order to attain them". Through this lens, we see that interviewees became exposed daily (perhaps sometimes even without consciously realising it) to new leisure activities and interpersonal relations, which enabled the acquisition of a new habitus; this, in turn, shaped new positions in the social structure, paving the way for desistance to occur.

For instance, since less serious crimes (such as theft and pickpocketing) are normally offences committed by individuals acting alone, those resorting to such crimes established a significant distance from their antisocial peers and helped them to rid themselves of the lifestyle associated with robberies – for instance, the use of drugs to help achieve an appropriate state of mind to commit the crimes and facilitate the use of violence (Droppelmann, 2017). Most importantly, while robberies generally imply the immediate seizure of cash assets, theft of items necessarily postpones the ultimate goal and gratification of the crime – accrual of wealth – since the items must first be sold. This thereby encourages individuals to dispel fantasies about "easy money" and reconsider the rewards of crime.

Although there is a paucity of research into the relationship between an individual's age and how they perceive the risks and rewards of criminal activity, there are some studies that have produced valuable evidence which demonstrates that, with age, perceptions of the risks and costs of crime increased or remained flat, and that the perception of the rewards associated with crime decreased (Ayers et al., 1999; Loughran et al., 2012; Shover & Thompson, 1992). Giordano, Schroeder and Cernkovich (2007), working instead within the field of emotions, argued similarly: in the transition from adolescence to adulthood, the negative emotions connected with crime increased and the positive ones decreased. Other studies have shown that, during the transition from crime to conformity, individuals engage in more utilitarian and less hedonistic activities (Kazemian & LeBlanc, 2004).

Consistently, during periods in which individuals experienced a deceleration of their criminal behaviour, their need for possessing and incorporating (in real and symbolic ways) material goods such as drugs, clothes, cars, and electronic devices decreased as well (Droppelmann, 2017). They experienced a transition from ambition to need, in which crime started to occur sporadically as a means to assure only economic survival, as the following narrative illustrates:

> Now I only commit crimes when I have no job and I need money for my daily survival, when I have to bring money home, to pay the bills and to eat. When you are in need, you have to forget about the law and do what you know how to do best.
>
> (Axel, persister, age 19)

Axel was a prolific offender who committed around 20 robberies and burglaries per month but had decreased them to an average of 2 per month in the year before the interview. Another interviewee also indicated the same pattern of change:

> Before I committed crimes just out of ambition. I was addicted to money; money was a vice for me. Then, I started to commit crimes only when I needed to. I went out once a week, I made 80,000 pesos and I made this last the whole week or even the whole month. Before that, it was different. If I had 200,000 pesos, I wanted 400,000 and so on.
>
> (Yerko, desister, age 18)

By contrast, interviewees argued that their most prolific periods in terms of crime frequency coincided with times during which they were deeply engaged with consumerism, characterised by the acquisition of luxury goods to display power and acquire social mobility. During these periods, their offending was almost compulsive, since consumerism relies on a promise of gratification that is never fulfilled and "remains seductive only as long as the desire stays ungratified" (Bauman, 2013:46), exacerbating the perception of relative deprivation in the long term (Young, 2007). This transition might be crucial for the desistance process, since, according to Fromm (1979), it is only by the abandonment of the "passionate drive to retain and keep" that individuals can achieve self-realisation and develop a life project that gives direction and meaning to their existence.

Bottoms and Shapland (2014:7) have argued that "desistance is the process of learning to live a non-criminal life when one has been leading a largely criminal life". This means that, when desisting from crime, individuals have to change their routine, lifestyles, and friends and generally resist the several temptations that they will encounter during their attempts to leave crime behind. In order to do so, according to Bottoms and Shapland (2011), offenders adopt tactics of "diachronic self-control" through which they purposely engage or avoid certain situations that might lead them to failure in their attempts to change. Indeed, actively staying away from former friends and risky places has been noted as a viable strategy that allows offenders to avoid the temptations associated with an antisocial lifestyle.

Nevertheless, the earlier cases illustrate that it is not just the changes in routine, lifestyle, and activities but also exposure to such settings that matters in the desistance process; the meanings that individuals impute are also relevant in the process of leaving crime behind (Hunt & Farrall, 2015). Routines, the places a person visit and the people with whom they associate all in some ways communicate the sort of person that they are (Goffman, 1963; Meisenhelder, 1977). Moreover, the subjective explanations that individuals ascribe to their criminal behaviour are also strongly relevant in the process of crime abandonment. In that sense, it was interesting to note how changes in the violence that accompanied crime paved the way in several cases for the restoration of social bonds and the reconstruction of a new sense of self. For individuals seeing themselves as "good thieves" through the avoidance of hurting others, this provides a starting point from which they may be able to build a conformist identity when moving towards prosocial roles.

There were also cases in which individuals decreased the seriousness of their criminal activities when they began to realise that their use of violence was increasing, or that their methods of intimidation were going too far (Droppelmann, 2017). Most of the time, this was triggered by a shocking event during a robbery in which they observed the victims' terror, or in which they had threatened children, old people, pregnant ladies, or – in one case – even a Catholic priest. Although they experienced this as a point at which they definitely crossed the boundary between crime and evil and violated the code of honour, this realisation did not affect all interviewees in the same way. Some simply used justifications to preserve a sense of moral decency, arguing that violence was needed because it prevented something more dangerous from occurring:

> Sometimes I really have to intimidate through violence, because people value their possessions more than their lives and they don't understand that resistance makes the situation worse.
>
> (Cristian, desister, age 19)

Others found that this dissonance between values and behaviour opened the way for reflection:

Interviewer (I): Was there any occasion on which you realised that you went too far?

Francisco: Yes … actually yes, once. We were robbing a mobile phone store … I saw a lady sitting on the floor, she looked at me and started to cry … she had urinated. Immediately I said to my friends, "Okay, let's go – we stop here, no more …" And after that I thought, "Fuck, she was so scared …" When I am working I transform myself, you wouldn't have recognised me.

I: And what did you feel in that moment?

Francisco: Fuck … I looked at my gun and I thought, "Oh, this is the kind of person that I am going to be at the end of all of this."

(Francisco, persister, age 20)

In this last example, the brutal nature of the experience encouraged Francisco to reflect upon more than the violent act itself: it was not so much the moral norm of "using violence is bad" that resonated with him, but rather the recognition of himself as the individual who was actively perpetrating the violence ("this is the kind of person that I am going to be at the end of all of this") (Droppelmann, 2017). As mentioned before, Shapland and Bottoms (2011) have claimed that desistance involves a process of "active maturation" in which individuals start thinking about their goals and ethical norms, reflecting on what sort of person they feel they should be. This kind of ethical reflection, described in virtue ethics theory, stresses that individuals approach moral dilemmas not simply by considering the moral rule itself but also by their own dispositions and beliefs within a certain context. From a neuro-criminological perspective, decreases in impulse control and suppression of aggression have been linked with desistance in several studies (Forste, Clarke, & Bahr, 2011; Forrest & Hay, 2011; Morizot & Le Blanc, 2007; Piquero, Moffitt, & Wright, 2007). Monahan et al. (2009), using data from the Pathways to Desistance Study, observed that adolescents who decreased their criminal activities across a follow-up period of three years showed higher levels of psychosocial maturity, and that suppression of aggression was also the component that best distinguished between individuals who followed different criminal trajectories.

From a gender perspective, the abandonment of the use of violence might be interpreted as a way of exploring more adaptive forms of masculinity – or, in Mosher and Tomkins' (1988:82) words, to learn "how to be a man – a mensch – without being a macho man".

> Now I'm more focussed, less impulsive, I avoid fights … I have evolved, I am responsible for my family and I have future projections.
>
> (Felipe, desister, age 20)

As Felipe's narrative evidences, the alternative identity of the male provider might help him transcend socio-economic marginalisation and explore an alternative identity. In capitalist societies, such as the Chilean society, which has strongly embraced capitalism in the last three decades, aggressiveness is not the only way of performing masculinity: pursuing a productive life and assuming gendered family roles through rationality and responsibility – "the power of reason" – are also expressions of hegemonic masculinities (Connell, 2005:164). This is consistent with Deuchar, Søgaard, Kolind, Thylstrup and Wells (2015 11), who observed in a study conducted in Denmark with adolescent offenders that the "performance of broader versions of local hegemonic masculinity" helped them to desist from crime.

The process: trapped within liminality

Desistance may not imply an absolute, clean-cut, and final break with criminal activity (Shover, 2004): some offenders, even if they have stopped committing crimes for a long period of time, may never reach an absolute lifestyle of conformity – or may never achieve the deep and radical internal transformation noted in some desistance studies (Leibrich, 1996; Maruna, 2001). Even after being away from crime for a year or more, over a quarter of the individuals who did not commit any crimes in the period prior to the second wave were either ambivalent about their decision to stay out of crime or felt able to commit crimes again if the opportunity were to arise.

Although the great majority of the desisters had well-defined conformist aspirations for the future, they did not have a clear idea of themselves, their lives, or their preferences in the present. They were characterised by ambivalence, uncertainty, and contradiction – and, from their facial expressions, body language, and emotional tone, it was possible to infer that talking about their conformist futures was not only boring but also distressing. By comparison, when reflecting back on the times when they were actively offending, their narratives became more alive, vibrant, and exciting (Droppelmann, 2017). This corroborates the conclusion drawn by Irwin (1970:202), who, when describing what he called "marginal" offenders, noted, "… there is no denial of, or regret for, the past. In fact, past criminal life is locked back upon with pleasure and excitement".

Participants were capable of talking about their (antisocial) achievements, telling stories about success, and taking pride in their criminal skills. The following example comes from Cristian's narrative, who was 19 years old at the time of the interview, studying to become a chef, and had desisted for more than 1 year after continual engagement with crime and drugs since childhood. He had been the leader of a violent gang, known for their efficiency in robbing pharmacies and petrol stations.

INTERVIEWER (I): *How were you when you were committing robberies?*
CRISTIAN: *I was very clever … Even today I wonder how good I was, to think about every single detail …*
I: *And how often did you [rob petrol stations]?*
CRISTIAN: *Very often. It didn't matter how much money I got; I went back again.*
I: *Why did you come back?*
CRISTIAN: *Because I loved it, I really enjoyed it, 'specially the excitement of doing it again and again …*
I: *And if you had the opportunity of doing something big again, would you do it?*
CRISTIAN: *Mmmmm … Yes, I guess I would …*
I: *Can you say that you have stopped completely?*
CRISTIAN: *I am not sure if I can say completely. There will be always something left, a kind of thread that linked you to crime … Like a murderer who killed someone; he will always have this instinct of being aggressive …*

For a late adolescent such as Cristian, crime was difficult to surrender not only because it was their way of life – and, for most, the only thing they knew – but also because it was a source of pleasure, enjoyment, and satisfaction (Droppelmann, 2017). Crime was embedded in the pleasure of transgression as a source of control and identity reassurance (Matthews, 2002; Young, 2007). For several participants of the study, the emotional attachment to crime was so strong that they were experiencing grief and were still "bargaining" with crime,[4] trying to delay or even undo their decision to leave it behind. As happens in any other mourning process, they secretly wanted to postpone their loss by leaving open the possibility of a return. Moreover, several desisters from the study dreamed about a re-encounter with crime and fantasied about having a farewell episode in which they would commit their last and biggest offence.

The future: desisting into what?

Mc Neill (2012:16) has argued that the process of crime abandonment is not just the absence of offending, it is an ongoing process of reintegration in which "people desist into something". Indeed, desistance is a prospective process, in which hope has been identified as key in projecting a possible future and the way in which it can be realised (Anderson, Weiss, & Oselin, 2020; Farrall, 2005). However, when exploring the idea of a possible future with the participants, it was clear to observe their inability to really project it. Their lack of a possible future, unlike what was stated in other studies with adult participants, was not simply associated with multiple individual experiences of failures (Nugent & Schinkel, 2016; Standing, 2011) – and nor with the need to live in the present, typical of the adolescent period. Rather, the lack of a future orientation was experienced by them as structural blockage; as Patton and Farrall argue (2021), to facilitate hope and promote life beyond desistance, a kind of society and social order is needed.

When desisters from the in-depth interviews were asked if they would commit crimes in the future, most were unable to give a straightforward answer (Droppelmann, 2017). They argued that, although they did not want to relapse, they could not say never, because they did not know what the future held:

> *Future? What future? I have never thought about my future … I have always been so poor that I live from day to day.*
>
> (Daniel, persister, age 18)

This is consistent with what Messerschmidt (1986:63) has suggested, "individuals become aware of their position in society by perceiving what future is possible for them […] To the individual male in marginalised community, his lack of future reflects the fate of his class." Only 14% of the participants of the study, who had worked in the year before the second-wave interview, had a formal job, while the rest were involved in sporadic jobs with no contracts or social security. Moreover, they were constantly confronted with enormous social distress. In the year prior to the second-wave interview, 48% of the interviewees experienced at least one stressful event in their families and immediate social environment, such as death, mental health or a drug abuse problem among their families or partners (Droppelmannn, 2017). Since almost all the individuals from the study lived in households with interdependence among the residents in terms of livelihood strategies, these events might have devastating consequences. Accordingly, if one of the members lost their job, went to prison, fell ill, got involved with drugs, or decided to leave home, the rest of the members would be affected in some way. Experiences such as these reinforce the imaginary idea that they have of their lives as being driven by "destiny" (see also Irwin, 1970; Maruna, 2001; Zemel, Ronel, & Einat, 2016) and highlight the fact that desistance is not only an individual process driven by personal agency, but a collective process that needs interpersonal support.

Desisting *into something* could also be interpreted as desisting *into normality,* to be recognised as a "conventional"/"normal" person (Barry, 2012; Martinez, 2009; Maruna, 2001; Maruna et al., 2009). Nevertheless, recognition could be one of the most difficult aspects to achieve. The following narrative illustrates how one interviewee in the present study showed his sense of distress at not being recognised as a non-offender after having desisted from crime for almost two years:

I: *How much have you changed?*

ALBERTO: *Completely, even physically. Look how I was before: [Shows a photograph from an old ID card.][5]*
Nevertheless, sometimes, in my neighbourhood people walk away from me. I tell them, "Lady, don't panic, I am working now, I am not stealing anymore," but they don't believe me. Also, in the shopping malls, guards always follow me; they don't believe that a guy like me would have money to buy stuff.

I: *And how do you feel when this happens?*

ALBERTO: *Ashamed and afraid. Every time I go to the supermarket, unconsciously I check my pockets, because I am scared that the guards will accuse me of stealing. Sometimes it is easier to continue stealing as before and give them what they want.*

(Alberto, desister, age 20)

This was commonly observed among the interviewees, especially when they were under strong pressure for maintaining themselves away from crime, such as the "fuck it moments" described by Halsey, Armstrong and Wright (2017). They were mostly afraid of failing in conformist settings, and, for several offenders, it was easier to live a life of failure than to fail after an attempt at success. Interestingly, participants experienced fear as an emotion that was extremely difficult to cope with, since fear is forbidden in the masculine culture of crime; it is believed to be an "inferior feminine emotion" (Mosher & Tomkins, 1988:67) that brings failure and dishonour. Among those participants, ambivalence operated here as a self-protection strategy in order to avoid the sense of failure that would arise from their failed attempts at societal integration. This is consistent with the idea of fearing success, which was introduced by Freud more than a century ago in his 1916 essay "Those wrecked by success".[6] From Freud's perspective, the guilt and shame of achieving what is believed to be an unmerited success can be so strong that individuals can even boycott themselves in their attempts to change.

Nevertheless, there was also a group of desisters who, even during times when they were very criminally active, always kept social attachments in conformist settings and experienced tertiary desistance much more easily. Similar to what was observed by Terry and Abrams (2017) with former incarcerated young men in California, they socialised intermittently with a small cohort of friends from school, a successful cousin who went to university, neighbours who prospered in their business, or a partner who was not involved in crime. Some individuals lived parallel lives, never disclosing their criminal behaviour to their families. This way of life was not easy to maintain, however, and several individuals stated that they lost significant prosocial attachments when their criminal behaviour was exposed. In order to avoid that eventuality, interviewees reported restricting their criminal behaviour to less serious crimes that did not threaten their status in conventional settings. Some engaged in crimes that were more "accepted" in their social environments, such as selling stolen goods. Others limited their behaviour to thefts: since they are committed during the day and conventional clothing is required in order to pass unnoticed, it was far more possible for them to deceive their family, friends, and neighbours through the illusion of going to work. The previous strategy has been called "circumscribed deviance", a duality of lifestyle that allows individuals to maintain bonds in both criminal and prosocial settings, and gain recognition and success on both sides (Glaser, 1969; Nagin, Farrington, & Moffitt, 1995). For those individuals, the process of crime abandonment was easier, because they had a social environment *into which they could desist.*

Persistence

Failures: not giving up in their attempts for change

Consistent with previous research (Anderson, Weiss, & Oselin, 2020; Bottoms & Shapland, 2011; Burnett, 2004), it was a common pattern to observe that, although the individuals of the present study were optimistic about desisting from crime in the first wave of interviews, several persisted in the second wave. Indeed, 57% of those who persisted in the second wave wanted to abandon crime, and, in the first wave, were sure of their capacity to do so. Moreover, 70% of the persisters argued the same thing during the second wave, even after one year of failing in their attempts to abandon crime. The fact that several persisters wanted to change and found they could not is easily understandable and will be explored in the next chapter. One could argue that these individuals' prosocial values were not robust or strongly held enough to prevent crime from occurring, or that they encountered several obstacles with capacity to impede their success, such as societal constraints in the changing process, lack of opportunities, and/or economic pressures (among others).

Although these are plausible explanations regarding the impossibility of changing faced by individuals, it is still not clear why their intentions and sense of self-efficacy remained apparently unaffected after their failed attempts to leave crime behind. Why do they not give up their intentions to change after realising that the obstacles are too hard to overcome? And why do they not become more realistic regarding their capabilities to change? One simple explanation could be that they did not have the intention to abandon crime in the present or in the short term, but that they wanted to desist at some point in the future. Indeed, 74% of the persisters from the study argued that they did not want to be offenders in the long term, and most of them wanted to pursue a conventional life in the future. Thus, in a context in which a crime-free life is a long-term rather than an immediate goal, their current failures would not affect their perceptions about their capabilities to change in the future. It could also be the case, as it was observed by Vidal, Ouellet and Dubois (2020), that success in criminal activities does not always hinder the intentions to desist from crime.

Nevertheless, considering that human agency is imbued with notions of gender, it could be argued that this exacerbated and decontextualised self-reliance would be better explained by an attempt at "doing masculinities". As mentioned earlier, the individuals in the study were embedded in contexts of great uncertainty, with lack of control in every single domain of their lives except crime, as the following narrative illustrates,

> **I:** *Did you want to come back to crime when you were in prison?*
> **JONATHAN:** *No, I decided to stop committing crimes then. There are people who decide to stop, others want to continue when they are in prison, it gives you time to think. Some decide to stop using drugs; it all depends on you, you are the one who decides.*
> **I:** *Do you think that it just depends on you?*
> **Jonathan:** *Yes, no one can tell me what to do. I'm not going to rob a car because someone tells me to do that. I decide what to do.*
> **I:** *Do you feel afraid of going back to crime?*
> **JONATHAN:** *No, not at all, I made a decision already.*
>
> (Jonathan, desister, age 22)

Here, Jonathan is expressing power of will, bravery, and independence – all features of the "macho" stereotype in the Latin American culture. Indeed, it is not just about crime, but about who commands the individual's life; self-efficacy operates here as a strategy to preserve a sense of power in a context of complete powerlessness.

Persisters who violate the laws in which they believe

When we think about those who persist in crime, one immediately pictures individuals who identify themselves with antisocial values and aspirations, and who are strongly involved in a delinquent culture. One might believe that persisters are the radical opposite of desisters in terms of their orientations towards conformity. The differences between persisters and desisters in terms of their identity, values, and aspirations were explored through a set of questions and scales. Logistic regression analysis presented in the next chapter shows that the two groups differ, and that these differences were statistically significant. Indeed, persisters have lower moral standards and see themselves more as delinquents than desisters.

Nevertheless, more detailed analysis reveals that – despite these differences – there was a group of persisters who performed in a very conformist way. Indeed, it was observed that half (50%) of the persisters did not see themselves as delinquents and, when asked about the future, 74% did not see themselves as offenders in the long term. Moreover, similar to what Doekhie and Van Ginneken (2019) observed, the vast majority of the persisters had conventional future aspirations. More than 90% of them wanted to have a job, finish school, and work hard to get ahead. Regarding their moral orientations, only 26% were against the statement "People should follow the law" (see Figure 3.1) – with only 25% of the persisters arguing instrumental reasons (avoid being punished) (see Figure 3.2).

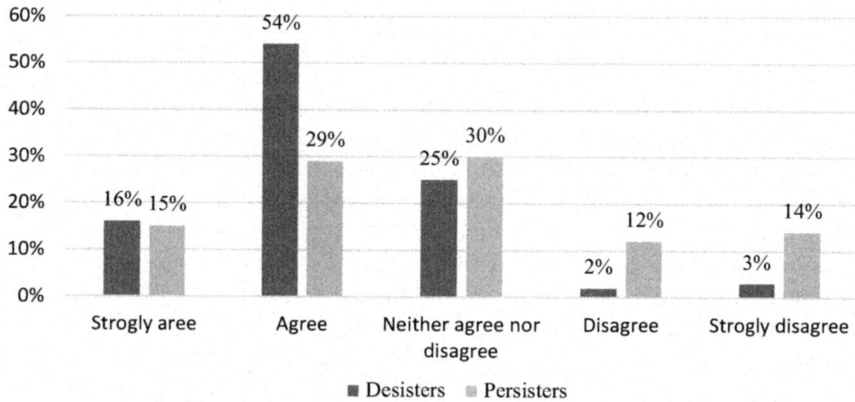

Figure 3.1 Law obedience among desisters and persisters.

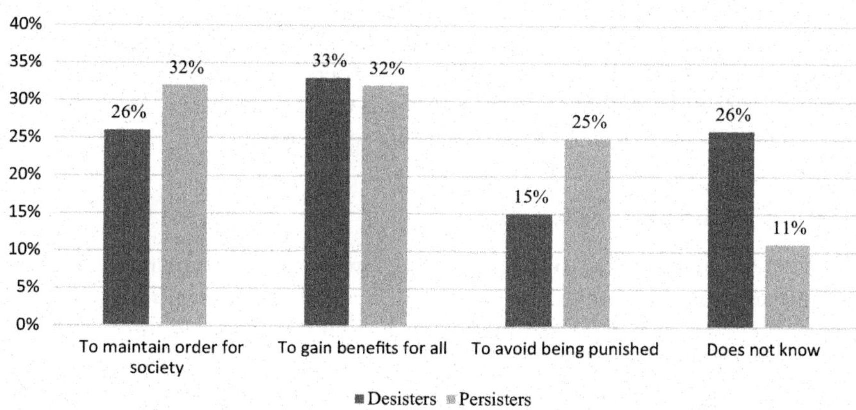

Figure 3.2 Reasons for obeying the law among desisters and persisters.

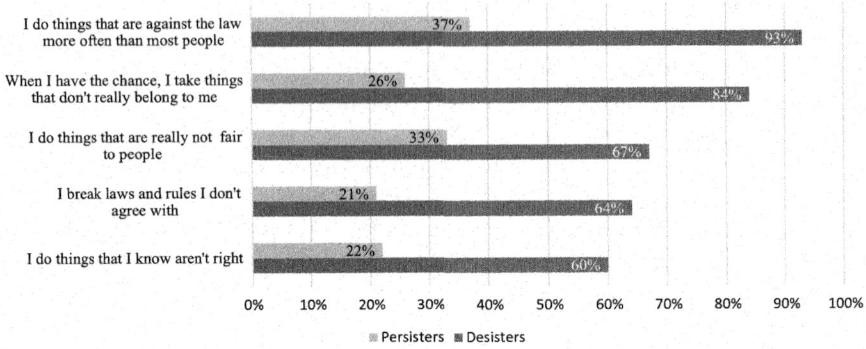

Figure 3.3 **Responsibility scale.**

Sykes and Matza (1957:666) developed the neutralisation theory to explain why individuals violate the laws in which they believe, arguing that individuals use mechanisms such as denials and justifications to relieve themselves from their own moral constraints to continue offending. Although this study did not test and explore neutralisation techniques specifically, almost all the individuals who committed robberies or assaults acknowledged the amoral character of their behaviour. Moreover, techniques of neutralisation were mainly used by desisters in order to reconstruct their sense of self and re-signify their past behaviour. Among persisters, these techniques were used only infrequently; it was clear from their narratives that the majority acknowledged their criminal behaviour yet did not try to neutralise it. Indeed, when comparing desisters' and persisters' mean scores on the responsibility scale (see Figure 3.3) using an independent sample t test,[7] it is clear that, on average, persisters (M=20, SD= 4.76) do acknowledge more of their antisocial behaviour than desisters (M= 26, SD=4.93) ($t(331) = -12.24, p < .001$). One might argue that these results are to be expected given that desisters are experiencing a crime-free gap; nevertheless, since this scale does not merely measure crime, it is still indicating the fact that – in general – the majority of the persisters acknowledge their amoral behaviour. Indeed, only around a third of them (with some variation according to the question) denied their behaviour (see Figure 3.3).

Resisting secondary deviance

The question therefore remains as follows: how do these conformist persisters manage the inconsistencies between their internal dispositions towards crime and their external behaviour? Why do they continue offending if they have conformist future aspirations? One plausible explanation could be that these individuals were engaged in the initial process of crime abandonment and experiencing a process that Merton (1957) described as "anticipatory socialisation" (discussed in Chapter 1). In this case, individuals identify themselves with values, norms, and orientations of social groups in which they aspire to participate, but of which they are not yet members. If this was indeed the case, one might expect to observe changes in the measures of identity, values, and aspirations as individuals became more conformist over time. Since we know that desistance is a long process, however, more than two waves of data would be needed. Indeed, when comparing the mean figures of these key measures among the persisters in the first and the second waves, no significant changes were found. It is therefore not possible to confirm or discount our conjecture with the available data.

Another plausible explanation may be that interviewees were trying to resist secondary deviance (Lemert, 1967) by rejecting the delinquent label as their only and single identity. Indeed, when exploring identity issues in the in-depth interviews, persisters felt quite uncomfortable with the "delinquent" label, and their immediate reaction was to reject it. However, when confronting them with the fact that they were still committing crimes, several individuals recanted, "Yes, I guess that I am delinquent ... but I am a good person as well". Instead of using justifications and denials (i.e. "I have to steal because I am poor"), as the neutralisation theory (Sykes & Matza, 1957) would have predicted, they tried to symbolically erase or balance the bad (being a delinquent) with the good (being a good person) (Droppelmann, 2017).

This process, that Maruna (2001) called "redemption script" and which Healy (2010) denoted as "integrated narrative", operates as a unification method that allows individuals to re-establish their previous prosocial roles and actions in order to "deemphasise the centrality of crime in the life story" (Maruna, 2001:89). Nevertheless, it was observed in the present study that even persisters experience such a process – not in order to reconstruct their selfhood but to construct or maintain a current self that rationalises inconsistent forms of being in the present (Droppelmann, 2017). Greenberg and Pyszczynski (1985) called this process "compensatory self-inflation", arguing that individuals inflate their self-image in an attempt to counteract and regulate negative emotions of inferiority that arise when the self is in jeopardy and under public scrutiny. Thus, it can be argued that the fact that almost half of the persisters do not see themselves as delinquents should not be interpreted as a denial of their criminal behaviour (Sykes and Matza, 1957), or a sign of their belonging to a criminal subculture in which crime is normative (Agnew, 2003; Cohen, 1955; Hayward, 2004; Schwendinger & Schwendinger, 1985). Rather, it should be seen as an individual's attempt to avoid the centrality of the delinquent identity and make sense of their inconsistencies in order to align their present self with their future conformist aspirations.

Persistence as reintegration

As mentioned earlier, persisters wanted to achieve the same mainstream societal goals as a "normal" (i.e. socially conformist) person – but, when exploring these in more detail in the in-depth interviews, it was apparent that they were strongly embedded in materialistic accumulation (Droppelmann, 2017). Indeed, when posing the question of "How do you want to be in the future?" during the in-depth interviews, only a few individuals answered using the verb "to be", saying, for example, that they wanted to be a father or a student; instead, most of the individuals phrased their answers using "to have", asserting that they wanted to have a house, money, a car, a business, etcetera:

I: What kind of future do you want to have?
MICHAEL: I don't know … I want to have my own house; to have all that you need to live a peaceful and quiet life.
I: What do you mean by a quiet life?
MICHAEL: To live in peace, because you have everything that one must have, a car, a house, a refrigerator, a washing machine.

(Michael, persister, age 20)

I: Regarding your future: how would you like to be in the future?
DANIEL: I don't know, just having everything.
I: What does this mean?
DANIEL: My house, my car, providing all that my son needs. I don't want him to have any needs, to have to ask someone for stuff. I want to give him all that he needs. This is the only thing that I care about, I don't think and I don't care where this money will come from, I just think about having all of that.

(Daniel, persister, age 19)

As Patton and Farrall argued (2021: 11), "The social role of 'homeowner' provided a sense of pride and stability for their family but also of appearing normal and respectable and communicating to others that they had changed and had somehow made it". Success was defined here in monetary terms: having material goods was the interviewees' main life goal, and an indication of an efficient and productive life in which money was not wasted but invested in symbolic sources of pride and status.

Economic growth accompanied by high levels of income inequality, experienced in Chile since the 1980s, has changed the social mobility strategy used by the lower classes. In fact, the rise of consumerism made possible by an increasing access to credit has created a situation wherein individuals' aspirations are no longer centred on occupational status or income, but on their consumer capacity and lifestyles (Franco et al., 2011). Individuals no longer exist in the postmodern consumer culture as workers or citizens, but as consumers (McIntyre, 1992), and the symbolic value of material goods has a compensatory effect, alleviating individuals from the humiliation and disrespect that arises from the dynamics of deprivation (Van Bavel & Sell Trujillo, 2003; Young, 2007). Consumerism also allowed interviewees to distinguish themselves from the rest of the young people in their neighbourhoods, acquire and experience social mobility and progress, and at the same time, feel themselves to be part of mainstream society.

Since, for most of the individuals of the sample, the opportunities to achieve material success have been blocked by different sources of social disadvantage and societal constraints, the only available means of accessing a consumer lifestyle was through so-called "aspirational crime" (Merton, 1957; UNDP, 2014). This was exemplified by one interviewee, Daniel: "I don't care where this money comes from, I just think about having all of that". His mainstream goals and aspirations pushed him towards crime instead of pulling him away from it. Therefore, consistent with Carlsson (2013) and Lindegaard and Jackes (2014), persistence in crime can be seen here as an agentic move in the direction of transforming one's life through the acquisition of power, status, and control. These interviewees were pursuing quick social mobility and had no interest in waiting for it – or, perhaps, did not believe that education and work could have benefitted their lives, evidencing that sometimes poverty encourages short-term thinking.

Conclusions

Throughout this chapter, it has been shown that desistance and persistence categories are far from absolute and are rather two ends of a continuum that individuals can move along fluidly. Indeed, 34% of the interviewees changed categories between the first and the second wave, challenging the dichotomous argument and the fact that desistance necessary implies clean-cut with crime. It has been demonstrated that changes in seriousness and frequency of crime offer interesting insights to explore the process of moving away from crime. A total of 43% of the youths who persisted in crime in the second wave had lessened the seriousness of their offences, and 36% of them committed crimes less frequently than in the first wave. These downward changes would be, for several individuals, the furthest they can go in terms of desistance. As was shown, crime remains a possible alternative for several desisters: occasional thefts for need, fights for self-defence, recreational drug use, and vandalism as an expression of social discontent are part of a lifestyle that is almost impossible to surrender, especially considering the structural restrictions of a society that has not much to offer in terms of welfare, employment, opportunities, and social participation and mobility.

This chapter has also shown that, in several cases, the process of crime abandonment started as a strategy of crime *avoidance* rather than abandonment, and that several desisters experienced it not as a radical transformation, but through the impetus to continue offending without being caught or despised by pro-social significant others. The beginnings of this process were marked not only by changes in routines and lifestyles but also in the meanings that individuals ascribe to crime. These young desisters started perceiving fewer rewards from crime, and their criminal behaviour started to be less expressive and hedonistic and became more instrumental. Leaving behind violent crimes was experienced as a way to explore other forms of expressing masculinity, through willpower and responsibility, which might trigger identity reconstruction in the long term. Indeed, *masculine transitions* (Glynn, 2018) might be crucial in the desistance process among young men.

Nevertheless, as Hunter and Farrall (2018) have argued, especially in early stages of desistance, emotions might be in conflict with individuals' attempts to desist – and, for the participants of the study, crime was profoundly difficult to surrender not only because it was their way of life but also because it was a way to reaffirm their identities and exercise control. Participants experienced structural blockages to developing a possible future and struggled immensely with tertiary desistance, perceiving their lives as marked by the delinquent label and driven by fate. Despite multiple failures, several persisters kept a strong sense of agency and were strongly confident in their capacity to leave crime behind, which can be interpreted as a way to exercise power within a life and future under which they had very low levels of control. Several persisters navigated through the inconsistencies between their internal orientations towards conformity and their criminal behaviour, resisting secondary deviance and trying to integrate themselves into mainstream society.

Although these findings offer interesting contributions, they must be considered with caution. When exploring desistance in this chapter, I am most precisely referring to a period of temporary desistance in which interviewees *stayed away from crime* or *continued committing crimes*. Whether those changes might stop, or last for another period or a lifetime, is a question that remains unanswered. Moreover, if we consider the age of the participants (16–21), it is very likely that the periods in which they stayed away from crime or showed qualitative changes in their criminal patterns reflect early states of desistance or simple zigzag periods within their criminal career, and therefore the salience of ambivalence and liminality might be overstated. The implications of the findings presented in this chapter for the ways in which we understand, theorise, and research desistance are presented in Chapter 6.

Notes

1 For Wolfgang et al. (1985), minor delinquency consists of shoplifting, vandalism, and fraud; moderate delinquency includes theft, gang fighting, carrying weapons, and joyriding; and serious delinquency consists of car theft, strong-arming, selling drugs, breaking and entering, forced sex, homicide, and assault.

2 In order to classify the level of seriousness of offending for the individuals who did not commit any crime during the year previous to the first wave (desisters, first wave), I used the most serious offence that they declared in the life calendar prior to them stopping committing crimes.

3 Nevertheless, in the long term, maintaining desistance entails a more active process in which individuals exercise their will and make choices to shape and reorientate their own lives towards the future (Carlsson, 2016; Farrall, 2002).

4 For a description of the bargaining stage of grief, see Kübler-Ross (1969), 'On death and dying'.
5 Maruna (2001:178), in the Liverpool Desistance Study, also experienced desisters showing him pictures "to appear respectable and present oneself in a conventional manner ...".
6 In this essay, Freud analysed how, in Shakespeare's *Macbeth*, the character of Lady Macbeth collapsed when reaching success.
7 This scale was adapted from the Weinberger Adjustment Inventory (WAI), Weinberger and Schwartz (1990). It consists of seven items. α=.81.

References

Agnew, R. (2003). An integrated theory of the adolescent peak in offending. *Youth & Society*, 34(3): 263–299.

Anderson, A. Y., Weiss, D. B., and Oselin, S. S. (2020). When I grow up: Exploring the link between future expectations and criminal trajectories. *Journal of Developmental and Life-Course Criminology*, 1: 43–66.

Ayers, C., Williams, J., Hawkings, J. D., Peterson, P., Catalano, R. and Abbot, R. (1999). Assessing correlates of onset, escalation, deescalation, and desistance of delinquent behavior. *Time*, 15(3): 277–306.

Barry, M. (2012). 'Young woman in transition: From offending to desistance'. In: Losel, F., Bottoms, A. and Farrington, D. P. (eds.) *Lost in Transition: Young Adult Offenders in the Criminal Justice System*. Collumpton: Willan Publishing, pp. 113–127.

Bauman, Z. (2013). *Liquid Modernity*. Cambridge: Polity Press.

Bottoms, A. and Shapland, J. (2011). 'Steps towards desistance among male young adult recidivists'. In: Farrall, S., Hough, M., Maruna, S. and Sparks, R. (eds.) *Escape Routes: Contemporary Perspectives on Life after Punishment*. Oxon: Routledge, pp. 43–80.

Bottoms, A. and Shapland, J. (2014). Can persistent offenders acquire virtue?. *Studies in Christian Ethics, 27*(3): 318–333.

Bourdieu, P. (1990). *The Logic of Practice*. Cambridge: Polity Press.

Burnett, R. (2004). 'To re-offend or not re-offend? The ambivalence of convicted property offenders'. In: Maruna, S and Immarigeon, R. (eds.) *After Crime and Punishment: Pathways to Offender Reintegration*. Cullompton: Willan Publishing, pp. 152–180.

Carlsson, C. (2013). Masculinities, persistence, and desistance. *Criminology, 51*(3), 661–693.

Carlsson, C. (2016). 'Human agency, criminal careers, and desistance'. In: J. Shapland, S. Farrall and T. Bottoms (eds.) *Global Perspectives on Desistance*. Abingdon: Routledge, pp. 28–49.

Cohen, A. K. (1955). *Delinquent Boys: The Culture of the Gang*. New York: The Free Press.

Connell, R. W. (2005). *Masculinities*. Berkeley: University of California Press.

Deuchar, R., Søgaard, T. F., Kolind, T., Thylstrup, B., and Wells, L. (2015). When you're boxing you don't think so much': Pugilism, transitional masculinities and criminal desistance among young Danish gang members. *Journal of Youth Studies, 19*(6): 725–742.

Doekhie, J., and Van Ginneken, E. (2019). House, bells and bliss? A longitudinal analysis of conventional aspirations and the process of desistance. *European Journal of Criminology,* 17(6): 744–763.

Droppelmann, C. (2017). 'Leaving behind the deviant other in desistance-persistence explanations'. In: Hart, E. and van Ginneken, E. (eds.) *New Perspectives on Desistance*. Palgrave Macmillan, London, pp. 213–240.

Farrall, S. (2002). *Rethinking what works with offenders*. Collompton, Devon: Willan Publishing.

Farrall, S. (2005) On the existential aspects of desistance from crime. *Symbolic Interaction*, 28: 367–86.

Forrest, W., and Hay, C. (2011). Life-course transitions, self-control and desistance from crime. *Criminology and Criminal Justice*, 11(5): 487–513.

Forste, R., Clarke, L., and Bahr, S. (2011). Staying out of trouble: Intentions of young male offenders. *International Journal of Offenders Therapy and Comparative Criminology*, 55(3): 430–444.

Franco, R., Hopenhayn, M. and León, A. (2011). Crece y cambia la clase media en América Latina: una puesta al día. *Revista Cepal*, 103: 7–26.

Fromm, E. (1979). *To Have or to be?*. London: Abacus.

Giordano, P. C., Schroeder, R. D. and Cernkovic, S. A. (2007). Emotions and crime over the life course: A neo-median perspective on criminal community and change. *American Journal of Sociology*, 112(6): 1603–1661.

Glaser, D. (1969). Introduction. *Journal of Research in Crime and Delinquency*, 6(2): 109.

Glynn, M. (2018). 'A framework model of black masculinities and desistance'. In: *New Perspectives on Prison Masculinities*. Cham, Chicago, IL: Palgrave Macmillan, pp. 169–195.

Goffman, E. (1963). *Stigma: Notes on the Management of Spoiled Identity*. New Jersey: Prentice-Hall.

Greenberg, J. and Pyszczynski, T. (1985). Compensatory self-inflation: A response to the threat to self-regard of public failure. *Journal of Personality and Social Psychology*, 49(1): 273–280.

Halsey, M., Armstrong, R., and Wright, S. (2017). 'F* ck It!': Matza and the mood of fatalism in the desistance process. *British Journal of Criminology*, 57(5): 1041–1060.

Hayward, B. (2002). 'The vilification and pleasures of youthful transgression'. In: Muncie, J., Hughes, G., and McLaughlin, E. (eds.) *Youth Justice: Critical Readings*. London: Sage, pp. 80–94.

Healy, D. (2010). *The dynamics of desistance: Charting pathways through change*. USA: Willan Publishing.

Hunt, B. and Farrall, S. (2015). Space, place and desistance from drug use. *Oñati Socio-Legal Series*, 5(3): 954–968.

Hunter, B. and Farrall, S. (2018) 'Emotions, future selves, and the process ofdesistance', *British Journal of Criminology*, 58, 291–308.

Irwin, J. (1970). *The Felon. Englewood Cliffs*. NJ: Prentice-Hall.

Kazemian, L. and Le Blanc, M. (2004). Exploring patterns of perpetration of crime across the life course offense and offender-based viewpoints. *Journal of Contemporary Criminal Justice*, 20(4): 393–415.

Kazemian, L., Farrington, D. P. and Le Blanc, M. (2009). Can we make accurate long-term predictions about patterns of de-escalation in offending behavior? *Journal of Youth and Adolescence*, 38(3): 384–400.

Kübler-Ross, E. (1969). *On death and dying*. New York: Macmillan Company.

Le Blanc, M. L. (2002). The offending cycle, escalation and de-escalation in delinquent behavior: A challenge for criminology. *International Journal of Comparative and Applied Criminal Justice*, 26(1): pp. 37–41.

Leibrich, J. (1996). 'The role of shame in going straight: A study of former offenders'. In: B. Galaway and J. Hudson (eds.) *Restorative Justice: International Perspectives*. Monsey, NY: Criminal Justice Press, pp. 283–302.

Lemert, E. M. (1967). *Human Deviance, Social Problems, and Social Control.* Englewood Cliffs, NJ: Prentice Hall.

Lindegaard, M. and Jacques, S. (2014). Agency as a cause of crime. *Deviant Behavior,* 35(2): 85–100.

Loeber, R. and Le Blanc, M. (1990). Towards a developmental criminology. *Crime and Justice,* 12: 375–473.

Loeber, R., Stouthamer-loeber, M., and Ahonen, L. (2016). 'Key behavioral aspects of desistance from conduct problems and delinquency'. In J. Shapland, S. Farrall and T. Bottoms. *Global Perspectives on Desistance,* Abingdon: Routledge, pp. 85–98.

Loughran, T. A., Piquero, A. R., Fagan, J., and Mulvey, E. P. (2012). Differential deterrence: Studying heterogeneity and changes in perceptual deterrence among serious youthful offenders. *Crime & Delinquency,* 58(1): 3–27.

Martinez, D. J. (2009). 'Former prisioners, their family members, and the transformative potencial of support'. In: Veysey, B. M., Christian, J. and Martinez, D. J. (eds.) *How Offenders Transform Their Lives.* London: Willian Press, pp. 56–71.

Maruna, S. (2001). *Making Good: How Ex-Convicts Reform and Rebuild their lives.* Washington, DC: American Psychological Association.

Maruna, S., LeBel, T., Naples, M. and Mitchell, N. (2009). 'Looking-glass identity transformation: Pygmalion and Golem in the rehabilitation process'. In B. Veysey, J. Christian and D.J. Martinez (eds.) *How Offenders Transform Their Lives.* Cullompton: Willan Publishing.

Matthews, R. (2002). Crime and control in late modernity. *Theoretical Criminology,* 6(2): 217–226.

McIntyre, R. 1992. Consumption in contemporary capitalism: Beyond Marx and Veblen. *Review of Social Economy,* 50(19): 40–60.

McNeill F. (2012) Four forms of "offender" rehabilitation. *Legal and Criminological Psychology,* 17(1): 18–36.

Meisenhelder, T. (1977). An exploratory study of exiting from criminal careers. *Criminology,* 15: 319–334.

Merton, R. (1957). *Social Theory and Social Structure.* New York: Free Press.

Messerschmidt, J. (1986). *Capitalism, Patriarchy, and Crime: Towards a Socialist Feminist Criminolgy.* Totowa: Rowman & Littlefield.

Monahan, K. C., Cauffman, E. and Steinberg, L. (2009). 'Affiliation with antisocial peers, susceptibility to peer influence, and antisocial behavior during the transition to adulthood'. *Developmental Psychology,* 45(6): 1520–1530.

Monahan, K. C., Steinberg, L., Cauffman, E. and Mulvey, E. P. (2009). Trajectories of antisocial behavior and psychosocial maturity from adolescence to young adulthood. *Developmental Psychology,* 45(6): 1654–1668.

Morizot, J. and Le Blanc, M. (2007). Behavioral, self, and social control predictors of desistance from crime: A test of launch and contemporaneous effect models. *Journal of Contemporary Criminal Justice,* 23(1): 50–71.

Mosher, D. and Tomkins, S. (1988). Scripting the macho man: Hypermasculine socialization and enculturation. *Journal of Sex Research,* 25(1): 60–84.

Nagin, D. S., Farrington, D. P. and Moffit, T. E. (1995). Life course trajectories of different types of offenders. *Criminology,* 33: 111–139.

Nugent, B. and Schinkel, M. (2016). The pains of desistance. *Criminology and Criminal Justice, 16*(5): 568–584.

Patton, D., and Farrall, S. (2021). Desistance: A utopian perspective. *The Howard Journal of Crime and Justice, 60*(2): 209–231.

Piquero, A., Hawkins, J. D. and Kazemian, L. (2012). 'Criminal career patterns'. In: Loeber, R. and Farrington, D. P. (eds.) *From Juvenile Delinquency to Adult Crime: Criminal Careers, Justice Policy and Prevention*. New York: Oxford University Press, pp. 14–46.

Piquero, A., Moffitt, T. and Wright, B. (2007). Self-control and criminal career dimensions. *Journal of Contemporary Criminal Justice*, 23(1): 72–89.

Sampson, R. J. and Laub, J. H. (2003). Life-course desisters? Trajectories of crime among delinquent boys followed to age 70. *Criminology*, 41(3): 555–592.

Schwendinger, H., and Schwendinger, J. S. (1985). *Adolescent Subcultures and Delinquency*. New York: Praeger.

Shover, N. (2004). 'Foreword'. In: Maruna, S., and Immarigeon, R. (eds.) *After Crime and Punishment: Pathways to Offender Reintegration*. New York: Willan Publishing, pp. vii–xii.

Shover, N. and Thompson, C. Y. (1992). Age, differential expectations, and crime desistane. *Criminology*, 30(1): 89–104.

Standing, G. (2011) *Precariat: New Dangerous Class*. London: Bloomsbury Academic.

Sykes, G. and Matza, D. (1957). Techniques of neutralization: A theory of delinquency. *American Sociological Review*, 22(6): 664–670.

Terry, D., and Abrams, L. S. (2017). Dangers, diversions, and decisions: The process of criminal desistance among formerly incarcerated young men. *International Journal of Offender Therapy and Comparative Criminology*, 61(7): 727–750.

UNDP (2014). *Citizen Security with a Human Face: Evidence and Proposal for Latin America*. New York: United Nation Development Programme.

Van Bavel, R. and Sell-Trujillo, L. (2003). Understanding of consumerism in Chile. *Journal of Consumer Culture*, 3(3): 343–362.

Vidal, S., Ouellet, F., and Dubois, M. È. (2020). Walking into the sunset: How criminal achievement shapes the desistance process: Criminal achievement and the desistance process. *Criminal Justice and Behavior*, 47(11): 1529–1546.

Weinberger, D. A. and Schwartz, G. E. (1990). 'Distress and restraint as superordinate dimensions of self-reported adjustment: a typological perspective'. *Journal of Personality*, 58(2): 381–417.

Wolfgang, M. et al. (1985). *The National Survey of Crime Severity*. Washington, DC: U.S. Government Printing Office.

Young, J. (2007). *The Vertigo of Late Modernity*, London: Sage.

Young, J. (2011). *The Criminological Imagination*. Cambridge: Polity Press.

Zemel, O., Ronel, N. and Einat, T. (2016). The impact of introspection and resilience on abstention and desistance from delinquent behavior among adolescents at risk'. *European Journal of Criminology*, 13(1): 111–128.

Chapter 4

Triggers within the liminal space of crime and conformity

The previous chapter discussed the process of crime abandonment, showing inter alia that the categories of desistance and persistence are far from absolute – and indeed that several individuals vacillated in the liminal space between crime and conformity. Moreover, completely reformed desisters and categorically antisocial persisters were rarely found among the interviewees, and ambivalence was a constitutive issue throughout the process of crime abandonment.

The aim of this chapter is to explore the factors that might be associated with the process of moving away from crime among the young offenders of the study, offering a preliminary identification of those factors which specifically facilitate or hinder its process. The following questions will, therefore, be addressed: (1) which factors increase the probability of desistance? and (2) do these factors change when different explanatory models and operationalisation of desistance are used?

The first section of this chapter discusses methodological issues. The second and third sections then present the results of logistic regression models and a discussion thereof. Last, the conclusion brings together final insights from the findings, considering their implications for research and policy.

Data, measures and analytical strategy

To answer the abovementioned questions, binary logistic regressions were conducted to test three models explaining desistance. The first model tested the association between factors from social control explanations and desistance from crime; to this, the second-added factors coming from routine activities explanations; the third synthesised factors from both previous models with psychosocial factors. Specifically, to explore the second question further, the third integrated model (including social control, routine activities and psychosocial factors) was tested using a different operationalisation of desistance. The results are integrated with information collected from the in-depth interviews.

The data used for the analyses later come from the prospective questionnaire in two waves, conducted over one year described before, that was administered

DOI: 10.4324/9781003160809-5

to a sample of 334 late-adolescent offenders (males aged 16–20) who were sentenced to probation in 2012 in Santiago. In addition, 35 in-depth interviews were conducted with a subsample of individuals from the panel in the first wave of interviews. For detailed information of the data set and characteristics of the sample, see Chapter 2. The variables for the analysis were selected according to three criteria: theoretical relevance, reliability, and availability in the data set (the latter imposes some limitations that are discussed at the end of the chapter).

Dependent variables

As discussed in Chapter 2, desistance rates vary considerably when different operationalisations are used; therefore, desistance is here operationalised in two ways (see Table 4.1 for descriptive statistics). Unfortunately, the data available did not allow the assessment of desistance as a continuous variable, because frequency was measured in a categorical way. Furthermore, although the data set allowed the assessment of changes in the seriousness of crime between the first and second wave, this measure could not have been used as a dependant variable because of methodological restrictions.

Behavioural desistance: Self-reported crime was assessed in the second wave, asking the interviewees if they had committed at least one crime (out of a list of 23 criminal offences) in the last 12 months. Self-reported crime was cross-checked against official criminal data provided by the National Office of the Public Defender.

Intentional desistance: Intentional desistance was measured by responses to the statement "I have stopped committing crime completely during the past year", to which interviewees could answer "yes" or "no". Due to the nature of the statement, a positive answer to this question might include interviewees who committed crimes between the first and the second wave but were not committing crimes at the time of interview; it can be, therefore, understood as a relatively free operationalisation of desistance (not limited to a crime-free gap of 1 year), and as one that might capture some initial agentic moves towards the process of crime abandonment. In other words, this measure aims to capture an intentional position regarding crime abandonment.

Socio-demographic and control variables

Age: Age declared at the second wave, which was cross-checked with official data provided by the Chilean Youth Justice Board.

Age of crime onset: Using a life calendar, interviewees were asked the age at which they committed the first offense (regardless of whether they were arrested or not).

Independent variables

As discussed in Chapter 1, desistance is triggered by different factors recognised within diverse theoretical perspectives. Some scholars have argued for the supremacy of some factors over others (Bushway & Paternoster, 2013; Sampson & Laub, 1993), while others have tried to develop integrated models that consider a wider range of elements (Bottoms & Shapland, 2014; Farrall et al., 2014; Giodano, 2016). The independent variables included in the analysis come from three groups of theoretical explanations: social control, routine and lifestyle, and psychosocial explanations.

Social control variables[1]

Partner: This variable is derived from questions assessing whether, between the first and second wave, the interviewees had a partner for more than seven months who was against their criminal behaviour.
Parental influence: This variable denotes whether the interviewee always lived with at least one parent between the first and second wave, under the condition that the parent was not involved in crime.[2] Although this variable did not emerge in the literature review as a relevant one (but see Copp et al., 2019; Lee, Moon, & Garcia, 2019), it was decided to include it because several interviewees were living with their parents and it could operate as a protective factor against persistence.
Occupation: This dichotomous variable denotes whether the interviewees worked or were enrolled in school or other type of educational institution, between the two waves. Therefore, zero denotes the absence of any occupational activity during the year before the last interview.[3]

Routine and lifestyle variables

Antisocial peers: The effect of antisocial peers was measured using a three-item scale assessing: their presence ("Most of my friends commit crimes"); their influence ("In general I do more dangerous things when I'm with my friends than when I'm alone"); and the interviewee's participation in a gang ("I'm part of gang that get together to commit crimes"). The Cronbach's alpha was .663 at the second wave and a principal component analysis revealed a single factor (E=1.19 V=39.73%).
Risky behaviour: This dichotomous variable denotes whether the interviewee spent time in discos or pubs, at parties, or hanging around with friends on the street between the first and the second wave.
Drug misuse: This denotes whether the interviewee used *often* hard drugs (cocaine and/or crack) between the first and the second wave. Only hard drugs were included, because the prevalence of marijuana was very high among the interviewees (76%).

Psychosocial variables

Legal cynicism: Legal cynicism was assessed using the legal cynicism scale (Sampson & Bartusch, 1998). The Cronbach's alpha was .667 at the second wave and a principal component analysis revealed a single factor (E=2.00 V= 50.12%). This variable was considered in the model as the best proxy of morality available in the data set, despite its limitations. As discussed in the conclusion, the best way to measure morality is through scenarios or vignettes.

Consideration for others: Consideration for others was assessed through three items drawn from the Weinberg adjustment inventory (Weinberger & Schwartz, 1990): "I think about other people's feelings before I do something they might not like"; "I enjoy doing things for other people, even when I don't receive anything in return"; and "I often go out my way to do things for other people". The Cronbach's alpha was .577 at the second wave and a principal component analysis revealed a single factor (E=1.60 V=53.47%).[4]

Self-efficacy: Self-efficacy was measured using an adapted version of the Self-efficacy Scale for Adolescents developed by Prothrow-Stith (1987). The items assessed the interviewees' confidence in attaining educational and career goals, and in staying out of trouble through four items: "I am confident that I will graduate from school"; "I am confident that I will get the job that I really want"; "I am confident in my ability to stay away from fights"; and "I am confident that I can abandon crime whenever I want". The Cronbach's alpha was .699 at the second wave and a principal component analysis revealed a single factor (E=2.135 V=53.38%).[5]

Delinquent identity: Delinquent identity was measured using a three-item scale: "I see myself as a delinquent"; "My family sees myself as a delinquent"; and "People from my neighbourhood see myself as a delinquent". The Cronbach's alpha was .842.

Behavioural and intentional desistance

Table 4.1 presents the descriptive statistics of the variables used in the analysis. As it can be seen, desistance rates varied according to the two different methods used to operationalise desistance from crime. While the desistance rate is 43% when it is measured as a one-year crime-free gap (behavioural desistance), it increases to 65% when it is assessed as a positive response to the statement "I have abandoned crime completely in the past year" (intentional desistance).

The regression models presented in Table 4.2 examine the association between the independent variables and desistance from crime. Three models are presented, which include controls for age at the second wave and age of crime onset. The first model tests the association between social control variables and desistance from crime. All the social control variables included in the model are significantly correlated with desistance. The interviewees who lived with at least one parent (not involved with crime), who had a prosocial partner and who worked (or were enrolled in school or other type of educational institution between the two waves) were more likely to desist from crime.

The second model adds routine and lifestyle variables to the former model to tests the association between these variables and desistance from crime. The results show that, while social control variables remain significant, the three

Table 4.1 Description of variables

Variable	*Description*	*Coding*	*N*	*M*	*SD*	*Alpha*
Dependent variables						
Behavioural desistance	Self-reported criminal behaviour in the last year checked against official crime records	1=DES 0=PER	334	43%[1]	.496	
Intentional desistance	Answers yes to "I have abandoned crime completely in the last year"	1=YES 0=NO	334	65%	.478	
Socio-demographic and control variables						
Age	Age at second wave	16–21	334	18.09	1.086	
Crime onset	Age of crime onset	7–17	333	12.57	2.423	
Social control variables						
Occupation	Working or studying in the past year	1=YES 0=NO	334	81.7%	.386	
Parental influence	Consistently living with at least one parent in the last year who is not involved in crime	1=YES 0=NO	334	62.6%	.484	
Prosocial partner	Having a stable, prosocial (against criminal behaviour) partner in the last year	1=YES 0=NO	334	27.8%	.448	
Routine and lifestyle variables						
Risky activities	Spent time in discos/bars, at parties, or hanging around with friends on the street in the last year	1=YES 0=NO	334	85.3%	.354	
Antisocial peers scale[2]	Set of three questions that measure the presence and influence of antisocial peers, and participation in a gang	3–15	332	9.96	2.844	.663
Drugs	Drug use in the last year marked as "often" (hard drugs only)	1=YES 0=NO	334	22.5%	.417	
Psychosocial variables						
Consideration of others[3]	WAI (Weinberg Adjustment Inventory)	3–15	333	10.77	2.25	.577
Identity scale[4]	I see myself, or my family/parents see me, as a delinquent	0–3	334	.643	.99	.842
Legal cynicism[5]	Legal cynicism scale Sampson and Bartusch (1998)	3–15	331	9.22	2.72	.669
Self-efficacy[6]	Self-efficacy Scale (Prothrow-Stith, 1987)	10–30	328	22.95	3.85	.757

1 It is important to mention that the behavioural desistance rate here is 43%, while in the previous chapter it was 41%. This difference is due to the fact that the sample size for the present analysis was smaller (334 versus 341).

2 Higher values showing more involvement with antisocial peers.

3 Higher values showing higher levels of consideration for others

4 Higher values showing higher levels of antisocial identity.

5 Higher values showing higher levels of legal cynicism.

6 Higher values showing higher levels of self-efficacy.

Table 4.2 Logistic regression estimating desistance/persistence from crime

	Model 1: Social control variables			*Model 2: Routine and lifestyle variables*			*Model 3: Psychosocial variables*[1]		
	Beta	*SE*	*OR*	*Beta*	*SE*	*OR*	*Beta*	*SE*	*OR*
Socio-demographic variables									
Age	.205*	.116	1.23	.243*	.128	1.28	.326**	.146	1.38
Age of crime onset	.120**	.052	1.13	.084	.057	1.09	.039	.066	1.04
Social control variables									
Partner	.829***	.281	2.29	.525*	.306	1.69	.389	.345	1.47
Living with no criminal parents	1.19***	.267	3.29	1.32***	.302	3.75	1.58***	.340	4.84
Occupation	1.52***	.386	4.57	1.15***	.414	3.18	1.09**	.458	2.96
Routine and lifestyle variables									
Peers				–.232***	.057	.793	–.112	.070	.894
Risky activities				–1.35***	.437	.259	–1.44***	.518	.237
Drug misuse				–1.196***	.341	.302	–.876**	.374	.417
Psychosocial variables									
Consideration of others							.140*	.077	1.15
Self-efficacy							.029	.065	1.029
Antisocial identity							–.521**	.219	.594
Legal cynicism							–.289***	.072	.749
Constant	–7.802***	2.21		–8636	2.45		–6.504**	3.10	
N	334			331			326		
Cox and Snell R square	.170			.310			.403		
Nagelkerke R square	.229			.416			.540		

*p < .05. **p < .01. *** p < .001.

[1] The model correctly classifies 82% of the cases and the omnibus goodness of fit test indicates that overall the model is predictive of desistance (p<.001). The model does not violate the assumptions of linearity and multicollinearity (Tolerance<10 and VIF>.2).

routine and lifestyle variables added appear as significant as well. Indeed, more involvement with antisocial peers, being involved in risky activities and using hard drugs between the two waves, were negatively and significantly associated with desistance.

The third model added psychosocial variables to the second. Interestingly, when adding other theoretically relevant variables into this final model, some variables that were significantly associated with desistance in the former model did not appear significant in this final integrated model. This is the case of involvement with antisocial peers and having a partner. Nevertheless, the rest of the social control variables that were significant in the second model maintained their significance in the integrated model as well. Moreover, all the psychosocial variables included (aside from self-efficacy) were significantly associated with desistance. This is the case for consideration for others, which were positively and significantly correlated with desistance and antisocial identity and legal cynicism, which were negatively and significantly correlated with desistance.

It is also important to mention that the integrated model showed a better fit than the first and the second, better predicting the outcome (Nagelkerke R square .540). This might indicate that an integrated model which includes a wide range of variables drawn from diverse theoretical models could better explain desistance. Moreover, it might show that the integration of psychosocial variables, which are generally neglected in quantitative research on desistance, would be useful as a starting point for exploring key issues that might be involved in the changing process.

To properly analyse the marginal effects of the different independent variables over the dependent variable (desistance/persistence), the marginal probabilities (dy/dx) were calculated for the integrated model. Regarding the social control variables, the results show that the probability of desisting increases by 22.6% for those individuals who have lived with non-criminal parents in the last year, compared to their peers which did not during the last year. Also, individuals who have worked or studied in the last year have 15.1% more chances of desisting.

When analysing routine activities variables, data shows that those who have been involved in risky activities in the last 12 months have a 20.3% lower probability of desisting. Additionally, those who have "often" used hard-drugs in the last year are 12.6% less likely to desist from crime.

Finally, regarding psychosocial variables, the analysis shows that increases in one standard deviation in the score of the "antisocial identity" and "legal cynicism" scales are correlated to a 7.2% and 10.9% decrease, respectively, in the probabilities of desistance from crime. Finally, a standard deviation increase in the scale of "consideration for others" increases the chances of desisting from crime by 4.3%.

From the integrated model, it is possible to observe that the individuals who did not see themselves as delinquents, demonstrated less legal cynicism, and showed more consideration for others were those who were more likely to desist from crime. Although lower than the effect of social control and routine activities variables, this shows that the psychosocial factors that operate in the desistance processes do not do so in isolation from each other: rather, there is an orientation towards pro-sociality in a broad sense. Not only are they less likely to see themselves as criminals, but they realise that others also see them differently, and both their families and other people from their social contexts begin to trust and approach them. This is consistent with previous research showing that the desistance process is related to a reconciliation of familial attachments (Bottoms & Shapland, 2016) and the emergence of consideration for others (Porporino, 2010). That closeness to significant others may facilitate greater levels of empathy, enhancing a sense of social integration – as this narrative evidences:

I: How can you define yourself now?
ALBERTO: More like a person.
I: What does this mean?
ALBERTO: I don't know – now I am more social. For example, before people on the bus avoided me, changing seats. Now people do not get scared. I no longer feel like a danger to society.
I: How do you feel that?
ALBERTO: In so many ways, because I'm working, I was studying … Now they treat me well, I can talk to anyone. There are people who treat me with affection. People ask me for help.

(Alberto, desister, age 20)

Arnett (2004) has noted that learning consideration for others has been one of the key markers of adulthood in several studies. It opens the way to new forms of social demands, such as reciprocity and mutual care, which may be key in giving individuals the impetus to stop offending. Indeed, the belief that one can provide support and help is perhaps one of the deepest demonstrations of social recognition, since it implies the acknowledgement of one's capacity to perform according to the demands and standards from significant others.

The abovementioned is not to say that psychosocial factors precede social control or routine activities factors, as Bushway and Paternoster (2013) have argued. The available data do not allow such a conclusion to be drawn – and, in any case, this is not the aim of the chapter. Moreover, since it was not possible to assess changes with those measures, it is not clear if changes in identity, consideration for others or legal cynicism were associated with desistance, or if those individuals had those characteristics even when offending. What these findings suggest, consistently with Giordano (2016), is that although lifestyle factors (such as drug use, risky activities, and occupation) are strongly relevant to stay away from crime, the desistance process is not just related to key events that operate in individuals' lives. Although we may think that the achievement of transition events such as work and marriage are what define individuals as adults, research has shown that feelings of being an adult are based on more gradual and internal issues (Arnett, 2004, 2010).

This contention was confirmed through the in-depth interviews, in with, similar to what was observed by McCuish, Lussier, and Rocque (2020) with data from the Pathways to Desistance Study, interviewees experienced these internal changes in combination with lifestyle changes as a transformative process towards adulthood. Their narratives clearly identified two different selves: the adolescent and the adult. The adolescent self was impulsive, irresponsible, and selfish, while the adult self was more focused, hard-working, calm, organised, and mature.

Consistent with previous research (Maruna, 2001), most of the interviewees indicated that what they did in the past was necessary to become the kind of person they had become in the present. Indeed, the division between the adolescent and the adult self, allowed them to handle the guilt and to relegate the adolescent self to the past. Furthermore, similar to what Coyle (2019) observed among young offenders in Belfast, it was possible in several narratives to clearly differentiate between them *behaving* like a delinquent due to immaturity and having *been* a delinquent in the past. The relegation of delinquency to the adolescent period allowed these young people to develop and sustain a prosocial identity more easily, separating past actions and present self. Maturation among participants was seen as an incremental process of improvement, helping them to find forgiveness among significant others and become a reliable person who would never go back. As one individual stated:

> Before I was so silly, so immature. Now everyone on the programme is impressed with my change. They know that I would not return to the same thing for anything in the world.
>
> (Yerko, desister, age 18)

The abovementioned process of incremental change is consistent with the factors associated with the process of crime abandonment discussed in the previous chapter, such as the fact that the interviewees started exploring other forms of doing masculinities through rationality and responsibility, pursuing a productive life, assuming adult roles, and leaving expressive crime (caused by humiliation and the pursuit of identity and status) behind. Moreover, transitions towards a more prosocial self might be triggered by the dissonance some of them experienced between their values and their behaviour.

This might also be consistent with the other factors that appeared to be associated with desistance in the former analysis. Indeed, individuals who were less involved in risky activities, such as spending time in discos and bars, at parties, or hanging around with friends on the street, were more likely to desist from crime. They were likely engaged in what Bottoms and Shapland called "strategies of diachronic self-control", avoiding situations that would confront them with temptations they would struggle to resist. It could also be the case that they were occupied by conventional duties and, therefore, less exposed to risky activities. Indeed, "occupation" as a measure of being working or being enrolled in school or other type of educational institution between the two waves was also significantly associated with desistance. As Giordano (2016) argues, individuals manage their environments – they actively choose some activities over others, and more conventional routines start to be more consistent with their way of life.

This is not to say that their former lifestyles start to be completely neglected and lose all their appeal, as Paternoster and Bushway (2009) have suggested. Indeed, as discussed in the previous chapter, crime was not easy to surrender since it was still viewed as a source of pleasure, enjoyment, and satisfaction by several interviewees. The lack of alternative identities, roles, routines, and places that were available to them outside the criminal realm made the "crystallization of discontent" (pointed out by these authors) very difficult to experience. Social structure has a direct effect on role transitions and, consequently, a person with a lack of human and social capital would have access to very few new conventional social roles to replace or enrich the old ones (Farrall, 2010; Matsueda & Heimer, 2004; Bottoms & Shapland, 2011). Moreover, crime was for the interviewees, not merely related to life failures; it brought status, power, and money to their lives and – for several interviewees – was strongly rewarded within a social context which measures life success through individuals' consumption capacity.

Routine and lifestyle changes (which were found to be strongly associated with desistance) were perhaps the most challenging issues for the interviewees. Several interviewees described how their routines became structured and limited, since they could not inhabit the places around their work due to the strong social stratification of Santiago's neighbourhoods – not to mention that most of the places in their neighbourhoods were marked with strong temptations. They were trapped within their households, because hanging around on the street was no longer a possibility for them – and, at the same time, they were not able to cross the city limits to access wealthier areas as they did when they were committing crimes.

The fact that those who lived with at least one of their parents during the last year were 22.6% more likely to desist was not unexpected. If the abovementioned changes are to emerge, social support and exposure to prosocial models are needed. Furthermore, if we consider that 60% of these youths lived with their mothers all the time and 20% sporadically between the two waves, it may also be the case that they were supposed to assume the breadwinner role. Indeed, in low-class contexts in Chile, it is actually expected that young males start behaving as "respectable men" upon reaching the age of maturity, with a more structured life that is free of drugs and crime. Research has also shown that, in the transition towards adulthood, the relationship with parents improves and that this progress might be associated with desistance from crime (Copp et al., 2019; Johnson, Blum, & Giedd, 2009; Lee, Moon, & Garcia, 2019). Several interviewees reflected the ways in which individuals' relationships with their parents changed, becoming more mature, based on mutual acceptance and support. They also started having more realistic expectations regarding parental support, realising that their lives were to be forged by themselves.

Finally, the fact that having a prosocial partner did not emerge as a factor associated with desistance in the integrated model was not surprising; the evidence on the effects of intimate relationships on desistance has, after all, shown conflicting results (Horney, Tolan, & Weisburd, 2012; Wyse, Harding, & Moreonff, 2014). This is consistent with the interviewees' accounts of their romantic relationships. Whilst prosocial partners were a strong influence for some to leave crime behind, others found that being with a partner entailed financial pressures that were solved through crime. This was particularly the case for those who were unemployed or studying, as this narrative evidences:

> If you are a man, you are expected to have some cash ... If you go out with your girl to the shopping mall, you have to invite her for some food and buy her stuff – a present, you know – some clothes or make-up ... If not, you are not a real man.
>
> (Miguel, persister, age 19)

Contrary to the abovementioned factors, the fact that greater involvement with anti social peers was not associated with persistence was certainly unexpected. Nevertheless, in the case of deviant peers, consistent with Haynie et al. (2014), most of the interviewees expressed that they were involved in social networks that included delinquent as well as non-delinquent peers, and that they started to be more receptive to the conventional ones:

> I have friends who study, others who work, others who commit crimes, others who do nothing. Not everyone is doing only one thing. I still see those who commit crimes, but they respect my decision and I spend a little time with them, I smoke a cigarette and I leave, then they follow in other things, but I go home. I go out with my other friends now, the quieter ones, the ones who work.
>
> (Alvaro, desister, age 19)

Moving towards further exploration of the second question, and to remain consistent with the findings presented in the previous chapter, a different operationalisation of desistance was also tested. Table 4.3 compares the results of two models using logistic regression with the same predictors, but with two different dependent variables. The first model is the same integrated model presented in Table 4.2, where desistance was operationalised as the absence of crime in the last year (behavioural desistance). The second model tests the association between the same factors with intentional desistance, which was measured by a positive or negative response to the statement, "I have stopped committing crime completely during the past year".

As previously discussed, considering the fact that the intentional desistance rate is considerably higher than the behavioural desistance rate, it could be argued that this measure of desistance is likely to have captured interviewees in the first stages of crime abandonment as well, or individuals who have recently decided to abandon crime (it does not imply a one-year crime-free gap in the same way as behavioural desistance does).

Therefore, intentional desistance could be better interpreted as a measure reflecting the perceived capacity to stay away from crime, rather than as being

Table 4.3 Logistic regression estimating desistance/persistence from crime and intentional desistance

	Model 1: Behavioural desistance (persistence versus desistance)			*Model 2: Intentional desistance1 (persistence versus intentional desistance)*		
	Beta	*SE*	*OR*	*Beta*	*SE*	*OR*
Socio-demographic and control variables						
Age	.326**	.146	1.38	.097	.135	1.10
Age of crime onset	.039	.066	1.04	-.024	.061	.976
Social control variables						
Partner	.389	.345	1.47	.448	.336	1.56
Living with no criminal parents	1.58***	.340	4.84	.253	.289	1.29
Occupation	1.09**	.458	2.96	.389	.371	1.47
Routine and lifestyle variables						
Peers	–.112	.070	.894	–.043	.062	.958
Risky activities	–1.44***	.518	.237	–.090	.441	.914
Drug misuse	–.876**	.374	.417	–.444	.319	.641
Psychosocial variables						
Consideration for others	.140*	.077	1.15	131*	.068	1.14
Self efficacy	.029	.065	1.029	.162**	.064	1.175
Antisocial identity	–.521**	.219	.594	–.531***	.158	.588
Legal cynicism	–.289***	.072	.749	–.189***	.085	.828
Constant	–6.504**	3.10		–3.519*	2.98	
N	326			326		
Cox and Snell R square	.403			.260		
Nagelkerke R square	.540			.358		

*p < .05. **p < .01. *** p < .001.

1 The model correctly classifies 76% of the cases and the omnibus goodness of fit test indicates that overall the model is predictive of desistance (p<.001). The model does not violate the assumptions of linearity and multicollinearity (Tolerance<10 and VIF>.2).

a proxy for a proper crime-free gap. In that sense, it is interesting to note that only the psychosocial factors included in the model – all of them – were significantly associated with intentional desistance; the factors related to social control and routine activities theories, on the other hand, were not. This might reflect the early stages of desistance, during which – as Bottoms and Shapland (2014) pointed out – individuals start thinking differently about themselves and others. It is also interesting to note that only in the intentional desistance model did self-efficacy emerge as significantly associated with desistance – a fact that might reflect the aforementioned overemphasis of personal agency at the beginning of the desistance process.

Finally, the fact that social control and routine activities variables were not significantly correlated with intentional desistance might indicate that – as suggested in the previous chapter – the antisocial lifestyle was at the beginning of the desistance process particularly difficult to surrender, and these young offenders were probably still strongly embedded within their social settings, therefore, not yet benefiting from prosocial opportunities or investing in conventional activities such as work or family life.

Concluding remarks

This chapter aimed to investigate the factors that increase the probability of temporary desistance among the young offenders from the study, and to explore how these factors change when different models and operationalisations of desistance are used. Despite some limitations (discussed below), the findings give rise to some preliminary insights that must be further explored through future research.

The factors associated with temporary desistance from crime among the participants of the study vary according to the theoretical model and the operationalisation of desistance used. While some factors emerged as significantly associated with behavioural desistance in models based on social control and routine activities approaches, for instance, they were not associated with behavioural desistance in the final integrated model that included psychosocial factors as well. The integrated model, shows definitively that the process of moving away from crime is not simply associated to social control factors that appear in life and promote changes without individuals being aware of it. As Giordano (2016) pointed out, the most effective hooks for change are not the ones that operate as sources of social control, but the ones that provide a roadmap to trigger the development of a new identity. Individual orientations towards conformity may be also relevant throughout the process, opening individuals to the influence of other factors and supporting daily decisions of routine and lifestyle changes that allow them to avoid crime, facilitating the coherence and sense of purpose that orients behaviour.

Although the data available for the present analysis do not allow me to completely answer the second question (Do these factors change when different explanatory models and operationalisation of desistance are used?), it is possible to offer the preliminary conclusion that, when comparing two different measures of desistance, the predictors differ. Indeed, while behavioural desistance was associated with social control factors, routine activities, and psychosocial variables, intentional desistance was only associated with psychosocial factors. Bearing in mind that this measure could reflect the perceived capacity to avoid crime (as opposed to being a proxy for a proper crime-free gap), a similar argument to that in Chapter 2 may be advanced: namely, that secondary desistance might not necessarily be a long-term achievement that arises as a consequence of crime abandonment. This might demonstrate early stages of desistance in which, as Bottoms and Shapland (2014) pointed out, individuals start thinking differently about themselves, and gradual changes in identity occur.

Unfortunately, due to sample size and other methodological issues, it was not possible to test whether the predictors also differed when measuring desistance as a change in seriousness and frequency of crime. Nevertheless, as the qualitative data presented in the former chapter showed, it is likely that specific and different predictors would account for these two processes as well, most probably reflecting ambivalence and ambiguity.

These findings have clear implications for research and practice. In terms of research, the role played by psychosocial factors in the process of moving away from crime paves the way to continue exploring them longitudinally with larger samples comprising also female offenders. Moreover, better measures of these types of factors must be developed. These measures must be informed by the findings of qualitative studies to better capture psychosocial processes – especially regarding identity changes. Moral orientations must be assessed using scenarios or moral dilemmas instead of scales, enabling a more detailed capture of individuals' strategies for resolving moral conflicts in specific situations. This might further inform knowledge regarding offenders' management of ambivalence and how it interacts with the development of a sense of self.

Consideration of others measures should include interpersonal dynamics of support exchange, accounting for the reciprocal aspects of this construct that are not captured when we conceptualise it simply as a proxy of empathy. Although there are aspects of these psychosocial factors that might be only captured through qualitative methods (and perhaps they are the best way of doing so), quantitative approaches might complement them by incorporating factors that have been mostly neglected in quantitative research.

Regarding implications for practice, these findings enable consideration of factors that could be easily woven into correctional practice: people cannot, of course, be forced to radically change their daily routine – but it is possible to work with offenders on developing a new sense of identity, a sense of empathy, and on improving their moral orientations to reorient their routines and to help them to take advantage of social opportunities. Research on desistance and probation has shown that relationships between probation officers and offenders can play a crucial role in the desistance process, promoting and supporting the development of prosocial narratives (Barry, 2006; Burnett & McNeill, 2005; Farrall, 2014; King, 2013; McNeill et al., 2005).

This might be important to counteract the "bureaucratic positivism", characterised by an excessive orientation towards compliance based only on decision-making that has captured probations in many countries (King, 2013:147). It might also be of great importance in developing countries, where social protection mechanisms are weak and access to social opportunities (such as formal employment, education, housing, and health) is not always guaranteed. Indeed, research on life-course transitions in Latin America has shown that the most disadvantaged young people move towards adult life in an unclear way, with a high degree of indeterminacy towards the future which sometimes prevents turning points. Moreover, some scholars (e.g. Machado Pais, 2007; Rausky, 2014) have argued that, due to poverty and inequality in Latin America, the specific rituals that indicated the path to adulthood now hold less weight.

Last, these findings facilitate consideration of how contact with the criminal justice system hinders not only the transition towards adulthood, blocking the occurrence of specific turning points or social control factors, but also the development of prosocial sense of self. In that sense, civic reintegration through voluntary work, restorative practices, the restoration of civil rights, and the redemption rituals advocated by Maruna (2001) might support transitions towards conformity, de-labelling of individuals, and the promotion of social integration.

Notes

1 The variable of "Having children" was included in the initial model – however, it was not significant and did not affect the model, so it was excluded from the final model.

2 "Parental influence" was checked by introducing the interaction variable: parents*parents no crime. The interaction was not significant. The model fit improved when including in the model the variable "parental influence", which denoted living continually with at least one parent in the last year that was not involved in crime.

3 It was decided to include this variable instead of assessing school attainment separately, since, at the first interview all the youths from the sample were on probation or semi-prison and in Chile it is mandatory to attend school when serving a sentence in the Youth Justice System. In fact, the offenders who served a prison sentence (and those were more seriously involved in crime) had achieved higher educational levels for that very reason.

4 The original version of the scale was not used, because in the pilot phase of the questionnaire it was observed that the rest of the items were difficult to understand by the interviewees and a factor analysis showed that the reliability improved if considering only the three items that were finally selected.

5 It is important to mention that a "self-efficacy" scale was included instead of a "self-control" scale, due to lower correlation with a "legal cynicism" scale (r=.12 instead of r=.33). Also, the "self-control" scale was checked by introducing the interaction variable: self-control *age. The interaction was not significantly correlated with desistance.

References

Arnett, J. J. (2004). *Emerging Adulthood: The Winding Road from the Late Teens Through the Twenties*. New York, NY: Oxford University Press.

Arnett, J. J. (2010). *Adolescence and Emerging Adulthood: A Cultural Approach (4th ed.)*. Boston, MA: Prentice Hall.

Barry, M. (2006). *Youth Offending in Transition: The Search for Social Recognition*. London: Routledge.

Bottoms, A. and Shapland, J. (2011). 'Steps towards desistance among male young adult recidivists'. In: Farrall, S., Hough, M., Maruna, S. and Sparks, R. (eds.) *Escape Routes: Contemporary Perspectives on Life after Punishment*. Oxon: Routledge, pp. 43–80.

Bottoms, A. and Shapland, J. (2014). Can persisten offenders acquire virtue?. *Studies in Christian Ethics,* 27(3): 318–333.

Bottoms, A. and Shapland, J. (2016). Learning to desist early adulthood: the Sheffield Desistance Study. In: Shapland, J., Farrall, S. and Bottoms, A. (eds.) *Global Perspective on Desistance: Reviewing what We Know, Looking to the Future.* London: Routledge, pp. 99–125.

Burnett, R. and McNeill, F. (2005). The place of the officer-offender relationship in assisting offenders to desist from crime. *Probation Journal,* 52(3): 221–242.

Bushway, S. D. and Paternoster, R. (2013). Desistance from crime: A review and ideas for moving forward. In: Gibson, C. L. and Krohn, M. D. (eds.) *Handbook of Life-Course Criminology.* New York, NY: Springer, pp. 213–231.

Copp, J. E., Giordano, P. C., Longmore, M. A., & Manning, W. D. (2019). Desistance from crime during the transition to adulthood: The influence of parents, peers, and shifts in identity. *Journal of Research in Crime and Delinquency,* 57(3): 294–332.

Coyle, B. (2019) 'What the f**k is maturity?': Young adulthood, subjective maturity and desistance from crime. (2019). *The British Journal of Criminology,* 59(5): 1178–1198.

Farrall, S. (2010). European criminal careers research: An introduction to the special issue. *European Journal of Criminology,* 7(6): 419–423.

Farrall S. (2014) The spatial dynamics of desistance. In: Farrall S, Hunter B, Sharpe G, et al. (eds.) *Criminal Careers in Transition: The Social Context of Desistance from Crime.* Oxford: Oxford University Press, pp. 159–186.

Farrall, S., Hunter, B., Sharpe, G., and Calverley, A. (2014). *Criminal Careers in Transition: The Social Context of Desistance from Crime.* Oxford: Oxford University Press.

Giordano, P. (2016). 'Mechanism underlying the desistance process: reflections on A theory of Cognitive Transformation'. In: Shapland, J., Farrall, S. and Bottoms, T. (eds.) *Global Perspectives on Desistance.* Abingdon: Routledge, pp. 11–27.

Haynie, D. L., Doogan, N. J., & Soller, B. (2014). Gender, friendship networks, and delinquency: A dynamic network approach. *Criminology,* 52(4): 688–722.

Horney, J. D., Tolan, P. and Weisburd, D. (2012). 'Contextual influence'. In: Loeber, R. and Farrington, D. P. (eds.) *From Juvenile Delinquency to Adult Crime: Criminal Careers, Justice Policy and Prevention.* Oxford: Oxford University Press, pp. 86–117.

Johnson, S., Blum, R. and Giedd, J. (2009). Adolescent maturity and the brain: the promise and pitfalls of neuroscience research in adolescent health policy. *The Journal of adolescent health: official publication of the Society for Adolescent Medicine,* 45(3): 216–221.

King, R. D. (2013). Assisted desistance and experience of probation supervision. *Probation Journal,* 60(2): 136–151.

Lee, W., Moon, J., & Garcia, V. (2020). The pathways to desistance: A longitudinal study of juvenile delinquency. *Deviant Behavior,* 41(1): 87–102.

Machado Pais, J. (2007): *Chollos, chapuzas y changas. Jóvenes, trabajo precario y futuro.* Barcelona: Antrhopos.

Maruna, S. (2001). *Making Good: How Ex-Convicts Reform and Rebuild Their Lives.* Washington, DC: American Psychological Association.

Matsueda, R. L. and Heimer, K. (2004). 'A symbolic interactionist theory of role-transitions, role-commitments, and delinquency'. In: Thornberry, T. P. (ed.) *Advances in Criminological Theory. Developmental Theories of Crime and Delinquency* (Vol. 7). New Brunswick, NJ: Transaction Publishers, pp. 163–213.

McCuish, E., Lussier, P., & Rocque, M. (2020). Maturation beyond age: Interrelationships among psychosocial, adult role, and identity maturation and their implications for desistance from crime. *Journal of Youth and Adolescence, 49*(2), 479–493.

McNeill, F., Batchelor, S., Burnett, R. and Knox, J. (2005). 21st century social work: reducing re-offending – key practice skills. Preprint / Working Paper. Scottish Executive, Edinburgh. Available from: https://strathprints.strath.ac.uk/38070/1/21st_c.pdf.

Paternoster, R. and Bushway, S. D. (2009). Desistance and the "Feared Self": Toward an identity theory of criminal desistance. *Journal of Criminal Law and Criminology*, 99(4): 1109–1156.

Porporino, F. (2010). 'Bringing sense and sensitivity to corrections: From programmes to 'Fix' offenders to services to support desistance'. In: Brayfor, J., Cowe, F. and Deering, J. (eds.) *What Else Works? Creative Work With Offenders*. Collompton: Willan, pp. 1–48.

Prothrow-Stith, D. (1987). *Violence prevention curriculum for adolescents*. Newton, MA: Educational Dvelopment Center. Radloff LS. (Unpublished).

Rausky, M. E. (2014). '¿Jóvenes o adultos? Un estudio de las transiciones desde la niñez en sectores pobres urbanos'. *Última década*, 41: 11–40.

Sampson, R. J. and Bartusch, D. (1998). Legal cynicism and (subcultural?) tolerance of deviance: The neighborhood context of racial differences. *Law and Society Review*, 32: 777–804.

Sampson, R.J. and Laub, J.H. (1993) *Crime in the making: Pathways and turning points through life*. London: Harvard University Press.

Shapland, J., & Bottoms, A. (2011). Reflections on social values, offending and desistance among young adult recidivists. *Punishment & Society*, 13(3): 256–282.

Weinberger, D. A. and Schwartz, G. E. (1990). Distress and restraint as superordinate dimensions of self-reported adjustment: a typological perspective. *Journal of Personality*, 58(2): 381–417.

Wyse, J. J., Harding, D. J., & Morenoff, J. D. (2014). Romantic Relationships and Criminal Desistance: Pathways and Processes. *Sociological forum (Randolph, N.J.)*, 29(2), 365–385.

Chapter 5

Housewife, mother, or thief

Gendered desistance and persistence

Criminology has almost ignored women – not only in their deviance but also in their conformity (Heidensohn & Silvestri, 2012). A number of writers have offered critiques that empirical studies on desistance from crime have been based on men, and that their conclusions and explanations have thus excluded women's accounts. Those few studies that have researched women's desistance have mainly been oriented towards exploring the differences in factors triggering crime abandonment between men and women, but little has been done (with some notable exceptions described later) to disentangle the dynamics of the process and discuss the gender particularities that must be considered when theorising about desistance.

In the first section of the chapter, I discuss some of the gender gaps in the literature available regarding women's desistance. Then, I present the results and conclusion of the study, drawing out implications for reflection on gendered transitions and processes that could inform correctional practices for women.

Assessing the gender gap in women's process of crime abandonment

The studies reviewed in Chapter 1 regarding women's desistance have mainly limited their focus to defining the factors that trigger, impede, or have no effect on the process of women's desistance, and the differences compared to desistance among men. Little attention, however, has been paid to understanding how gender might explain why these factors operate as they do. Nevertheless, emerging work in the last years representing a critical feminist approach has contributed to highlight structural and gender aspects involved in the process of leaving crime behind among female offenders (Barr, 2019; Barr & Christian, 2019; Gålnander, 2019; Hart, 2017; Hart & Van Ginneken, 2017; Österman, 2018).

Relationships and motherhood are without doubt the factors involved in women's desistance that have deserved more attention. Most research has uncritically assumed the importance of a caring role in the process of crime abandonment, without considering its implications in terms of gender inequalities (but see Gålnander, 2019; Hale, 2020). This has strongly impacted correctional

DOI: 10.4324/9781003160809-6

practices, which have been mainly oriented towards regulating women's relationships based on the misleading idea that women's risk factors arise from their choices to associate with the wrong people (Opsal, 2014).

The conflicting evidence regarding the effect of the traditional turning points (i.e. marriage and employment) on women's desistance might be in part a consequence of the fact that most studies have assessed them based on the assumption of direct causality, without taking into account the role of other auxiliary factors that might be implied in "desistance as a complex process of incremental change" (Skardhamer & Savolainen, 2016:180). As mentioned before, Giordano (2016) has argued that effective hooks for change are not the ones that operate as sources of social control, but the ones that provide a roadmap for triggering the development of a new identity. In that sense, it might be important to question whether marriage and employment operate in such a way among women – especially considering the strong influences of socialised gender roles, structural oppression, and female responses to male domination (Barr, 2019; Belkamp, 2006).

Explanations of women's desistance have also assumed that the performance of conventional roles brings social rewards that support the development of a non-criminal identity (Bachman et al., 2016; Barry, 2012; Leverentz, 2006; Leverentz, 2011). Women have to commit themselves to an "ethical code of conduct" (Rumgay, 2004) by which the normative feminine identity is governed, recognised, and rewarded. Although some scholars have discussed the struggle of negotiating a feminine identity within the restrictions of gender (Barr, 2019; Gålnander, 2019; Hart, 2017), little attention has been given to reputation and status as salient elements of young women's identities (Laidler & Hunt, 2001). The strong focus on the development of normative feminine identities as key factor triggering desistance has ignored the exploration of other sources of identities, serving to reify constraining gender binaries (Miller, 2002).

Following the limited scholarship on female crime, there does not seem to be a straightforward association between the process of women's desistance and traditional social control factors such as employment, conventional partner, and military service (Barr, 2019; Giordano, Deines, & Cernkovich, 2006). Indeed, it is difficult when researching women's desistance to depart from the notion of social control without perpetuating oppressive assumptions of what constitutes women's "normal behaviour" or reproducing gendered social hierarchies (Heidensohn & Silvestri, 2012:336). Simply adding women to traditional male explanations of desistance is not enough to account properly for women's experiences during the process of crime abandonment (Daly, 2010). Therefore, this chapter aims to reclaim the importance of gender for desistance, exploring how it shapes, limits, and structures women's pathways out of crime.

The sources of information used for this analysis are 30 retrospective semi-structured interviews conducted with a sample of late adolescent women offenders (aged 16–20 years old) who were sentenced to probation or semi-prison in 2012 in Santiago, Chile.[1] These interviews were conducted between November 2012 and February 2013 in the probation and semi-prison centres and lasted approximately one hour. They explored the experiences, norms, identities, institutions, and relations involved in the process of crime abandonment – whether successful or not. For a detailed description of the methodological issues relevant for the present chapter and the characteristics of the interviewees, see Chapter 2.

Temporary desistance and persistence

A life calendar with a detailed list of crimes and life events was used to explore the criminal trajectory of interviewees and assess changes in the patterns of their criminal behaviour along their lives. Temporary desistance was operationalised as the absence of self-reported crimes in the year prior to the interview, and this response was crossed-checked with official criminal records.[2] The study found that 14 young women had stopped crime completely in the year before the interview, while 16 were still engaged in it. A more nuanced analysis showed that, from the 16 interviewees classified as persisters, 3 did not commit any crime in the six months prior to the interview and 8 had decreased the severity and/or frequency of their offending in the last year. Nevertheless, most of these women – who persisted but significantly decrease their offending – were still labelling themselves as offenders:

I: Why did you say that you see yourself as a delinquent?
MITZI: Because I'm here on probation. Although I stopped committing crimes, I'm still here where the delinquents are.
I: And what about your neighbours? How do they see you?
MITZI: They see me as a delinquent as well; they will always see me like that.
I: Was there any period in which you have not seen yourself like that?
MITZI: Yes, when I was working – then I saw myself as a hard-working woman.
(Mitzi, desister, age 20)

Consistent with previous research, family issues (i.e. having a child or prosocial partner, or not wanting to hurt their parents) were the most common reasons given for desistance in their narratives. Occurring with less frequency were instrumental reasons (i.e. being arrested or the fear thereof) and moral reasons (i.e. realising that crime was wrong); these were mainly found in reference to violent crimes. The interviewees who persisted argued that they did so because crime was the only source of money to which they had access, and some even claimed that stealing was the only thing they knew to do well.

The process of crime abandonment: desistance and gendered redemption

For most of the interviewees, temporary desistance was triggered by and/or related to a transition towards traditionally feminine caring roles as mothers, housewives, or dutiful daughters. Most of the desisters argued that after they stopped committing crimes, they became more passive, domestic, caring, and "feminine":

> Now I look less slutty, less vulgar, more caring, I look more like a lady.
>
> (Raquel, desister, age 18)

Motherhood generally played a central role in interviewees' self-identity from the time of pregnancy, and its impact on desistance was immediate for almost all the interviewees. Nevertheless, assumption of the maternal role occurred progressively after birth for the two young women who were strongly involved in drug use, and the process was marked by strong contradictions and shame. Beyond traditional social control theories which argue that maternity restructures daily routines and increases the costs of crime, here it was observed that maternity triggers desistance through other mechanisms as well. First, it provides a sense of purpose in life through taking care of and being devoted to their children, as these two narratives evidence:

RAQUEL: Immediately after knowing that I was pregnant, I stopped committing crimes. I left everything – drugs, parties, everything – because I always wanted to have a child.

I: Why did you always want to have a child?

RAQUEL: To have a motivation in life, something that helps me to go on in life … how can I explain it to you? I needed something strong that helped me put my feet on the ground, because for many years I took care of my little sister, but now she has grown and she doesn't need me anymore.

I: And now your son needs you …

RAQUEL: Yes, now I have a motive to be here in this world. I left everything I was because of him.

(Raquel, desister, age 18)

I: What would you like to do in the future?

ALEJANDRA: Lots of nice things.

I: Like what?

ALEJANDRA: Nice things for my son, positive things, provide him with stability.

(Alejandra, desister, age 18)

Being a mother brought female offenders a sense of belonging, emotional stability, and future orientation, since they saw their children as a permanent source of unconditional love that could restore and heal previous experiences of abandonment and neglect:

> He makes me feel full, complete; I always felt so empty, so lonely. At least he [her son] won't abandon me – we will always be together.
>
> (Darlyne, desister, age 18)

Threat of separation and abandonment inhibited behaviour – such as crime – that might have hurt or dishonoured their children. These women felt that they had to be a role model for their children and perform the right behaviour – particularly because most of them were convinced that their own criminal involvement originated from the criminal families in which they grew up. Moreover, most interviewees argued that the threat of imprisonment prevented them from committing crimes, since they were scared of losing their children.

Second, motherhood was an opportunity to comply with gendered social imperatives and thus to gain social recognition and integration through the practice of traditional caring roles. Indeed, for all interviewees, maternity was their most important life attainment – and, for some, getting pregnant was a purposeful decision to achieve maturity and acquire the status of an adult woman. This is consistent with previous research conducted in Latin America which has shown that, in socially deprived contexts, pregnancy is viewed as a source of prestige and as a way to achieve social mobility, elevating young women's sense of responsibility and morality (Azevedo & Bouillon, 2009; Becker, 2009; Llanes, 2012; Marcus, 2006).

Maternity not only directly affected them and their partners but also brought positive indirect outcomes to their whole families: it reunited them, healed past conflicts, compensated for negative past familial experiences, and gave young women the opportunity to demonstrate that they could perform the expected domestic gender roles:

> Now I'm closer to my mother. They are all proud of me. I was the only female in the family left without a child, so I really had to be a mother.
>
> (Darlyne, desister, age 18)

> After having my child, I learnt everything: to clean, to cook … I'm more mature, I learnt how to be a housewife. Now, every day when my family arrives home everything is ready, the house is clean and there is food on the table.
>
> (Alejandra, desister, age 18)

Becoming mothers also facilitated the acquisition of a new status regarding welfare policies in Chile, making the women eligible for cash transference and social protection programmes – and thus achieving the rank of citizen. This is consistent with Barry's (2012) finding among Scottish women' offenders that gaining access to state benefits became an alternative source of income that helped women to stop committing crimes.

Third, maternity led interviewees to forego their own desires – viewed by them as selfish and antisocial – for the sake of their children. Motherhood freed them from the responsibility and conflicts that arose from their own life decisions; after pregnancy, there was nothing to choose – the only way possible was to perform the maternal duties, which were incompatible with the anti-social lifestyle:

> Now I take care of my son instead of me – I don't care about me anymore. I don't need money to go out, I need less stuff; everything I want is for him.
>
> (Tanya, desister, age 16)

> If I didn't have a son, I would continue offending, being just me, crazy and irresponsible ... taking care of myself only.
>
> (Alejandra, desister, age 18)

Previous research on the narratives of adolescent mothers has also highlighted the sacrificial face of maternity, through which young women achieve transformation and redemption leaving behind "irresponsible" lives (Becker, 2009; Cater & Coleman, 2006).[3]

Beyond the ethic of care

Among the interviewees' narratives, it was observed that the ethic of care operated beyond the maternal role. Temporary desistance among these women was accompanied by an increase in familial duties: they began not only to take care of their own children but also their parents, siblings and partners, and the children of other family members. They assumed all the household duties – cleaning, cooking, and doing the shopping – and sometimes adopted the task of visiting the family members that were in prison. They restored social and family bonds, redeemed themselves from their criminal past, and found a place in the social structure through the ethic of care.

Redemption through the provision of care and support is not something that has been highlighted only within female desisters. Maruna (2001) observed among his male sample in the Liverpool Study what he called the "wounded healers": offenders who actively construct a conforming identity that supports desistance through helping other offenders to achieve change. LeBel (2007) found empirical support for the abovementioned and observed no gender differences regarding the effect of a wounded healer orientation on personal well-being and further crime. Later, Heidermann et al. (2016) explored the effects of the desire and commitment to help other offenders among a sample of formerly incarcerated women. They found that adopting the wounded healer approach improved self-esteem and prosocial attitudes and enhanced social connectedness.

At a first glance, redemption through helping and supporting others seems a reasonable and adequate strategy to desist from crime (and has been treated as such in most research on women's desistance).[4] However, it is argued here that this strategy must be interpreted with caution. Indeed, although the young women of the study were caring, attentive and responsive to others – and this helped them to gain social acceptance, recognition and to manage shame – they were at the same time completely selfless, and thus unable to develop the identity shifts required to embrace new, crime-free roles in the long-term. As Maruna and Roy (2007:119) pointed out, "... knifing off alone, without the provision of new scripts for future identity development, may enhance pre-existing criminal tendencies rather than lead to desistance".

Whilst the interviewees improved and expanded their relationships, their own demands, desires, and expectations nevertheless remained invisible. This is consistent with the work of Giordano and colleagues (2002:1053) and Rumgay (2004) who observed among their interviewees that those who desisted crafted replacement selves that were strongly repressive, with women limiting themselves to traditional domestic roles. It is interesting to note that, while Bottoms and Shapland (2014:332) observed in their male-based study that desistance began with the virtue ethics question, "What kind of life should I lead?", the process clearly started among these women with the radically different moral question highlighted by Gilligan (2008) when describing women's moral development, of "How should I respond?". This strongly influenced their interpersonal relationships, which were markedly unilateral, based on dependence rather than reciprocity. These young women were expected to give a lot (almost their entire selves), but to ask and expect very little in return. For example, in the case of their partners, they qualified a relationship as good even when there was a complete absence of emotional support. Their expectations were centred on the provision of the minimum standards of respect and compliance with the breadwinner role:

> My partner is good. At least he doesn't treat me badly, and he brings money home.
>
> (Mitzi, desister, age 20)

> He is not a bad father, and he treats me OK.
>
> (Alejandra, persister, age 18)

Following Gilligan (1993:71), it can be argued that the desistance process for these women was bound up within the dilemma between "autonomy and compassion" – in this case the dilemma was: taking care of me versus taking care of others (see Table 5.1).

The first choice (taking care of me) was oriented towards following their own desires and enjoying the pleasures of life; it was anchored in the present without considering the consequences of their behaviour on others. In that sense, interviewees viewed this option as selfish, irresponsible, and irrational. The second option (taking care of others) was based on rationality and was seen as the "right" one – the way to desist from crime and became a "good woman".

Table 5.1 Desisters' dilemma

Taking care of me	*Taking care of others*
Crime	Desistance
Irrational	Rational
Impulsive	Responsible
Single/lonely	Mother/wife/daughter
Bad girl	Good girl
Selfish	Caring
Funny	Boring

Nevertheless, they realised at the same time that this decision made their lives less exciting, more routine, and boring, as Raquel (desister, age 18) pointed out:

> Now I don't go out anymore. If you go out and take drugs, one thing leads you to another and you end up forgetting that you are a mother. I'm quite boring right now. Everyone must think that I have become a sour and boring old lady.

This is consistent with De Meis (2002:6) study with prostitutes in Brazil, in which she also observed this dichotomy in the roles available for women: the "sanctified mother", "good woman", and "family girl" on the one hand, and the "depraved woman", "whore", and "street woman" on the other. This imposed binary impeded their attempts to find a legitimate identity and a place in the world.

The abovementioned is of pivotal importance within the Latin American context, where cultural constructions of femininity are strongly identified with motherhood – a state associated with moral virtue, altruism, and self-sacrifice (Jelin, 1990; Molyneux, 2000). From a cultural perspective, it has been argued that Latin American ideologies of motherhood have restricted women to private lives, influenced the gendered division of labour, and constrained their power to maternal love and caring practices. These conceptions, historically rooted in the Christian image of the Virgin Mary (central to the Chilean culture), relegate women to "roles" as mother and spouse, operating as a grounding model of the self-denying sacrificial woman who serves and depends on others (Legarde y de los Rios, 2005; Melero, 2015; Montecino, 1997).

Moreover, a key factor contributing to women's subordination within the household has been domestic detachment on the part of men, and their resistance to engage in child-rearing responsibilities (Chant, 2014). In Chile, while one-third of women are housewives, only 1% of men subscribe to the role of househusband and only 5.2% of women of low socioeconomic status share household chores with their partners (Stuven et al., 2013). Although social policies in Chile in the last decade have followed a gender-conscious approach, and reforms have been introduced to expand the provision of early childcare for low-income families and introduce better mechanisms for maternity/paternity leave, they are still strongly based on maternalism and male-breadwinner bias (Staab, 2012). Some scholars have argued that these reforms have even increased social control and surveillance of mothers' child-rearing performance (Luccisano & Wall, 2009).

As can be seen, the ethic of care holds a fundamental place in women's life within the Chilean context, leaving them in a passive position of dependence in which their desires and actions are confused with the expectation of others. This was the case for those interviewees who had desisted from crime, who were compliant, who practised abnegation and were responsible for others, but were not responsible for or consistent with themselves. As Gilligan (1993:84) pointed out, they had engaged in a transition from "selfishness to goodness" yet lacked a transition from "goodness to truth" that encompasses the needs of self and others.

This is not to say that the inclusion of others in their lives and the engagement in the ethic of care did not trigger desistance in the first place. This first step was useful not only to stop committing crimes but also to manage shame and to start building a new sense of self. Nevertheless, research suggests that they must recognise themselves within these relationships in a mutual sense. Interdependence plays here a crucial role, allowing them to take the position of a person that not only has something to give but also of someone with needs that orient her own choices. Indeed, it is only from this position that the virtue ethics question (key for the desistance process in the long term) highlighted by Bottoms and Shapland (2014) – "How should I lead my life?" – can arise.

Developing a sense of self and recognising one's own desires is highly relevant in the process of desistance and would have allowed the women to make stronger transitions based on the acquisition of new roles beyond gender restraints. It would also have helped them to avoid crime relapses triggered by perceiving crime as an opportunity to reclaim their authentic selves and to escape the societal constraints of their gender and their class (of which see more further). Consistent with former research (Gålnander, 2019; Hart, 2017) the possibilities for transformative action among interviewees were also limited by the intersectionality of gender, class, age, education, and available occupational roles. The position they occupied in society did not permit an awareness of or access to other choices, narrowing their windows of opportunities in other domains:

I: What would you like to do now in your life?
ROSA: I don't know.
I: But you must be good at something, or there must be something that you like.

ROSA: Yes, I'm good at cooking, cleaning and I'm very good doing the household chores.

I: And perhaps something else as well?

ROSA: Mmmmmm ... Yes, when I attended school in fourth grade, I was very good at maths. That is why if you ask me to remember a phone number, I never fail. I could finish my studies, I would love to, but I don't think that I'm smart enough.

(Rosa, desister, age 19)

As this extract demonstrates, the only instance of socialisation paving the way for these women to think beyond gender and class constraints was the school system. Since 20 of them abandoned school before eighth grade, however, these memories were distant, and it was hard to drag them back to inform and broaden their repertoire of possible identities and roles. Across the whole study, there were only two interviewees who engaged in transitions out of crime that were less constrained by gender and class (one a mother, one not). In these two cases, it was the pursuit of higher education that helped them to abandon crime. This is consistent with research on women's empowerment, which has highlighted that women with more access to education have fewer constraints on agency – even in social contexts where gender norms are restrictive (The World Bank, 2014).

Mother/housewife or thief: a narrow and tight liminal stage

Although this analysis used the narratives of interviewees precisely to avoid getting trapped and biased by male-based explanations of desistance, it was impossible to avoid comparing these women's experiences with those ones highlighted by men – both in the literature on desistance and my own research presented in the former chapters. For instance, as noted before, it has been highlighted in the research based on male offenders, that offenders regularly oscillate in the liminal space or continuum between crime and conformity (Bottoms et al., 2004; Healy, 2010). As shown in Chapter 3, this finding has been particularly helpful in understanding not only the zigzag pattern that most offenders follow, but also situating those individuals that cannot be constrained by the narrow binary categories of "persister" and "desister". That said, although the female interviewees in this study were experiencing contradictions and ambivalence as well, they mostly situated themselves at one or other extreme of the continuum, and the liminal stage between crime and conformity was narrow and tight.

Contrary to what Hale (2020) found in her study with former incarcerated women in Australia, the participants of the study who were still sporadically committing crimes (even those who strongly reduced the frequency and seriousness of their offending) still labelled themselves as offenders, whereas the ones who stopped assumed a non-offender self-conception immediately, devoting their lives to the caring roles discussed earlier and avoiding any temptation that could pull them back to crime. This is not to say that these women had more or less agency than men, but rather to evidence further that their social contexts did not provide them with enough possibilities for being and doing to exercise their agency, thereby limiting their choices. It was, therefore, rare to find non-binary possibilities of being; their transitions were quite radical. They saw themselves as housewives/mothers at one extreme of the continuum or as thieves/drug addicts at the other, assuming the identities, behaviours, and the characteristics of the role to which they ascribed themselves.

This is consistent with previous research in Latin America, showing that there is a marked rigidity in the identities possible for women in the hegemonic culture. Latina women are mainly focused on being mothers and wives, docile and self-sacrificing to live for others (Valdés, 1995). Or, more precisely they are contextualized agents constrained within the limits imposed by gendered social expectations, subordination, and social class. Nevertheless, this finding seems to be cross-cultural as well, since Graham and Bowling (1995) also observed that women's desistance was more abrupt than men. Similarly, Fredriksson and Gålnander (2020) with data from a Swedish study observed that women ex-offenders have restricted narratives to reconstruct their selves and that not belonging to either their past or future lifestyles leads to the development of negative feelings and anguish.

Among the interviewees who desisted, it was possible to observe three main issues that accelerated their transitions or, in other terms, that narrowed the liminal stage. First, the strong presence of shame and remorse (especially among violent offenders) was often compounded by limited ability to manage these negative emotions. Unlike men who "rewrite a shameful past into a necessary prelude to a productive life" (Maruna, 2001:87), arguing that crime made them stronger or wiser, these women engaged in a process closer to what Maruna and Roy (2007) termed "knifing off" their past, believing that this was the only way to move on. The experience of the sampled women was also inconsistent with Hundleby, Gfellner, and Racine (2007), who observed that women who desisted from crime explored their past identities and integrated them with their new selves to get directions for their current and future behaviour. Here, women argued that thinking about their previous criminal behaviour made them weak and vulnerable and jeopardised their mental health:

> I regret some of these crimes, but I try not to think about it; I try to forget and not feel ashamed about my past, because if not my memories drive me crazy and I get depressed.
>
> (Susana, persister, age 17)

As Maruna (2001:143) argued,

> shame may create as many problems as it solves ... Being ashamed of one isolated act or two is one thing, but it is quite a different thing to be ashamed of one's entire past identity, of who one used to be.

Accordingly, the interviewees wanted to get rid of their pasts as fast as they could, and thus (unlike the males of the study), "neutralisations" and other strategies to justify their criminal behaviour were strongly present in their narratives:

> I only stole stuff from posh ladies ... I didn't do any harm because they had everything they wanted and could easily replace what I stole from them ... Once, a well-dressed lady looked down on me, like thinking, "What is this slut doing here?". I felt bad, because I was dressed like a lady to pass unnoticed in this posh neighbourhood, but she detected that I was not one of them. When she turned around, I stole her bag. I laughed after that.
> (Darlyne, desister, age 18)

It is interesting to note how this justification was not only based on the lack of harm inflicted against the victim but also on gender rivalry and on the unfair different access that she and the victim has to symbols of status and prestige.

Second, it was difficult for the women in the study to find lucrative activities in the overlap of legality and illegality. Male desisters, for instance, capitalise on their previous antisocial experiences and transform them into transferable skills that can be strategically used during the transition from crime to conformity (Sanders, 2007). Some work in illegal bars, offering protection to prostitutes or drug dealers, helping in transactions of stolen goods, among others activities. This allows them to take advantage of their previous delinquent skills and social capital to survive economically while they try to find a job and to embrace roles in the conventional world. This also helps them, as discussed in previous chapters, to distance themselves from the antisocial world gradually and, therefore, manage the emotional and social cost of leaving crime behind. Among the young women, however, these halfway possibilities were absent; they could not transfer their delinquent skills into a productive and lucrative activity outside the subordination of gender.

Third, the women's awareness and acknowledgement of their vulnerability also accelerated their transitions. Unlike men, they were not ashamed of their weakness and lack of capacity to control themselves in risky situations. Self-isolation was their main strategy to avoid the risk of relapsing into crime. Self-isolation was easier, because it was consistent with the domestic role (i.e. staying at home, taking care of the house and the children) and it was strongly socially rewarded. Nevertheless, it was actually this self-imposed reclusiveness which prevented them from associating with new prosocial individuals in other settings (co-workers, friends of friends, classmates, employers, etc.), forging new roles, or otherwise exploring new identities beyond the domestic sphere. This is consistent with previous research on women's desistance conducted in developed countries as well (Giordano et al., 2003; McIvor, 2016; Nugent & Schinkel, 2016).

Persistence: resisting and accomplishing gender

On the contrary, persistence was found to be a way of resisting gender subordination and patriarchy. First and foremost, the financial independence that the interviewees acquired through crime allowed them to achieve the sense of supporting themselves. For some, crime assured daily survival and the possibility of avoiding the streets and prostitution; for most, however, it was a way to escape from economic dependency.

Around the age of 13, most interviewees started having needs that their parents or caregivers either could not or did not want to cover, such as clothes, beauty products, public transport costs, or money to socialise or buy drugs with. Crime, which in most cases had started as a way to have fun and defy conventional norms, was therefore transformed into a source of money and independence.

Most of the interviewees developed stable romantic relationships through adolescence, and some moved to live with their partners – starting to depend on them economically. The ones who did not find a partner ended up at a stage where they could not depend on their parents anymore (because they assumed that they had to work and bring money home), and crime was their only way to make a life. Believing themselves to be either lazy or not clever enough to find a job, participants' economic survival followed a pattern in which they relied on their parents/caregivers, their partners, or on crime:

ANDREA: A job? I've never thought about it. I don't know how to find a job either … I'm lazy and I didn't finish school.
I: But what would you like to do?
ANDREA: Perhaps to work in a factory – it must be easier than other jobs.

(Andrea, desister, age 17)

Given the subordinate position that woman occupy in the Chilean familial structure, it was expected for the partners of interviewees to perform the role of breadwinner (through legal or illegal means); the women, meanwhile, behaved as traditional housewives in return, performing all the domestic and caring duties. Indeed, the "bad partner influence" asserted by some feminist scholars (e.g. Mullins & Wright, 2003) was not present in the narratives of most interviewees. Partners here operated as a source of social control in a similar way to the male sample studied by Sampson and Laub (2003). Although some sporadic thefts were accepted, most interviewees' partners were against their criminal involvement:

> I am not committing crimes right now, because I am with a narco[5] and it is not well regarded for a narco's partner to be engaged in crime. I have to behave as a lady now to support him in his business. He also provides me with everything – clothes, perfumes – I don't have any needs now.
>
> (Susana, persister, age 17)

Among the interviewees who were living with their partners, sporadic crime relapses after long periods of desistance were mainly triggered by their partners' absence. Alejandra, a vulnerable woman who had been engaged in crime from the age of 14, argued that it was impossible for her to stop committing crimes – even though she wanted to – because every time her partner was sent to prison, she felt abandoned and helpless and was suddenly forced to assume the role of breadwinner without the skills needed to get a job:

ALEJANDRA: I'm lazy, I've never worked. Every time I start a new job, I don't last more than a week … When my husband goes to jail, the only way to get money is by going back to crime.

I: But you mentioned that he was against it, right?

ALEJANDRA: Yes, but he believes that I'm working as a cleaner. He can commit crimes, but I can't, this is the way it is.

(Alejandra, persister, age 17)

Nevertheless, the influence of partners on crime was strongly shaped by the degree of autonomy and economic independence that they could exercise within the relationship. Some women committed sporadic thefts in order to get things that their partners did not provide or to get some extra money to afford costs beyond daily survival. Others sporadically engaged in crime to experience autonomy outside the household and to liberate themselves from the oppressive relationships they had with their partners through the exciting experience of shoplifting.

Persistence also allowed them to avoid taking the limited occupational roles that were structurally available for them. Crime was the only alternative to an occupation anchored in the ethic of care, such as being a maid, servant, hairdresser, or cook. Poor women in Latin America, with narrow windows of opportunity and lack of training and education, generally engage in home-based enterprises that routinely revolve around domestic activities (Chant, 2014). In Chile, according to 2018 figures, domestic service represents 8.2% of the female labour force (ILO, 2018), and 44% of the women who work in domestic service come from the first and second lowest income quintiles (Comunidad Mujer, 2012). This type of work reproduces gender and class inequalities in different ways. While upper class' women are integrated into the social life through work, women from lower classes are invisibilised within familial dynamics that do not belong to them.

Furthermore, through persistence in crime, they maintained a sense of self-efficacy and exercised agency. Crime was a source of control and pride for the persisters, since it was the only instance in which they could do well, transform their choices into actual practices, show their talents and capabilities, and gain recognition as being good at something:

> I felt so good when I was doing well in crime, I got everything I wanted. It was not easy, but I always managed to do well.
>
> (Mitzi, desister, age 20)

Persistence was also the only way to venture towards masculine ground and be recognised as an autonomous, brave, and determined woman. This is exemplified in the story of Cristina, a 19 year-old girl, who joined a well-known and prominent male gang at the age of 12. She engaged with the gang on an equal footing, sharing all the roles with her friends:

> I was one of them – I was never scared, I wasn't vulnerable like the other girls. After I learnt all I needed to know, I formed my own gang with three young boys, who learnt everything from me. Since they saw me as stronger, they did everything I said.
>
> (Cristina, desister, age 20)

Her narrative evidences how "gender crossing", defined as a way of distancing oneself from degrading feminine attributes through the adoption of masculine attitudes (Daly, 2010; Miller, 2002), helped her not only to be part of the gang but also to acquire the independence to abandon it and to subordinate men. Gender crossing did not only bring rewards, however; there were several costs as well, the most relevant one being her failure to fulfil the caring female role:

> The time I felt worst committing a crime was several years ago, when I went into a house with my friends to commit a burglary and two little children were there. I said, "This is a robbery", holding my gun – and the youngest child, who was around three years old, thought I was playing; he laughed and came up to me. I pushed him back, and he realised that it wasn't a game and started crying … That broke my heart.
>
> (Cristina, desister, age 20)

It was extremely difficult for these women to navigate the conflicting dynamics of gender crossing and effectively resist patriarchy without losing all their female attributes. At the time I interviewed Cristina, she had started a course to become a cook. Run by a very prestigious middle-class cooking institute, the course was significantly helping her to cross the borders of her class, to acquire a new sense of self, to get to know new people, and to leave crime behind. Nevertheless, she was not entirely satisfied with her new life: she was strongly missing the excitement of crime, and most of the time she felt very bored. She was aware that it would not be possible to transpose most of the elements that she liked from her previous life into her new role as a cook. Moreover, this role did not allow her to engage in gender crossing practices in the way that she was used to; she was not afforded the opportunity to construct an identity outside normative femininity and differentiate herself from the rest of the girls of her neighbourhood:

> I know more about stealing than cooking ... I'm never going to be as good at this as I have been at crime ... Sometimes I get bored with this life, with being a student, not going out ... How much more should I change? What do they expect from me? That I become a nun?
>
> (Cristina, desister, age 20)

Yet, further to the abovementioned, it was also observed that persistence was not only a way to resist gender inequality; persistence was a way to accomplish gender as well. This was strongly evident in the case of the interviewees who, although they had decreased their criminal activity, were still engaged in occasional thefts to contribute to the household income. Interestingly, several desisters relapsed only on specific celebration days (such as Christmas, birthdays, and the Chilean independence commemoration day) to give presents to their children or comply with the cultural practice of being well dressed for celebration festivities.[6]

Crime was the only way to cover needs associated with vanity and to get access to the products they felt they must have to be recognised as a beautiful women and thus fulfil the idealised standard of appearance and style that was imposed on them. As with the boys' behaviour described previously in Chapter 3, in which displays of financial capital (through their capacity to buy expensive clothes and drive stylish cars) reflected their acquired status, women without any access to other sources of social pride and status relied instead on social recognition resulting from the "attractiveness capital" described by Miller and Mullins (2006:60). Natural beauty, as well as their own capacity for self-embellishment, was experienced as a way to gain control, distinction, and status. As Bourdieu (2000:204) wrote, "beauty can thus be simultaneously a gift of nature and a conquest of merit ... associating aesthetic value and moral value, they [women] feel superior". The beautifying process among the interviewees operated through crime as a ritual of emancipation and empowerment, confounding freedom from beauty with freedom of choice. Interviewees mostly stole things that were appealing to them but sold them to get money and buy what they wanted directly from the shops. They not only wanted to have jewellery, clothes, and cosmetics but wanted to experience the status of being a consumer and accessing the symbolic profits that arose from it. They aspired to be like a girl from the movies, who happily and carelessly strolls along carrying bags from expensive brands around the shopping mall.

In a similar way, it was found that criminal relapses were related to infidelity and jealousy –not as observed by Kruttschnitt and Carbone-Lopez (2006), i.e. inflicting violence against their partners or other women, but to restore their dignity and reinforce their attractiveness capital and beauty through stealing or buying products (with stolen money) to embellish themselves and feel superior to other women.

Although the "gaining of attractiveness" capital helped acquisition of status and differentiation from other young women in the neighbourhood, it was not effective in helping them to desist from crime. For most interviewees, the only productive way they had to take financial advantage of this capital (which several believed was the only capital they had) was through crime. This was the case for the young women who were recruited by male gangs to pass unnoticed using their "traditional beauty" and shoplifters who used their "lady-like" appearance in shops to make security guards believe that they were just shopping. In the first case, women were accomplishing gender through their subordinate positions in the gang, and in both cases, they were using their resources precisely as women to succeed at crime.

Concluding remarks

As has been discussed throughout this chapter, the process of crime abandonment is strongly gendered; temporary desistance among women was related to a transition towards traditional feminine caring roles, and persistence operated as a way both to resist and affirm gender subordination and patriarchy.

Although some of the triggers for temporary desistance that had been highlighted in previous research were also relevant in these young women's transition out of crime,[7] the dynamics they followed did not always operate in the expected way. For example, the positive influence of a partner only worked if women had a degree of economic independence within the relationship. Shame was found to accelerate the desistance process – not because the interviewees reconfigured or re-signified its impact and meaning to develop a new sense of self, but because it precipitated the acquisition of new roles to leave past memories behind. Most importantly, it was found that a number of these factors were strongly anchored in the ethic of care. This was the case for motherhood, familial bonds, and self-isolation, which – although they proved useful as initial triggers – were shown to be problematic for sustaining desistance in the long term, keeping these young women trapped within gender constraints which could afterwards be contested and resisted through crime relapses and persistence.

The fact that employment did not emerge as a relevant factor in the triggering of temporary desistance was not surprising, especially if we consider these women's young age, their self-perception of a lack of capacity to work, and also the fact that the jobs available for them routinely revolved around domestic and caring activities. The only factor that operated in the expected way was education, which was observed to be a source of social mobility and gender emancipation.

Although at a first glance the tightness of the liminal phase in these young women's transitions could be interpreted as a positive issue that sped up the desistance process, it was observed to be the result of strong constraints within the limits imposed by patriarchy and social class, blocking access to other choices and narrowing the women's opportunities in domains beyond traditional gender roles.

Persistence, on the other hand, was found to be a way to resist patriarchy and subordination through facilitating financial independence, avoiding the acquisition of roles anchored in the ethic of care and allowing them to engage in so-called cross gendering practices. Yet, persistence was a way to accomplish gender as well. Some interviewees committed occasional crimes to contribute to the household income and thus to comply with the expected familial demands of providing a nurturing environment and meeting the physical survival needs of their children, such as clothing, medicines, and education. Moreover, through crime they were able to maintain and take advantage of their attractiveness capital, using it strategically within the gangs they were engaged with, and thus reproducing gender status subordination through their criminal behaviour.

Some limitations must be considered before discussing the implications of the findings in the final chapter. First, the fact that these young women were on probation or semi-prison at the time of the interview impeded the assessment of the effect of imprisonment on the process of crime abandonment. Second, although their young age was an advantage for delving into natural life transitions triggering desistance, it curtailed the implications that may be drawn from this study only to include young female offenders, thereby excluding possible dynamics that might follow women with longer crime trajectories and a deeper crime involvement. Third, the short period of observation and the fact that desistance was assessed retrospectively could have biased women's emotional accounts of their experiences; it could also be the case that the findings were reflecting a crime-free gap instead of a full and proper transition out of crime. Fourth, because the study was conducted in Latin America, relevant cultural differences that influenced these young women's lives and criminal trajectories must be considered when comparing these results with research conducted in developed countries, where most of the research of desistance has been carried out. Indeed, the fact that the process of crime abandonment was found to be strongly gendered could in part be the result of the high levels of gender inequality affecting women in Chile – particularly those from low socio-economic strata. While the United Kingdom is ranked 23rd and the United States 30th of 145 countries in the Gender Gap Index, Chile is ranked 78th (World Economic Forum, 2018). This evidences the relevance not only of conducting research in developing countries, but also how structural circumstances might play a crucial role in the process of crime abandonment.

Notes

1 Semi-prison is a type of sanction in which youth offenders spend the night in custody, and leave the youth training centre to work or study under close supervision during the day. It is an intermediate sanction that stands between probation and custody.

2 Interviewees' criminal records were obtained with their informed consent. The National Office of the Defence Attorney provided information regarding their arrests and convictions during the year of observation.

3 The term "ethic of care" as used in this research study is informed by Carol Gilligan's early argument that female morality, due to gender differences, is based on responsiveness to others (i.e. empathy and caring), assuming that care is mainly the role of the woman. Gilligan (1993) divides women's moral development into three stages: (1) self-interest; (2) overemphasising the interests of others; and (3) balancing the interests of the self and of others. It has been argued that, due to structural gender constraints, several women cannot move beyond the second stage.

4 Research based on males has also highlighted that the acquisition of "more virtuous dispositions" is a key factor when desisting from crime (Bottoms & Shapland, 2014:332).

5 Taken from the Spanish Word *narcotraficante*, which means "drug trafficker" or "drug dealer".

6 The tradition of dressing well for the independence commemoration dates from the 19th century, with its origins traced to the fact that, during these festivities, Chilean farmers went to the capital city to attend the national celebration activities. Since this occasion was the most important annual instance of socialising in the year, they bought new clothes and shoes in order to improve their appearance and help them seduce a woman.

7 E.g. motherhood, re-establishment of familial bonds and other social interactions based on empathy, the pursuit of education, a partner who disapproves of their criminal involvement, shame, remorse, and self-isolation.

References

Azevedo, V. and Bouillon, C. (2009). Social mobility in Latin America: A review of existing evidence. *Revista de Analisis Economico – Economic Analysis Review*, 25: 7–42.

Bachman, R., Kerrison, E., Paternoster, R., Smith, L., & O'Connell, D. (2016). The complex relationship between motherhood and desistance. *Women & Criminal Justice*, 1–20.

Barr, U. (2019). *Desisting sisters gender, power and desistance in the criminal (in)justice system*. Palgrave Macmillan.

Barr, Ú, & Christian, N. (2019). A qualitative investigation into the impact of domestic abuse on women's desistance. *Probation Journal*, 66(4): 416–433.

Barry, M. (2012). 'Young woman in transition: From offending to desistance'. In: Losel, F., Bottoms, A. and Farrington, D. P. (eds.) *Lost in Transition: Young Adult Offenders in the Criminal Justice System*. Cullompton: Willan Publishing, pp. 113–127.

Becker, J. (2009). Young mother in late modernity: Sacrifice, respectability and the transformative neo-liberal subject. *Journal of Youth Studies*, 12(3): 275–288.

Belknap, J. (2006). The gendered nature of risk factors for delinquency. *Feminist Criminology*, 1(1): 48–71.

Bottoms, A. and Shapland, J. (2014). Can persistent offenders acquire virtue?. *Studies in Christian Ethics*, 27(3): 318–333.

Bottoms, A., Shapland, J., Costello, A., Holmes, D. and Muir, G. (2004). Towards desistance: theoretical underpinnings for an empirical study. *The Howard Journal*, 43(4): 368–387.

Bourdieu, P. (2000). *Masculine Domination*. Stanford, CA: Stanford University Press.

Cater, S. and Coleman, L. (2006). 'Planned' teenage pregnancy: Views and experiences of young people from poor and disadvantaged backgrounds. *Journal of Youth Studies*, 9(5): 593–614.

Chant, S. (2014). Exploring the "feminisation of poverty" in relation to women's work and home-based enterprise in slums of the global South. *International Journal of Gender and Entrepreneurship*, 6(3): 296–316.

Comunidad Mujer. (2012). Mujer y trabajo: tres años en perspectiva. Series Comunidad Mujer (Vol. 19). Available from: http://dev.comunidadmujer.cl/biblioteca-publicaciones/wp-content/uploads/2012/11/BOLETIN-NOV-2012-baja.pdf.

Daly, K. (2010). 'Feminist perspectives in criminology: A review with Gen Y in mind'. In: McLaughlin, E. and Newburn, T. (eds.) *The Handbook of Criminological Theory*. London: Sage, pp. 225–246.

De Meis, C. (2002). House and street: Narratives of identity in a liminal space among prostitutes in Brazil. *Ethos 30*(1/2): 3–24.

Fredriksson, T. & Gålnander, R. (2020). Fearful futures and haunting histories in women's desistance from crime: A longitudinal study of desistance as an uncanny process. *Criminology*, 58(4): 599–618.

Gålnander, R. (2019. Desistance from crime – To what? Exploring future aspirations and their implications for processes of desistance. *Feminist Criminology*, 15(3): 255–277.

Gilligan, C. (1993). *In a different voice: Psychological theory and women's development*. Cambridge: Harvard University Press.

Gilligan, C. (2008). 'Moral orientation and moral development'. In: Bailey, A. and Cuomo, C. (eds.) *The Feminist Philosophy Reader*. Boston, MA: McGraw-Hill, pp. 463–467.

Giordano, P. (2016). 'Mechanism underlying the desistance process: reflections on A theory of Cognitive Transformation'. In J. Shapland, S. Farrall and T. Bottoms. *Global Perspectives on Desistance,* Abingdon: Routledge, pp. 11–27.

Giordano, P. C., Cernkovich, S. A. and Holland, D. D. (2003). Changes in friendship relations over the life course: Implications for desistance from crime. *Criminology*, 41(2): 293–2003.

Giordano, P. C., Cernkovich, S. A., & Rudolph, J. L. (2002). Gender, Crime, and Desistance: Toward a Theory of Cognitive Transformation 1, *107*(4), 990–1064.

Giordano, P. C., Deines, J. A. and Cerknovic, S. A. (2006). 'In and out of crime: A life course perspective on girl's delinquency'. In: Heimer, K. and Kruttschnitt, C. (eds.) *From Gender and Crime: Patterns in Victimization and Offending*. New York, NY: New York University Press, pp. 17–40.

Graham, J. and Bowling, B. (1995). *Young People and Crime, Home Office Research Study N° 145*. London: Home Office.

Hale, R. (2020). Good intentions: Women's narratives of post-release anticipatory desistance in the context of historical and contemporary disadvantage and trauma. *Feminist Criminology*, 15(5): 519–544.

Hart, E. L. (2017). Women prisoners and the drive for desistance: Capital and responsibilization as a barrier to change. *Women & Criminal Justice*, 27(3): 151–169.

Hart, E. L., & Van Ginneken, E. F. J. C. (2017). *New Perspectives on desistance theoretical and empirical developments*. Palgrave Macmillan.

Healy, D. (2010). *The Dynamics of Desistance: Charting Pathways through Change*. Portland, OR: Willan Publishing.

Heidensohn, F. and Silvestri, M. (2012) 'Gender and crime'. In: Maguire, M., Morgan, R. and Reiner, R. (eds.) *The Oxford Handbook of Criminology*. Oxford: University Press, pp. 336–369.

Heidemann G, Cederbaum JA, Martinez S, LeBel TP (2016). Wounded healers: How formerly incarcerated women help themselves by helping others. *Punishment & Society*, 18(1): 3–26.

Hundleby, J. D., Gfellner, B. M. and Racine, D. (2007). Desistance and identity change among aboriginal females. *Identity*, 7(3): 225–253.

ILO (2018). World Employment and Social Outlook: Trends for Women 2018 – Global snapshot International Labour Office – Geneva: ILO, 2018. Available at: www.ilo.org/wcmsp5/groups/public/---dgreports/---dcomm/---publ/documents/publication/wcms_619577.pdf

Jelin, E. (Ed.) (1990). *Women and Social Change in Latin America*. London: Zed Books.

Kruttschnitt, C. and Carbone-Lopez, K. (2006). Moving beyond the stereotypes: Women's subjective accounts of their violent crime. *Criminology: An Interdisciplinary Journal*, 44(2): 321–351.

Laidler, K. J. and Hunt, G. (2001). Accomplishing femininity among the girls in the gang. *British Journal of Criminology*, 41: 656–678.

LeBel, T. (2007). An examination of the impact of formerly incarcerated persons helping others. *Journal of Offender Rehabilitation*, 46(1–2): 1–24.

Legarde y de los Rios, M. (2005). *Los cautiverios de las mujeres. Madresposas, monjas, putas, presas y locas*. Ciudad de México: UNAM ediciones.

Leverentz, A. M. (2006). The love of a good man? Romantic relationships as a source of support or hindrance for female ex-offenders. *Journal of Research in Crime and Delinquency*, 43(4): 459–488.

Leverentz, A. (2011). Being a good daughter and sister: Families of origin in the reentry of African American female ex-prisoners. *Feminist Criminology*, 6(4): 239–267.

Llanes, N. (2012). Theoretical approaches to teen maternity as a subjective experience. *Sociológica*, 27(77): 235–266.

Luccisano, L. and Wall, G. (2009). 'The shaping of motherhood through social investment in children: Examples from Canada and Mexico'. In: Ruckert, A. and MacDonald, L. (eds.) *Post-Neoliberalism in the Americas*. London: Palgrave Macmillan, pp. 199–214.

Marcus, J. (2006). Ser madre en los sectores populares: una aproximación al sentido que las mujeres le otorgan a la maternidad. *Revista Argentina de Sociología*, 4(7): 100–119.

Maruna, S. (2001). *Making Good: How Ex-Convicts Reform and Rebuild their lives*. Washington, DC: American Psychological Association.

Maruna, S. and Roy, K. (2007). Amputation or reconstruction? Notes on the concept of "knifing off" and desistance from crime. *Journal of Contemporary Criminal Justice*, 23(1): 104–124.
McIvor, G. (2016). 'Offending and desistance among young women'. In: Kruttschnitt, C. and Bijleveld, C. (eds.) *Lives of Incarcerated Women: An International Perspective. Routledge Frontiers of Criminal Justice, 28*. New York, NY: Routledge, pp. 159–175.
Melero, P. (2015). *Mythological Constructs of Mexican Femininity*. London: Palgrave Macmillan.
Miller, J. (2002). The strengths and limits of 'doing gender' for understanding street crime. *Theoretical Criminology*, 6(4): 433–460.
Miller, J. and Mullis, C.W. (2006). 'Stuck up, telling lies and talking too much: The gendered context of young women's violence'. In: Heimer, K. and Kruttschmidt, C. (eds.) *Gender and Crime: Patterns of Victimization and Offending*. New York, NY: Routledge, pp. 44–66.
Molyneux, M. (2000). *Women's Movements in International Perspective: Latin America and Beyond*. Basingstoke: Palgrave Macmillan.
Montecino, S. (1997). *Palabra dicha: estudios sobre género, identidades, mestizaje*. Chile: Universidad de Chile, Facultad de Ciencias Sociales.
Mullins, C.W. and Wright, R. (2003). Gender, social networks, and residential burglary. *Criminology*, 41(3): 813–840.
Nugent, B., & Schinkel, M. (2016). The pains of desistance. *Criminology and Criminal Justice, 16*(5): 568–584.
Opsal, T. D. (2014). "It's their world, so you've just got to get through": Women's experiences of parole governance. *Feminist Criminology*, 10(2): 188–207.
Österman, L. (2018). Penal cultures and female desistance. London: Routledge.
Rumgay, J. (2004). Scripts for safer survival: Pathways out of female crime. *The Howard Journal of Criminal Justice*, 43(3): 405–419.
Sampson, R. J. and Laub, J. H. (2003). Life-course desisters? Trajectories of crime among delinquent boys followed to age 70. *Criminology*, 41(3): 555–592.
Sanders, T. (2007). Becoming an ex – Sex worker a deviant career. *Feminist Criminology*, 2(1): 74–95.
Skardhamer, T. and Savolainen, J. (2016). 'Timing of change: Are life course transitions causes or consequences of desistance?'. In: Shapland, J., Farrall, S. and Bottoms, T. (eds.) *Global Perspectives on Desistance*. Abingdon: Routledge, pp. 170–184.
Staab, S. (2012). Maternalism, male-breadwinner bias, and market reform: Historical legacies and current reforms in Chilean social policy. *Social Politics: International Studies in Gender, State and Society*, 19(3): 299–332.
Stuven, A. M., Cabello, T., Crisóstomo, B. and Lozier, M. (2013). La mujer ayer y hoy: un recorrido de incorporación social y política. *Temas de La Agenda Pública*, Available from: https://politicaspublicas.uc.cl/wp-content/uploads/2015/02/serie-no-61-la-mujer-ayer-y-hoy-un-recorrido-de-incorporacion-social-y-politica.pdf
The World Bank. (2014). Voice and Agency: Empowering Women and Girls for Shared Prosperity. Available from: www.worldbank.org/content/dam/Worldbank/document/Gender/Voice_and_agency_LOWRES.pdf.
Valdés, T. (1995). Women, Education and Work in Latin America. Diálogo N°17, septiembre, UNESCO, Caracas.

World Economic Forum. (2018).The Global Gender Gap Report 2015.World Economic Forum. Available from: www.weforum.org/reports/the-global-gender-gap-report-2018.

Wright, E., DeHart, D., Koons-Witt, B. and Crittenden, C. (2013). Buffers' against crime? Exploring the roles and limitations of positive relationships among women in prison. *Punishment and Society*, 15:71–95.

Chapter 6

Conclusions and implications

As argued before, the process of moving away from crime is not just the cessation of criminal activity itself, but a process of acquiring roles, identities, and virtues; of developing new social ties, and of inhabiting new spaces. Such a framing of desistance is undoubtedly affected by structural, cultural, and gender issues. This book attempted to fill some of the gaps in our knowledge of desistance in a developing country and contribute to an intercultural dialogue with mainstream explanations. By way of summary, this chapter recapitulates the aim of the research and discusses its main conclusions, before presenting the theoretical and practical implications of the findings, and finally the study's limitations and the implications for future research.

Liminality, transitions, and contributions from a Southern Criminology perspective

The aim of this book was to explore the transition from crime to conformity among a sample of Chilean juvenile offenders and identify theoretical, policy, and practice implications from the findings. For these purposes, the research was focused upon the examination of three main areas: (1) the process of moving away from crime, its obstacles and challenges; (2) possible factors involved in the transition from crime to conformity; and (3) the particularities of gender in the process of moving away from crime, focusing on young female offenders. The data used in the present study came from the Trajectories Study, a longitudinal research project that used mixed methods to explore the criminal and life trajectories within a sample panel of young male and female offenders in Chile. The present research contributes to the ways in which we understand, explain, and research desistance. Perhaps the most crucial finding is that, by researching the process of moving away from crime among late adolescent offenders, the liminal space of ambivalences and inconsistencies that most individuals experience on their path to desistance from crime acquires a pivotal relevance.

This is supported by the first major finding of the study, that desistance and persistence categories are far from absolute and are rather two ends of a

DOI: 10.4324/9781003160809-7

continuum that individuals can move along fluidly. In several cases, the process of crime abandonment started as a strategy of crime avoidance rather than abandonment, marked not only by changes in routines and lifestyles but also in the meanings that individuals ascribe to crime. Despite multiple failures, several persisters kept a strong sense of agency and were strongly confident in their capacity to leave crime behind and navigated through the inconsistencies between their internal orientations towards conformity and their criminal behaviour, resisting secondary deviance and trying to integrate themselves into mainstream society.

Second, the factors associated with the process of moving away from crime among the young offenders of the study varied according to the theoretical model and the operationalisation of desistance used. While some factors emerged as significantly associated with temporary desistance in models based on social control and routine activities approaches, for instance, they were not associated with temporary desistance in the final integrated model that included psychosocial factors as well. The integrated model shows definitively that the desistance process is not simply associated with social control factors that appear in life and promote changes without individuals being aware of them. Psychosocial factors might also be relevant throughout the process and they do not operate in isolation from each other: rather, there is an orientation towards prosociality in a broad sense. The process of crime abandonment was experienced by the participants as a transformative process towards adulthood, in which internal changes in combination with lifestyle changes incrementally trigger maturation and reintegration.

Third, it has been shown that the process of crime abandonment is strongly gendered. In the case of the young men from the study, it was observed through the changing process that they learned new forms of doing masculinities by exerting control over themselves, restraining from violence, pursuing a productive life, assuming adult roles, and leaving behind expressive crime (caused by humiliation and the pursuit of identity and status). This is consistent with Connell (2005), who has argued that, in capitalist societies (such as the Chilean society, which has strongly embraced capitalism in the past three decades), aggressiveness is not the only way of performing masculinity: pursuing a productive life and assuming gendered family roles through rationality and responsibility are also expressions of hegemonic masculinities.

The process of moving away from crime among women was related to a transition towards traditional feminine caring roles and persistence operated as a way both to resist and affirm gender subordination and patriarchy. It was found that a number of the factors triggering crime abandonment were strongly anchored in the ethic of care and were shown to be problematic for sustaining desistance in the long-term. The ethic of care kept these young women trapped within gender constraints, which could afterwards be contested and resisted through crime relapses and persistence. The liminal phase in these young women's transitions was observed to be tight, due to the narrow spectrum of opportunities they had in domains beyond traditional gender roles. Persistence, on the other hand, was found to be a way to resist patriarchy and subordination through facilitating financial independence, avoiding the acquisition of roles anchored in the ethic of care and allowing them to engage in so-called "cross gendering" practices. Yet persistence was a way to accomplish gender as well, comply with some gender demands, and reproduce gender status subordination through their criminal behaviour.

Although cultural particularities were found in the present study, several results were consistent and confirmed findings from previous research conducted in developed and Anglophone countries. This might be due to the fact that, in societies with similar market-based economic systems and liberal welfare regimes, several structural factors operate in similar ways. Moreover, Chile – as distinct from Central American countries – does not have high violence rates, and crime is mainly concentrated on property offences: the same as occurs in developed countries. For instance, consistent with previous research, the present study confirms that psychosocial factors are strongly relevant throughout the process of moving away from crime, and they do not operate in isolation from each other: rather, there is an orientation towards prosociality in a broad sense. The findings shed light into the way in which these factors operate and how they not only trigger desistance, but also pull individuals back into crime. In terms of gender issues, the study puts together evidence coming from previous feminist studies on crime with the desistance paradigm, offering a novel analysis of the way in which gender shapes, limits, and structures women's pathways out of crime. Finally, the fact highlighted in previous research that offenders regularly oscillate in the liminal space or continuum between crime and conformity (Bottoms et al., 2004; Healy, 2010) was also confirmed. This space, as mentioned earlier, acquired pivotal salience in the present study, most probably due to the age of the participants (16–21 years of age) and due to several structural constraints that influenced the process of moving away from crime among them.

Perhaps the main differences with studies conducted in Anglophone countries and the main contributions from a Southern Criminological perspective are found in the intensity by which some structural constrains operate in participants' lives, strongly shaping the process of moving away from crime. This was certainly the case for the powerful effect of consumerism in participants desistance and persistence processes. As mentioned in Chapter 3 (see also Droppelmann, 2017), interviewees did not exist as workers or citizens, but as consumers: success was defined in monetary terms. Having material goods was the interviewees' main life goal, and an indication of an efficient and productive life in which money was not wasted, but invested in symbolic sources of pride and status. Structural changes experienced in Chile since the 1980s, such as economic growth accompanied by high levels of income inequality, have changed the social mobility strategy used by the lower classes. In fact, the rise of consumerism made possible by an increasing access to credit has created a situation wherein individuals' aspirations are no longer centred on occupational status or income, but on their consumer capacity and lifestyles (Franco et al., 2011). Since the opportunities for most individuals in the sample to achieve material success had been blocked by different sources of social disadvantage and societal constrains, the only available means of accessing a consumer lifestyle was through so-called "aspirational crime"; desistance, therefore, was not available to them (Merton, 1957; UNDP, 2014).

The great salience observed of psychosocial factors, and the fact that ambivalence, attachment, consumerism, and masculinity emerged as pivotal in the process of moving away from crime, might also be interpreted as a reflection of structural particularities. In developing countries (such as Chile), social protection mechanisms are weak and access to social opportunities (such as formal employment, education, housing, and health) are not always guaranteed. Indeed, research on life-course transitions in Latin America has shown that the most disadvantaged young people move towards adult life in an unclear way, with a high degree of indeterminacy towards the future which sometimes prevents turning points. As mentioned in Chapter 3, the *lack of future* of the participants from the study hindered the development of hope and perspective, both aspects crucial for leaving crime behind. Moreover, in these contexts of great uncertainty, crime operated as a strategy to preserve a sense of control in an environment of complete powerlessness and was, therefore, extremely difficult to leave behind. For several interviewees, a criminal life was the only certainty available.

In the case of women, the fact that the process of crime abandonment was found to be strongly gendered could in part be the result of the high levels of gender inequality affecting women in Chile – particularly those from low socio-economic strata.[1] As discussed in Chapter 5, desistance among women was related to a transition towards traditional feminine caring roles and persistence operated as a way both to resist and affirm gender subordination and patriarchy. Although this may be extrapolated to other cultures as well, it is of great importance within the Latin American context, where cultural constructions of femininity are strongly identified with motherhood – a state associated with moral virtue, altruism, and self-sacrifice (Jelin, 1990; Molyneux, 2000). From a cultural perspective, it has been argued that Latin American ideologies of motherhood have restricted women to private lives, influenced the gendered division of labour, and constrained their power to maternal love and caring practices. These conceptions, historically rooted in the Christian image of the Virgin Mary (central to the Chilean culture), relegate women to "roles" as mother and spouse, operating as a grounding model of the self-denying sacrificial woman who serves and depends on others (Legarde y de los Rios, 2005; Melero, 2015; Montecinos, 1997). Poor women in Latin America, with narrow windows of opportunity and lack of training and education, generally engage in home-based enterprises that routinely revolve around domestic activities (Chant, 2014).

Theoretical implications

The findings of the present study entail several implications that might confirm, contradict, or enrich the current explanations of desistance. First, despite the pivotal role that identity plays in desistance explanations, there are no agreements regarding the scope and timing of these changes. As mentioned in Chapter 1, it is not clear how they interact with other factors involved in the desistance process. The findings of the present research indicate that the division between primary and secondary desistance imposes an artificial distinction and a concretised temporal order to the process of crime abandonment, which may not best reflect the way in which it actually occurs. It was shown that secondary desistance is not necessarily a long-term achievement that arises as a consequence of crime abandonment, and that even several persisters do not see themselves as offenders. Indeed, while behavioural desistance was associated with social control factors, routine activities, and psychosocial explanations, intentional desistance was only associated with psychosocial factors.[2] This might indicate that, as Bottoms and Shapland (2014) pointed out, individuals start thinking differently about themselves in early stages of desistance, and gradual changes in identity occur. It also might support Giordano's (2016:15) argument that identity changes occurred simultaneously with behavioural changes, and that they are "mutually reinforce facets of the change process". Or it could simply highlight, as several scholars have noted, that some individuals maintained a non-offender identity alongside their criminal behaviour (see Gibbons, 1965; Healy, 2010; Irwin, 1970; Murray, 2009; Presser, 2008).

Second, the fact that only in the intentional desistance model did self-efficacy emerge as significantly associated with desistance might reflect the overemphasis of personal agency at the beginning of the desistance process. Moreover, the fact that social control and routine activities variables were not significantly correlated with intentional desistance might indicate that the antisocial lifestyle was (especially at early stages of desistance) particularly difficult to renounce, and these young offenders were probably still strongly embedded within their social settings, therefore not yet benefiting from prosocial opportunities or investing in conventional activities such as work or family life. Indeed, as it was observed in Chapter 3, crime was difficult to surrender not only because it was the participants' way of life – and, for most, the only thing they knew – but also because it was a source of pleasure, enjoyment, and satisfaction.

Third, although several authors have used the idea of liminality as a way of describing "half-way" offenders (Bottoms et al., 2004; Heally, 2010; Matza, 1964), little theoretical consideration has been given to the experiences of offenders within this space between crime and conformity. The findings of the present book confirmed that several individuals vacillated in that liminal space. Moreover, completely reformed desisters and categorically antisocial persisters were rarely found among the interviewees, and ambivalence was a constitutive issue throughout the process of crime abandonment. Conversely, in the case of young women offenders, it was found that the liminal stage between crime and conformity was narrow and tight. Although at a first glance the tightness of the liminal phase in their transitions could be interpreted as a positive issue that sped up the desistance process, it was observed to be the result of strong constraints within the limits imposed by patriarchy and social class, blocking access to other choices and narrowing the women's opportunities in domains beyond traditional gender roles.

Fourth, former research on desistance (see Paternoster et al., 2016) has addressed persistence as lack of agency and as a failure in the process of reintegration; in the present study, however, a different angle has emerged. In the case of several male persisters, consistent with Carlsson (2013) and Lindegaard and Jackes (2014), persistence in crime was also observed as an agentic move in the direction of transforming one's life through the acquisition of power, status, and control. Persistence for these men was a way to access consumer culture and, therefore, distinguish themselves from the rest of the young people in their neighbourhoods, acquire and experience social mobility and progress, and at the same time to feel themselves to be part of mainstream society. In the case of several young women of the study, persistence was found to be a way of resisting gender subordination and patriarchy, through facilitating financial independence, avoiding the acquisition of roles anchored in the ethic of care, and allowing them to engage in so-called "cross-gendering" practices.

Therefore, it could be argued that agency must be treated with caution in desistance research, because individuals' agentic moves are not always oriented towards crime abandonment. Indeed, although agency has been a pivotal concept in desistance research, some scholars (Carlsson, 2016; Healy, 2013; King, 2014; LeBel et al., 2008; Patton & Farrall, 2021) have warned against holding it in high regard. They have argued that neoliberalism may have led to an overemphasis on agency not only by researchers, but also in the narratives of the individuals who took part in the studies on desistance. In a culture which sees individuals as responsible for their own failures and successes, there is a danger of skewing interpretation to exclude consideration of relevant structural issues.

Indeed, consistent with Carlsson (2016), the present research demonstrated that agency was strongly imbued with notions of gender. As discussed in Chapter 3, several interviewees expressed an exacerbated and decontextualised self-reliance regarding their capability to abandon crime (even after several failures). Since the individuals in the study were embedded in contexts of great uncertainty, with lack of control in every single domain of their lives, except crime, this exacerbated sense of agency can be interpreted as an attempt of "doing masculinities". Beyond agency, these individuals were expressing power of will, bravery, and independence – all features of the "macho" stereotype in Latin American culture. For these individuals, it was not just about crime, but about and who commands the individual's life; agency operated here as a strategy to preserve a sense of control in a context of complete powerlessness.

Fifth, as mentioned in Chapter 1, late adolescence is a critical stage for the expression of resilience – particularly in the case of adolescent delinquents, who are normally immersed in contexts of high risks and adversities. During this period, different domains of maturation – such as changes in social roles, psychosocial, identity, civic, and cognitive domains – are additive in their effects on desistance. The present study confirmed that maturation was an incremental process of improvement, with interviewees experiencing these internal changes as a transformative process towards adulthood. Desisters relegated delinquency to the adolescent period, and this allowed them to develop and sustain a prosocial identity more easily, separating past actions and their current self.

Sixth, it was found that the desistance process is not simply associated with social control factors that appear in life and promote changes without individuals being aware of it. This contradicts Sampson and Laub's (2003:278) statement that offenders desist "by default", without experiencing any identity shift or cognitive transformation. Indeed, as mentioned earlier, the psychosocial factors that operate in the desistance processes did not do so in isolation from each other: rather, there was an orientation towards prosociality in a broad sense. Individual orientations towards conformity may be critical throughout the process, opening individuals to the influence of other factors and supporting daily decisions of routine and lifestyle changes that allow them to avoid crime, facilitating the coherence and sense of purpose that orients behaviour. What these findings suggest, consistent with Giordano (2016), is that the most effective hooks for change are not the ones that operate as sources of social control, but the ones that provide a roadmap to trigger the development of a new identity.

Nevertheless, consistent with other scholars (Bottoms & Shapland, 2011; Healy, 2010; Presser, 2008), it was also observed that the association of desistance with a prosocial orientation did not prevent all the individuals in the sample from continuing to offend. Indeed, almost half of the persisters in the study did not see themselves as delinquents. This finding should not be interpreted as a denial of their criminal behaviour (Sykes & Matza, 1957), or a sign of their belonging to a criminal subculture in which crime is normative (Agnew, 2003; Cohen, 1955; Hayward, 2002; Schwendinger & Schwendinger , 1985); rather, it should be seen as an individual's attempt to avoid the centrality of the delinquent identity and to make sense of their inconsistencies to align their present self with their future conformist aspirations and with the market-based values of mainstream society.

Finally, it is important to summarise how the research findings are consistent with, or different to, the *Integrated Theories of Desistance* discussed in Chapter 1. There are two main issues within Giordano, Cernkovich, and Rudolph's (2002) *Theory of Cognitive Transformation* that were confirmed by the present study. As previously mentioned regarding identity changes, it was shown that secondary desistance is not necessarily a long-term achievement that arises as a consequence of crime abandonment – a finding which concurs with Giordano's last updates of her *Theory of Cognitive Transformation* (2016), in which she argued that identity changes occur simultaneously with behavioural changes, and that insisting on disentangling a temporal order of transformations does not help to develop an accurate explanation of how the desistance process occurs.

Another finding in common with Giordano (2016) is that, although lifestyle factors (such as drug use, risky activities, and occupation) maintained strong relevance to avoidance of crime among participants of the study, the desistance process was not only related to key events in participants' lives. Although we may think that the achievement of transition events such as work and marriage are what define individuals as adults, the research findings showed that feelings of being an adult are based on more gradual and internal developments. As Giordano (2016) notes, the most effective hooks for change are not the ones that operate as sources of social control, but the ones that provide a roadmap for triggering the development of a new identity.

Nevertheless, the research findings do not support the role played by agency in the *Theory of Cognitive Transformation* (Giordano, Cernkovich, & Rudolph, 2002), in which desistance is strongly dependent on motivational and attitudinal changes. Here, it was observed that participants' agentic moves were not always oriented towards crime abandonment, and that agency was strongly imbued with notions of gender. Therefore, it is argued that the interpretation of failures in the process of crime abandonment simply as problems based on lack of self-control and/or motivation for change must be avoided in desistance explanations.

On the contrary, the research findings are more consistent with Farrall's *Structural and individual-level processes of desistance* approach (2014), in which desistance is the result of the interaction between individual choices and social forces. This gives special weight to the fact that individual agency is embedded within specific social contexts that affect it in several ways – a finding which was strongly present in the experiences presented in Chapter 5 with female participants, where it was observed that their social contexts did not provide them with enough opportunities for being and doing to truly exercise their agency, thereby limiting their choices. The transitions of these young women were quite radical: they saw themselves as housewives/mothers at one extreme of the continuum, or as thieves/drug addicts at the other, thereby assuming the identities, behaviours, and the characteristics of the role to which they ascribed themselves.

The role played by emotion in the desistance process highlighted by Farrall and Calverley (2006) was also supported by the research findings. Among women, it was observed how shame and remorse (especially among violent offenders) was often compounded by limited ability to manage these negative emotions. Unlike men – who "rewrite a shameful past into a necessary prelude to a productive life" (Maruna, 2001:87), arguing that crime made them stronger or wiser – the young women of the study engaged in a process closer to what Maruna and Roy (2007) termed "knifing off" their past, believing that this was the only way to move on.

As Farrall (2005) has argued, hope has been identified as key in the desistance process, projecting a possible future and the way in which it can be realised. In the participants' narratives, the lack of hope – rooted in an uncertainty regarding their future lives – was strongly present. By contrast with other studies of adult participants, the absence of a possible future was neither simply associated with multiple individual experiences of failures (Nugent & Schinkel, 2016; Standing, 2011), nor to the need to live in the present, as is typical of the adolescent period; rather, the lack of a future orientation and hope was experienced by the participants as a structural blockage. This is consistent with the findings of Patton and Farrall (2021): to facilitate hope and promote life beyond desistance, a kind of society and a kind of social order is needed.

Other emotions were also key in participants' processes of crime abandonment – namely, the anxiety of leaving crime behind, and fear. For several participants of the study, the emotional attachment to crime was so strong that they were experiencing grief, and were still "bargaining" with crime, trying to delay or even undo their decision to leave it behind. In the case of fear, they were mostly afraid of failing in conformist settings, and, for several offenders, it was easier to live a life of failure than to fail after an attempt at success. As per Hunter and Farrall (2018), emotions – especially in early stages of desistance – might be in conflict with individuals' attempts to desist. Many participants of the study had a strong emotional attachment to crime, making it profoundly difficult to surrender – not simply because it was their way of life, but because it was a way of reaffirming their identities and exercising control.

The main similarities between the research findings and integrated theories of desistance can be found by comparing the present study to the *Heuristic and interactive model of the early stages of desistance* (Bottoms & Shapland, 2016) – though this is perhaps to be expected, since this model explains the early stages of the desistance process, where most of the participants of the present study were situated. As mentioned before, confirming the findings of Bottoms and Shapland (2016), the present study demonstrated that maturation was an incremental process of improvement, with interviewees experiencing internal changes towards conformity as a transformative process towards adulthood. It also supported the fact that, within this process of active maturation, individuals start considering their goals and ethical norms through reflection on what sort of person they "should" be.

The findings also confirm the role played by changes in routines, lifestyles, and friends – as well as more generally resisting the inevitable temptations that individuals will encounter during their attempts to abandon a life of crime (Bottoms & Shapland, 2014). Indeed, the quantitative analysis showed that those participants who were involved in risky activities in the past 12 months had a 20.3% lower probability of desisting. Routine and lifestyle changes were perhaps the most challenging issues for the interviewees: several described how their routines became structured and limited, since they could not inhabit spaces around their work due to the strong social stratification of

Santiago's neighbourhoods – not to mention that most of the places in their neighbourhoods were marked with strong temptations.

Nevertheless, consistent with Hunt and Farrall (2015), the research findings also showed that it was not only the changes in routine, lifestyle, activities, and exposure to such settings that matter in the desistance process: the meanings that individuals impute to those activities and settings were also relevant to the process of crime abandonment – as were the subjective explanations they ascribed to their criminal behaviour. In that sense, it was interesting to note how, in several cases, changes in the violence that accompanied crime paved the way for the restoration of social bonds and the reconstruction of a new sense of self.

Several of the aforementioned theoretical insights open the way to discuss how desistance explanations might be enriched by the engagement with theories beyond mainstream Criminology and life-course explanations of crime. As it has been showed throughout this book, desistance is the interaction between structural, agentic, and subjective processes and, therefore, needs a wide range of interdisciplinary approaches to be appropriately addressed and explained. As Graham and McNeill (2017:15) have noted, "What desistance theory and research perhaps lacks, however, is a well-developed archaeology. Perhaps because it begins with the assumed problems of offending and of ending offending rather than with what lies behind these problems and their construction". Accordingly, and consistent with the findings of the present study, it can be argued that desistance explanations must move beyond the boundaries of the rehabilitative approach and start interacting with critical approaches – especially with Feminist and Cultural Criminology (among other approaches) – if it really aims to develop the archaeology mentioned earlier.

Feminist approaches are strongly needed to counteract the assumption (which was found to be problematic for the desistance process in this study) that the performance of conventional gender roles brings social rewards that support the development of a non-criminal identity. As shown in Chapter 5 and discussed later in the section on practical implications, the belief that women have to commit themselves to an "ethic of care" to abandon crime has strongly imprinted desistance explanations and women's correctional practices. Although some scholars have discussed the struggle of negotiating a feminine identity within the restrictions of gender (Barr, 2019; Gålnander, 2019; Hart, 2017), little attention has been given to reputation and status as salient elements of young women's identities (Laidler & Hunt, 2001). The strong focus on the development of normative feminine identities as a key factor triggering desistance has ignored the exploration of other sources of identities, serving to reify constraining gender binaries (Miller, 2002).

Cultural Criminology has also been excluded (or perhaps it has excluded itself) from desistance explanations, despite the fact that it can contribute insightfully regarding transgression and its attractions – especially among young offenders. Perhaps Cultural Criminology does not have much to offer precisely to explain desistance from crime, but it has a strong relevance when understanding persistence and the obstacles to leaving crime behind. Despite some scarce work on the pains of desistance (Nugent & Schinkel, 2016; Patton & Farrall, 2021), desistance explanations have not given much attention to the questions of why and how abandoning crime is a difficult process. Explanations for the above-mentioned have mainly been oriented towards highlighting structural constrains (lack of opportunities to exercise conventional roles) and lack of internal drifts (agency, self-efficacy, motivation, hope), without considering a key fact established by Cultural Criminology: crime is "the breaking through of restraints, a realisation of immediacy and a reassertion of identity and ontology" (Hayward & Young, 1999:8). Transgression is, therefore, a way to solve subcultural problems and emotional conflicts of contemporary life – especially the ones derived from consumerism and the absence of stimulation in marginalised neighbourhoods.

Towards a desistance's informed correctional practice

It is interesting to note that, although the study of desistance emerged as the explanation of a process that happens in spite of the intervention of the criminal justice system, its results have become a strong influence for the rehabilitation paradigm. It has challenged the traditional correctional model by showing that self-change is crucial, that the criminal justice intervention might block desistance processes that naturally occur in offender's lives, and that social interactions are key factors, highlighting the role of the probation officer as a therapeutic agent.

The design in 2007 of Chile's Youth Justice System responded to the aim of promoting the responsibility and reintegration of adolescents in conflict with the law. However, in its implementation process, the system has not been able to establish a re-entry narrative associated with change and rehabilitation, but rather one aimed at mere compliance. Accordingly, the expected results of the Youth Justice System – and its interventions in particular – are measured only through recidivism rates. Although this is expected – and is the way in which criminal justice systems generally assess their impact – using recidivism rates as the single way to assess interventions risks hiding crucial changes that occur during the process of desistance. Indeed, as mentioned earlier, it was observed in the present research that changes in seriousness and frequency of crime can activate several processes that might sustain desistance in the long term. These changes must be recognised, measured, and promoted through correctional interventions and have to be considered when assessing the impact of the Youth Justice System.

All this demonstrates the need to expand the ways of measuring the impact of interventions and, more importantly, to visualise and recognise the changes that young people experience throughout the process. This could open the way for the development of new reintegration measures and indicators that properly account for the progress in the process of leaving crime behind. The above-mentioned would entail an institutional recognition both of participants' achievements and the difficulties of the process. It would communicate a strength-based narrative and would favour a de-labelling process, in which the recognition of the desisting individuals' changes leads to a greater sense of self and, thus, supports desistance from crime in the long-term.

The institutional recognition of the difficulties of leaving crime behind is key not only when measuring the effectiveness of the system but also when implementing interventions with young offenders. Indeed, by moving forward from the binary categorisation of the process of crime abandonment (crime/no crime), we turn our focus instead to the liminal space of ambivalences and inconsistencies that most individuals in this study experienced on their path to desistance from crime.

The approach to drug addiction rehabilitation represents an interesting paradigm to discuss the inclusion of ambivalence as a focus of intervention. Before the 1990s, drug addiction suffered from a long tradition of moralistic condemnation, with drug use addressed through prohibition and interventions aimed at total abstinence. However, after the heroin crisis of the 1980s in several developed countries, the harm reduction paradigm began to be installed. This approach works to meet those with substance use disorder "where they are", accepting that drug use is their current reality, rather than forcing treatment or abstinence. Alongside this, important aspects associated with drug rehabilitation began to be highlighted, such as ambivalence, and the role of motivation throughout the process. This was possible thanks to the understanding and acceptance that forgoing drugs was difficult, that the changing process was not linear, and that complete abstinence was never going to happen for some individuals.

Nevertheless, such an approach has not yet permeated correctional practice (and perhaps never will), confronting crime as an undesired behaviour that must be eradicated – a symbolic representation of internal danger and interpersonal deficits. Accordingly, ambivalence towards desistance is not recognised, and offending desires and crime relapses are generally not therapeutically approached. If there is intervention, it is via strategies of self-control to address the problematic behaviour (crime) through the Cognitive Behavioural approach, which does not address the subjective, emotional, and cultural issues behind those desires to continue offending. In correctional settings, speaking about the pains of leaving crime behind and the losses incurred by this process are issues that are avoided, both by practitioners and by the young offenders themselves. Practitioners generally engaged in moral dialogues with offenders (Rowers, 2006; King, 2013), discussing what is bad or good, but forgetting to assist desistance by supporting individuals in the mourning process of leaving crime behind and helping them to recognise and manage the fear of failing in conventional settings.

As mentioned earlier, it was observed in the study that the antisocial lifestyle was particularly difficult to renounce, not only because it was the participants way of life – and, for most, the only thing they knew – but also because it was a source of pleasure, enjoyment, and satisfaction. Lifestyle is a very difficult aspect to modify, since it is intrinsically relational, and, therefore, does not solely depend on the individual who wants to change it. This is why several scholars have argued that, especially in the first stages of desistance, individuals avoid situations that would confront them with temptations they would struggle to resist and end up in situations of strong self-isolation (Bottoms & Shapland, 2011; Giordano, Cernkovich, & Holland, 2003; McIvor, 2016; Nugent & Schinkel, 2016; Wright et al., 2013). This situation was confirmed in the present study, especially among female ex-offenders. Nevertheless, since self-isolation is not sustainable in the long term, intervention must help individuals to inhabit new spaces, occupy different roles, and, sometimes, interact with new people. Of course, these kinds of interventions cannot be confined within the probation centres or prisons – they must occur within offenders' environments and social settings.

Correctional interventions are mainly oriented towards offering individuals opportunities for change, such as employment, education, drug treatment among others. Nevertheless, it was found in the present study that the desistance process is not simply associated with social control factors that appear in life and promote changes without individuals being aware of it. Accordingly, offenders' intervention must go beyond the simple provision of opportunities – it must support individuals' daily decisions of routine and lifestyle changes that allow them to avoid crime and promote a sense of purpose that orients behaviour. Nevertheless, as discussed in Chapter 3, the individuals in the study lacked a future orientation and had instead a feeling of their lives being driven by destiny. In that sense, interventions should promote a life project and an orientation towards a future that departs from the reflexion regarding the individuals' own identities, taking advantage of the fact (highlighted in the findings) that even several persisters defy the anti-social identity and do not see themselves as offenders.

The above-mentioned can only arise from a structural change in the system, which advances – as per Lewis (1990:923) – "from programmes to lives", in which the relational aspects of interventions are put at the centre, and the changing process is supported by the therapeutic alliance established between practitioners and offenders. To assist desistance, interventions must be located in new spaces: in the liminal space between crime and conformity, in the places and settings the participants inhabit, and in a possible future that must be constructed with new, mixed, or residual identities.

Finally, gender constraints must also be addressed through correctional practice. As has been shown throughout the book, the process of crime abandonment in the case of women is strongly shaped by the limits imposed by patriarchy and social class. Therefore, it is suggested that correctional practices must be based on solid grounds that challenge gender and class hierarchies, instead of making these young women accept their position within the social order. This is not to suggest that gender is the only thing that matters, but simply to make clear that, as Goodkind (2009) notes, if gender and class inequalities that have contributed to female crime involvement are not addressed, crime will be ultimately perpetuated.

Although in recent years, the inclusion of a gender-responsive approach in penal policies has been widespread, influencing the ways in which prison interventions and programmes must be delivered for female offenders (Hannah-Moffat, 2011), insufficient consideration has been given to the ways in which gender must be operationalised through incorporating the relevance of women's multiple sources of oppression; instead, a normative and stereotypical assumption of femininity has usually been adopted.

Concerns about women's vulnerability and their strong dependence on welfare benefits have been used as grounds for widespread penal intervention and practices have mainly been oriented towards supporting women's transition to "goodness", but they have not helped them to construct a better life for themselves. As Gelsthorpe (2010) pointed out, the paradigm has been strongly embedded in notions of redemption through normative femininity, moral tutelage, and gender conformity, putting the focus on relational issues – as if they were therapeutic per se – and merely reproducing the logic of the ethic of care. Therapeutic discourses of self-regulation have attributed women's lack of choices to an incapacity to take decisions based on their low self-esteem, fragility, and weakness, thereby diverting the attention from structural constraints and making the women responsible for their own rehabilitation (Hannah-Moffat, 2001). The "risk and need" approach has further worsened this situation by focusing on women's deficit, predominantly targeting psychological needs and omitting the interaction between agency and structure, which is crucial for supporting a long-term and sustainable process of crime abandonment.

Unfortunately, overcoming this situation is not easy: the conception of female offenders as risky and vulnerable is strongly embedded in current correctional narratives, particularly in Latin America. In that sense, and taking into account the findings of this study, it can be argued that correctional practice must move from a deficit-based model towards an approach that promotes young women's strengths, decision-making, and personal growth through their active participation in the definition of their needs and goals. Peer support services have been shown to work in this regard (Nixon, 2020), being more effective than expert-led interventions in decreasing feelings of isolation, and improving self-worth and autonomy. Helping other women who are at a much earlier stage in their desistance process also affords previous female offenders the opportunity to incorporate and re-signify the elements that emerged from their past lives and build a coherent narrative to explain and justify their change.

Furthermore, it is important to understand that the factors triggering desistance do not operate in a vacuum and are strongly shaped by gender, class, and age. In that sense, as mentioned earlier, interventions must be oriented not only towards providing "hooks for change" to trigger desistance but also to help young women recognise the existence and accessibility of the opportunities available to them beyond the norms of their gender. One must also be very careful when choosing the type of intervention to be implemented, its content, and the process by which it will be delivered to not continue reproducing the logic of the ethic of care through practices that encourage women's traditional roles. Interventions must rather support women to explore and inhabit multiple identities, beyond caring roles.

Finally, agency (a cornerstone in explanations of desistance discussed earlier) must be understood within a context of gender oppression (for males and females) to avoid both orienting correctional practices towards notions of self-triggered change alone and interpreting failures as problems based on lack of self-control and motivation towards change. Similarly, relapses in crime and persistence must be approached as ways to resist patriarchy and, thus, suitable alternatives to crime outside the realm of gender constraints must be offered. Agency has to be approached as "transformative action", challenging structures of patriarchy, enlarging individuals' choices, improving decision-making, promoting identity development, and providing genuine opportunities for change.

What I would do differently: limitations and implications for future research

During the design, implementation, and analysis phases of the present research, several methodological decisions were made, some of which entailed limitations that must be considered.

As mentioned in Chapter 2, I wanted to immerse myself deeply in the environments, routines, and cultures that provided the context for the life stories of young offenders. I, therefore, decided to embark personally on a primary data collection effort. Although this substantially enriched the present research, it prevented the possibility of having a larger sample size and, thus, impeded the possibility of conducting more advanced statistical analyses.

Despite the preceding fact, the time I spent collecting the data directly and the time I spent in the participants' own neighbourhoods, waiting for them in probation centres and listening to the informal conversations they had with each other, or talking with their families when trying to locate them, allowed me to gain a first-hand understanding of cultural meanings and resonances that were of strong relevance when interpreting the results. In this sense, I would say that future research should go beyond traditional research methods and should explore more sophisticated ways to collect the cultural aspects of desistance. As mentioned earlier, Cultural Criminology has much to offer to the exploration of the desistance process, opening the way to discover meanings, symbolism, lifestyles, and social practices, which might be part of the process of abandoning crime.

I also decided only to include young people who were serving community sanctions in the study to observe the desistance process and the obstacles they face in their lived experience; therefore, young people who were serving prison sentences were excluded. As a result, the present cohort of respondents has an unavoidable bias, in that it is composed of less serious offenders than the ones who were imprisoned. Despite this, however, the young people in the study were by no means first-time offenders: they all had a relevant criminal history and several previous convictions. The effect of sanctions and interventions was not assessed: since all the juveniles from the sample were serving the same programmes, it was considered a static factor. It was decided that the inclusion of those factors would have significantly enlarged the scope of the study. Nevertheless, the inclusion of those issues must be considered in further developments of the study. It is key for further studies on desistance-based practices to deeply understand how correctional practices and narratives hinder or facilitate the process of crime abandonment and how the relational dynamics between offenders and practitioners could support the changing process.

As mentioned in Chapter 2, the number of young female offenders who were serving community sentences in Santiago in 2012 was very small; it was, therefore, decided not to include them in the panel and instead to investigate their desistance process through in-depth interviews. The short period of observation and the fact that desistance was assessed retrospectively could have biased women's emotional accounts of their experiences; it could also be the case that the findings were reflecting a crime-free gap instead of a full and proper transition out of crime. This might have been the case for the males of the study as well, so it is important to clarify that, when talking about desistance in this book, I am referring to a one-year crime free period; perhaps it would, therefore, be more accurately define it as temporary desistance.

Although the young age of the participants was an advantage for delving into natural life transitions triggering desistance, it restricts the implications that may be drawn from this study only to include young offenders, thereby excluding possible dynamics that might follow individuals with longer crime trajectories and a deeper crime involvement. Further waves of the present longitudinal study are needed to properly understand the desistance process and to observe the impact of the transition to adulthood among the participants of the cohort.

The use of mixed methods was a key decision for the study. As noted in the introduction, there is a lack of large-scale quantitative criminological research in Latin America; developing a panel study with juvenile offenders was, therefore, essential not only for academic purposes but also more importantly as a means of informing public policy decisions. Nevertheless, quantitative methods have some limitations – especially when addressing phenomenological aspects linked to desistance, such as identities, emotions, tensions, and symbols that arise throughout the process of leaving crime behind (which the information drawn from qualitative sources was intended to overcome). Unfortunately, due to practical exigencies, it was not possible to conduct in-depth interviews prospectively – an unfortunate limitation of the study, since it would have been particularly interesting to reinterview the qualitative sample one year after the first interview.

Longitudinal qualitative studies are much needed to assess phenomenological issues and could strategically improve attrition, since they allow the development of a stronger bond with participants. Indeed, as mentioned before, establishing a way to approach the participants of the study (especially the women) was a great challenge. I intended to minimise the hierarchies between myself and the participants as much as possible, recognising their subjectivity and following a flexible approach, and constantly reflecting on my own assumptions about them that could bias or otherwise negatively impact on the interviews. This constant reflexivity is crucial when conducting research with offenders and must be considered not only for ethical reasons but also to avoid resistance and, thus, get properly immerse in the participants narratives.

One of the main challenges of the present research was formulating an approach to operationalise desistance from crime. As discussed in Chapter 1, in almost all the studies carried out before the 1990s (with the exception of Meisenhelder, 1977), desistance had continually been defined as a static end point of the criminal career (see Cusson & Pinsonneault, 1986; Farrington, 1986; Farrington & Hawkins, 1991; Glueck & Glueck, 1943). Although the research that followed has tried to be more sophisticated in its understanding of the ways in which desistance and persistence are operationalised, several limitations still remain. Therefore, considering all the limitations and methodological decisions described in Chapter 2, when using the terms desistance and persistence across this research, I am most precisely referring to a period in which interviewees **stayed away from crime** or **continue committing crimes**, respectively. If desistance would stop, would last for another period, or for a lifetime is a question that remains unanswered. Moreover, if we consider the age of the participants (16–21), it is very likely that the period in which they stayed away from the crime was reflecting temporary desistance, early states of desistance, or simple zigzag periods within their criminal career, and therefore, the concept of liminality (the space between crime and conformity) becomes of primary importance in the present study.

Although the operationalisations of desistance used in the present study were limited by the data available, several interesting issues emerged. It was observed that desistance rates vary considerably when different operationalisations are used. It was also discovered that, when comparing two different operationalisations of desistance, the predictors differ as well. Moreover, it was demonstrated that operationalising desistance as only considering crime-free gaps risks hiding crucial changes that occur during the process of leaving crime behind. Indeed, 43% of the youths who persisted in crime in the second wave had lessened the seriousness of their offences, and 36% of them committed crimes less frequently than in the first wave. Future research should consider and explore different ways to operationalise desistance, formulating adequate measures from the very inception of the research process (research design stage) to assure that the right type of data will be collected.

Finally, the sources of information of the present study were the narratives of the young people themselves. Again, the practicalities of this study meant that it was not possible to interview significant others, probation officers, or peers. Given that desistance is so strongly anchored in the so-called "looking-glass self-concept", this is undoubtedly an important limitation of the study that must be accounted for and corrected in future waves. Moreover, considering that places and routines are shown to have specific meanings that facilitate or hinder certain social interactions, in turn shaping individuals' desistance process, strategies to research those spatial dynamics must be developed.

The way in which one researches those interactions, lifestyles, and places where the desistance process takes place cannot be restricted by disciplinary boundaries and controls. In that sense, data collection strategies that are not widely used in Criminology must be integrated. Good examples might be: walking interviews, photo-box or auto-photography, participatory action research, and ethnography as a methodology of attentiveness,[3] as ways to explore the meaning and symbolism within criminal subcultures. Only by crossing the methodological and theoretical disciplinary boundaries of Criminology, will desistance research be able to overcome the constraints on intellectual enquiry and advance to a deeper understanding of the process of leaving crime behind.

Notes

1 While the United Kingdom is ranked 23rd and the United States 30th of 145 countries in the Gender Gap Index, Chile is ranked 78th (World Economic Forum, 2021).

2 Intentional desistance was a measure that could reflect the perceived capacity to avoid crime, as opposed to being a proxy for a proper crime-free gap as behavioural desistance does.

3 A systematic interpretive process in which an outside observer of a culture attempts to relate to it and understand others (Ferrell, 1997).

References

Agnew, R. (2003). An integrated theory of the adolescent peak in offending. *Youth & Society*, 34(3): 263–299.

Barr, U. (2019). *Desisting sisters gender, power and desistance in the criminal (in)justice system*. London: Palgrave Macmillan.

Bottoms, A. and Shapland, J. (2011). 'Steps towards desistance among male young adult recidivists'. In: Farrall, S., Hough, M., Maruna, S. and Sparks, R. (eds.) *Escape Routes: Contemporary Perspectives on Life after Punishment*. Oxon: Routledge, pp. 43–80.

Bottoms, A. and Shapland, J. (2014). Can persistent offenders acquire virtue?. *Studies in Christian Ethics*, 27(3): 318–333.

Bottoms, A. and Shapland, J. (2016). 'Learning to desist early adulthood: the Sheffield Desistance Study'. In: Shapland, J., Farrall, S. and Bottoms, A. (eds.) *Global perspective on desistance: reviewing what we know, looking to the future*. London: Routledge, pp. 99–125.

Bottoms, A., Shapland, J., Costello, A., Holmes, D. and Muir, G. (2004). Towards desistance: theoretical underpinnings for an empirical study. *The Howard Journal*, 43(4): 368–387.

Carlsson, C. (2013). Masculinities, persistence, and desistance. *Criminology*, 51(3): 661–693.

Carlsson, C. (2016). 'Human agency, criminal careers, and desistance'. In: Shapland, J., Farrall, S. and Bottoms, T. (eds.) *Global Perspectives on Desistance*. Abingdon: Routledge, pp. 28–49.

Chant, S. (2014). Exploring the "feminisation of poverty" in relation to women's work and home-based enterprise in slums of the global south. *International Journal of Gender and Entrepreneurship*, 6(3): 296–316.

Cohen, A. K. (1955). *Delinquent Boys: The Culture of the Gang*. New York, NY: The Free Press.

Connell, R. W. (2005). *Masculinities*. Berkeley, CA: University of California Press.

Cusson, M., and Pinsonneault, P. (1986). 'The decisión to give up crime. In D. Cornish and R. Clarke (eds.), *The reasoning criminal: Rational choice perspectives on offending*. New York: Springer-Verlag, pp. 72–82.

Droppelmann, C. (2017). 'Leaving behind the deviant other in desistance-persistence explanations'. In Hart, E. and van Ginnecken, E. (eds.) *New Perspectives on Desistance*. London: Palgrave Macmillan, pp. 213–240.

Farrall, S. (2005) On the existential aspects of desistance from crime. *Symbolic Interaction*, 28, 367–86.

Farrall S. (2014) The spatial dynamics of desistance. In: Farrall S, Hunter B, Sharpe G, et al. (eds.) *Criminal careers in transition: The social context of desistance from crime*. Oxford: Oxford University Press, pp. 159–186.

Farrall, S. and Calverley, A. (2006). *Understanding Desistance from Crime: Theoretical Directions in Resettlement and Rehabilitation*. Maidenhead: Open University Press.

Farrington, D. P. (1986). 'Age and crime.' In: Morris, N. and Tonry, M. (eds.) *Crime and Justice* (Vol. 7). Chicago, IL: Chicago University Press, pp. 189–250.

Farrington, D. P. and Hawkins, J. D. (1991). Predicting participation, early onset, and later persistence in officially recorded offending. *Criminal Behaviour and Mental Health*, 1: 1–33.

Ferrell, J. (1997) Criminological Verstehen. *Justice Quarterly* 14(1): 3–23.

Fowers, B. J. (2006). 'Psychotherapy, character, and the good life'. In: Slife, B. D. and Richardson, F. C. (eds.) *Critical Thinking about Psychology: Hidden Assumptions and Plausible Alternatives*. Washington DC: American Psychological Association, pp. 39–60.

Franco, R., Hopenhayn, M. and León, A. (2011). Crece y cambia la clase media en América Latina: una puesta al día. *Revista Cepal*, 103: 7–26.

Gålnander, R. (2019). Desistance from crime—to what? Exploring future aspirations and their implications for processes of desistance. *Feminist Criminology*, 15(3), 255–277.

Gelsthorpe, L. (2010). Woman, crime and control. *Criminology and Criminal Justice*, 10: 375–386.

Gibbons, D. C. (1965). *Changing the Lawbraker*. Englewood Cliffs, NJ: Prentice-Hall.

Giordano, P. (2016). 'Mechanism underlying the desistance process: Reflections on a theory of cognitive transformation'. In: Shapland, J., Farrall, S. and Bottoms, T. (eds.) *Global Perspectives on Desistance*. Abingdon: Routledge, pp. 11–27.

Giordano, P., Cernkovich, S. and Rudolph, J. (2002). Gender, crime, and desistance: Toward a theory of cognitive transformation. *American Journal of Sociology* 107(4): 990–1064.

Giordano, P. C., Cernkovich, S. A. and Holland, D. D. (2003). Changes in friendship relations over the life course: Implications for desistance from crime. *Criminology*, 41(2): 293.

Glueck, S. and Glueck, E. (1943). *Criminal Career in Retrospect.* New York, NY: The Commonwealth Fund.

Goodkind, S. S. (2009). Gender difference and offender reentry: A review of the literature. *Journal of Offender Rehabilitation*, 48(4): 314–335.

Graham, H. and McNeill, F. (2017). 'Desistance: Envisioning futures'. In: Carlen, P. and França, L. (eds.) *Alternative Criminologies*. London: Routledge, pp. 433–451.

Hannah-Moffat, K. (2001). *Punishment in Disguise: Penal Governance and Canadian Women's Imprisonment.* Toronto: University of Toronto Press.

Hannah-Moffat, K. (2011). Sacrosanct or flawed: Risk, accountability and gender-responsive penal politics. *Current Issues in Criminal Justice*, 22(2): 193–215.

Hart, E. L. (2017). Women prisoners and the drive for desistance: Capital and responsibilization as a barrier to change. *Women & Criminal Justice*, 27(3): 151–169.

Hayward, B. K. and Young, J. (1999). Cultural criminology: Some notes on the script. *Theoretical Criminology*, 8(3): 259–285.

Hayward, B. (2002). 'The vilification and pleasures of youthful transgression'. In: Muncie, J., Hughes, G. and McLaughlin, E. (eds.) *Youth Justice: Critical Readings*. London: Sage, pp. 80–94.

Healy, D. (2010). *The Dynamics of Desistance: Charting Pathways through Change.* USA: Willan Publishing.

Healy, D. (2013). Changing fate? Agency and the desistance process. *Theoretical Criminology*, 17(4): 557–574.

Hunt, B. and Farrall, S. (2015). 'Space, Place and Desistance from Drug Use'. *Oñati Socio-Legal Series*, 5(3): 954–968.

Hunter, B. and Farrall, S. (2018) 'Emotions, future selves, and the process ofdesistance'. *British Journal of Criminology*, 58: 291–308.

Irwin, J. (1970). *The Felon*. Englewood Cliffs, NJ: Prentice-Hall.

Jelin, E. (Ed.) (1990). *Women and social change in Latin America*. London: Zed Books.

King, R. D. (2013). Assisted desistance and experience of probation supervision. *Probation Journal*, 60(2): 136–151.

King, S. (2014) Desistance Transitions and the Impact of Probation. Abingdon: Routledge.

Laidler, K. J. and Hunt, G. (2001). Accomplishing femininity among the girls in the gang. *British Journal of Criminology*, 41: 656–678.

LeBel, T. P., Burnett, R., Maruna, S. and Bushway, S. (2008). The 'Chicken and Egg' of Subjective and Social Factors in Desistance from Crime. *European Journal of Criminology*, 5(2): 131–159.

Legarde y de los Rios, M. (2005). *Los cautiverios de las mujeres. Madresposas, monjas, putas, presas y locas*. Ciudad de México: UNAM ediciones.

Lewis, D. A. (1990). From programs to lives: A comment. *American Journal of Community Psychology*, 18(6): 923–926.

Lindegaard, M. and Jacques, S. (2014). Agency as a cause of crime. *Deviant Behavior*, 35(2): 85–100.

Maruna, S. (2001). *Making Good: How Ex-Convicts Reform and Rebuild their lives.* Washington, DC: American Psychological Association.

Maruna, S. and Roy, K. (2007). Amputation or Reconstruction? Notes on the concept of 'knifing off' and desistance from crime. *Journal of Contemporary Criminal Justice*, 23(1): 104–124.

Matza, D. (1964). *Delinquency and Drift*. New York, NY: Routledge.

McIvor, G. (2016). 'Offending and desistance among young women'. In: Kruttschnitt, C. and Bijleveld, C. (eds.) *Lives of Incarcerated Women: An International Perspective. Routledge Frontiers of Criminal Justice, 28*. New York, NY: Routledge, pp. 159–175.

Meisenhelder, T. (1977). An exploratory study of exiting from criminal careers. *Criminology*, 15: 319–334.

Melero, P. (2015). *Mythological Constructs of Mexican Femininity*. London: Palgrave Macmillan.

Merton, R. (1957). *Social Theory and Social Structure*. New York, NY: Free Press.

Miller, J. (2002). The strengths and limits of 'doing gender' for understanding street crime. *Theoretical Criminology*, 6(4): 433–460.

Molyneux, M. (2000). *Women's Movements in International Perspective: Latin America and Beyond*. Basingstoke: Palgrave Macmillan.

Montecino, S. (1997). *Palabra dicha: estudios sobre género, identidades, mestizaje*. Chile: Universidad de Chile, Facultad de Ciencias Sociales.

Murray, C. (2009). Typologies of young resisters and desisters. *Youth Justice*, 9(2): 115–129.

Nixon, D. (2020). 'Giving back and getting on with my life': Peer mentoring, desistance and recovery of ex-offenders. *Probation Journal*, 67(1): 47–64.

Nugent, B. and Schinkel, M. (2016). The pains of desistance. *Criminology and Criminal Justice*, 16(5): 568–584.

Patton, D. and Farrall, S. (2021). Desistance: A utopian perspective. *The Howard Journal of Crime and Justice*, 60(2): 209–231.

Paternoster, R., Bachman, R., Kerrison, E. and O'Connell, D. J. (2016). Desistance from Crime and Identity: An Empirical Test With Survival Time. *Criminal Justice and Behavior*, 43(9): 1204–1224.

Presser, L. (2008). *Been a Heavy Life: Stories of Violent Men*. Urbana, IL: University of Illinois Press.

Sampson, R. J. and Laub, J. H. (2003). Life-course desisters? Trajectories of crime among delinquent boys followed to age 70. *Criminology*, 41(3): 555–592.

Schwendinger, H., & Schwendinger, J. S. (1985). *Adolescent subcultures and delinquency*. New York: Praeger.

Standing, G. (2011) Precariat: New Dangerous Class, London: Bloomsbury Academic.

Sykes, G. and Matza, D. (1957). Techniques of neutralization: A theory of delinquency. *American Sociological Review*, 22(6): 664–670.

UNDP. (2014). *Citizen Security with a Human Face: Evidence and Proposal for Latin America*. New York, NY: United Nation Development Programme.

World Economic Forum. (2021). The Global Gender Gap Report 2021. World Economic Forum. Available from: www3.weforum.org/docs/WEF_GGGR_2021.pdf.

Wright, E., DeHart, D., Koons-Witt, B., and Crittenden, C. (2013). 'Buffers' Against Crime? Exploring the Roles and Limitations of Positive Relationships Among Women in Prison. *Punishment and Society* 15: 71–95.

Index

Redemption 4, 20, 22, 39, 59–60, 127, 149, 154, 157, 188